Praise for *The Wic[ked Boy]*

"Summerscale's ambitious literary goal . . . is to position her close study of a specific crime within the broader context of the social and political climate in which it was committed. When the novelist P. D. James turned to true crime . . . [she] share[d] that expansive vision. . . . Irresistible."
—Marilyn Stasio, *The New York Times Book Review*

"Ms. Summerscale has found a nifty literary specialty: resurrecting and reanimating, in detail as much forensic as it is novelistic, notorious true-life tales of the Victorian era. . . . Enjoyable as an atmospheric tale of crime and punishment from a distant era written in lucid, limber prose, *The Wicked Boy* also implicitly raises questions that remain with us today. . . . Ms. Summerscale's easy mastery of what turns out to be a complicated, at times surprising, narrative drives the book forward. . . . Ms. Summerscale draws no firm psychological conclusions, but instead leaves the mystery of the boy and the man to our imaginations, where it pricks at us throughout the book."
—Charles Isherwood, *The New York Times*

"Summerscale has taken her research to many levels of learning for the reader. It's more than [*An Infamous Murder in Victorian London*]—it's a tale about change. It belongs on every reader's bookshelf." —*New York Journal of Books*

"Summerscale specializes in revisiting scandals that reveal Victorians in the throes of their own morbid spells. She expertly probes the deep anxieties of a modernizing era. Even better, she brings rare biographical tenacity and sympathy to bear."
—*The Atlantic*

"A remarkable job of historical reconstruction . . . In the time-honored tradition of Victorian crime stories, *The Wicked Boy* is a compelling mixture of the gruesome and the perfectly ordinary, a brew uniquely British. . . . A feat of genuine detective work."
—*The Dallas Morning News*

"A chilling look at an infamous child murderer, *The Wicked Boy* will have you losing sleep."
—*Bustle*

"Kate Summerscale is deft at interweaving her narrative with extensive quotes from court proceedings and press accounts. Don't look to *The Wicked Boy* for either amped-up emotion or for sanitization of the facts. It reads like the successful and well-balanced offspring of a liaison between a crime novel and a scholarly paper."
—*The Florida Times-Union*

"In *The Wicked Boy* you'll think you're reading Dickens."
—NBC-2

"Summerscale's command of the detail of Victorian life is impressive; her grasp of the nuances and characters of the individual personalities complete. *The Wicked Boy* is an extraordinary tale of black tragedy and hard-won redemption. Not to be missed by devotees of the Victorian Era."
—*Daily Herald*

"Narrative nonfiction that reads like a novel."
—Omnivoracious Best History Books of July

"*The Wicked Boy* is an absorbing piece of true-crime investigation, and a surprising and satisfying tale of redemption. . . . A treat for true-crime fans."
—*Shelf Awareness*

"Summerscale bolsters her reputation as a superior historical true crime writer with this moving account of Victorian-age murder that is a whydunit rather than a whodunit. . . . [Her] dogged research yields a tragedy that reads like a Dickens novel, including the remarkable payoff at the end."

—*Publishers Weekly* (starred review)

"This well-written story is not so much a true-crime tale or murder mystery as an excellent sociological study of turn-of-twentieth-century England." —*Kirkus Reviews*

"No other writer could have made the Coombes case so fascinating and so vivid. . . . It would be impossible to read this dry-eyed." —Cressida Connolly, *The Spectator* (London)

"An extraordinary book which will stay with you."
—Vanessa Berridge, *Daily Express* (London)

"Gripping . . . Summerscale is an exquisite storyteller. She is judicious in her use of detail, subtle in her unspoken connections between the past and the present. . . . This is the story of one wicked boy, but it is also a plea for compassion and empathy."
—Daisy Goodwin, *The Times* (London)

"For her latest forensic investigation into the throttled passions of Victorian family life, Summerscale has moved forward thirty-five years to 1895 and turned away from the provincial bourgeois home to the working-class terraces of London's East End. . . . [A] fine account . . . Subtle and confident."
—Kathryn Hughes, *The Guardian* (UK)

"Unexpectedly touching . . . A fascinating account of a murder and its endless reverberations."
—Craig Brown, *The Mail on Sunday* (UK)

"As Kate Summerscale has proved before, she has a wonderfully sharp eye for stories which turn out not to be quite what they seem. . . . A remarkably heartening story."
—John Preston, *Daily Mail* (London)

"Compelling . . . It gripped and stoked the national imagination, just as it surely will again."
—Philippa Stockley, *Evening Standard*

"A work of social history that is as compassionate as it is absorbing . . . We almost feel we are wandering through these scenes ourselves."
—Rebecca Gowers, *The Oldie*

"Ultimately, the narrative is an exploration of Victorian attitudes to juvenile crime, and this pacy slice of social history acts as both hawk-eyed prosecution and gentle defense."
—Zoë Apostolides, *Financial Times* (London)

"An absorbing account of fin-de-siecle Britain . . . [and] a powerful story about vulnerable and neglected children, both then and now."
—Daisy Hay, *Daily Telegraph* (London)

"It's a fascinating story and Summerscale tells it beautifully. . . . [Her] sympathetic and intelligent study is full of social interest too. I can't imagine that it could have been done better."
—Alan Massie, *The Scotsman* (Edinburgh)

"The challenge, to which Ms. Summerscale rises wonderfully well, is to sustain the reader's interest in him for the remaining fifty-odd years of his life. . . . Evocative . . . Through a mixture of serendipity and meticulous research, Ms. Summerscale is able to add one final, heart-stopping twist." —*The Economist*

"Redemption comes twice in this account . . . An extremely touching twist . . . Scrupulous and occasionally startling." —Rachel Cooke, *The Observer* (London)

"Summerscale has performed a stunning post-mortem of 'the horror' at number 35 . . . Talk about bringing history alive." —*Sunday Express* (London)

"It is above all her skill in creating a context for the crime which makes *The Wicked Boy* so readable . . . The sounds and smells of the East End docks, from which their father set sail, are evoked with particular vividness. More fascinating still are the ideas of the age . . . An extraordinary tale of redemption." —*Tablet*

"Her research is needle-sharp and her period detail richly atmospheric, but what is most heartening about this truly remarkable book is the story of real-life redemption that it brings to light." —John Carey, *The Sunday Times* (London)

ABOUT THE AUTHOR

Kate Summerscale, formerly literary editor of the *Daily Telegraph*, is the author of *The Queen of Whale Cay*, which won a Somerset Maugham Award and was short-listed for the Whitbread Biography Prize. *The Suspicions of Mr. Whicher* was a number one bestseller in the UK, has been translated into more than a dozen languages, was short-listed for the CWA Gold Dagger for Non-Fiction and the Edgar Award for Best Fact Crime, and won the Samuel Johnson Prize for Non-Fiction and the British Book Awards Book of the Year. Summerscale lives in London.

katesummerscale.com

THE WICKED BOY

An Infamous Murder in Victorian London

Kate Summerscale

PENGUIN BOOKS

PENGUIN BOOKS
An imprint of Penguin Random House LLC
375 Hudson Street
New York, New York 10014
penguin.com

First published in Great Britain by Bloomsbury Publishing, 2016
First published in the United States of America by Penguin Press,
an imprint of Penguin Random House LLC, 2016
Published in Penguin Books 2017

Family tree, floor plan and map illustrations by Liane Payne

Acknowledgments on page 361 constitute an extension of this copyright page.

ISBN 9781594205781 (hardcover)
ISBN 9780143110460 (paperback)
ISBN 9780698135000 (e-book)

Printed in the United States of America
1   3   5   7   9   10   8   6   4   2

For Miranda and Keith

CONTENTS

PART V: WITH TRUMPETS AND SOUND OF CORNET

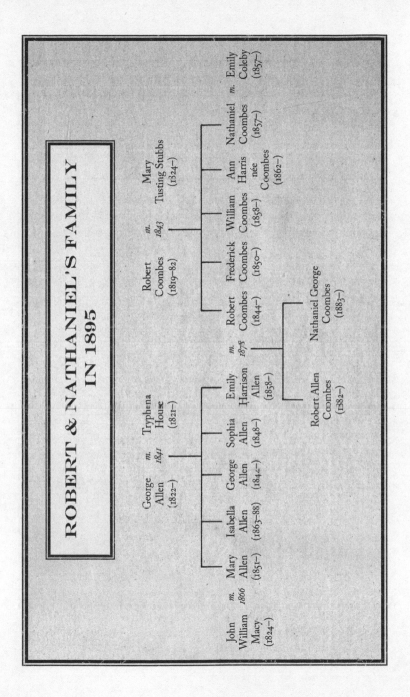

ROBERT & NATHANIEL'S FAMILY IN 1895

George Allen (1822–) *m.* *1841* Tryphena House (1821–)

Mary Allen (1851–) *m.* *1866* John William Macy (1824–)

Isabella Allen (1863–88)

George Allen (1844–)

Sophia Allen (1848–)

Emily Harrison Allen (1858–) *m.* *1878*

Robert Coombes (1844–)

Robert Allen Coombes (1882–)

Nathaniel George Coombes (1883–)

Robert Coombes (1819–82) *m.* *1843* Mary Tusting Stubbs (1824–)

Frederick Coombes (1850–)

William Coombes (1858–)

Ann Harris née Coombes (1862–)

Nathaniel Coombes (1857–) *m.* Emily Coleby (1857–)

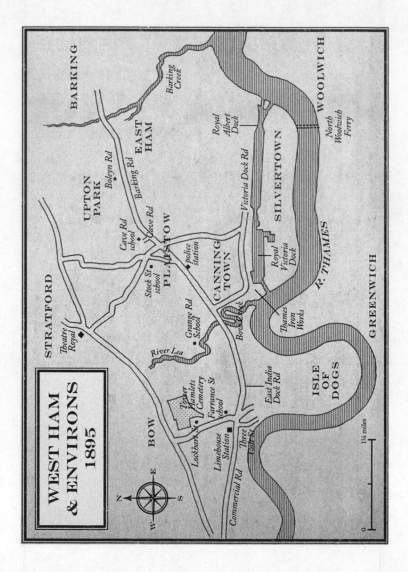

WEST HAM
& ENVIRONS
1895

¼ miles

STRATFORD

Theatre Royal

BOW

Tower Hamlets Cemetery

River Lea

Lockbart

Farrance St school

Limehouse Station

Three Colt St

Commercial Rd

East India Dock Rd

ISLE OF DOGS

Grange Rd School

Stock St school

Cave Rd school

Cave Rd

PLAISTOW

police station

Barking Rd

Boleyn Rd

UPTON PARK

EAST HAM

Barking Creek

BARKING

Bow Creek

CANNING TOWN

Thames Iron Works

Royal Victoria Dock

Victoria Dock Rd

SILVERTOWN

Royal Albert Dock

R. THAMES

North Woolwich Ferry

WOOLWICH

GREENWICH

N E S W

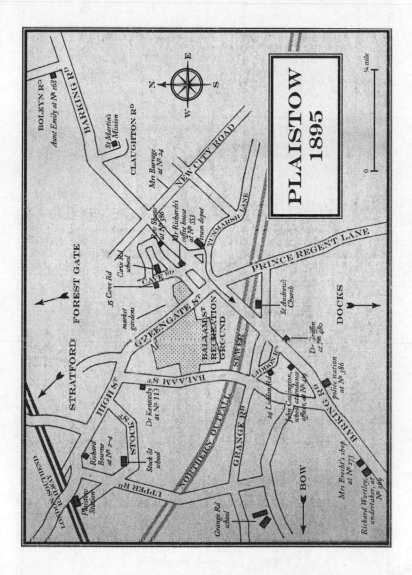

PLAISTOW
1895

BOLEYN RD

Aunt Emily at Nº 163

BARKING RD

St Martin's Mission

CLAUGHTON RD

Mrs Burrage at Nº 24

NEW CITY ROAD

Mrs Shaw at Nº 590

Mr Richard's coffee house at Nº 553

tram depot

TUNMARSH LANE

PRINCE REGENT LANE

FOREST GATE

35 Cave Rd

Cave Rd school

CAVE RD

market gardens

GREENGATE ST

BALAAM ST RECREATION GROUND

BALAAM ST

St Andrew's Church

DOCKS

D. Griffin at Nº 480

SEWER

LIDDON RD

24 Liddon Rd

John Cossington, school attendance officer, at Nº 409

Police station at Nº 386

BARKING RD

BOW

Mrs Erecht's shop at Nº 273

Richard Wortley, undertaker, at Nº 269

STRATFORD

HIGH ST

Dr Kennedy at Nº 113

Richard Bourne at Nº 2-4

STOCK ST

Stock St school

NORTHERN OUTFALL

GRANGE RD

UPPER RD

Plaistow Station

LONDON TILBURY & SOUTHEND RY

Grange Rd school

¼ mile

0

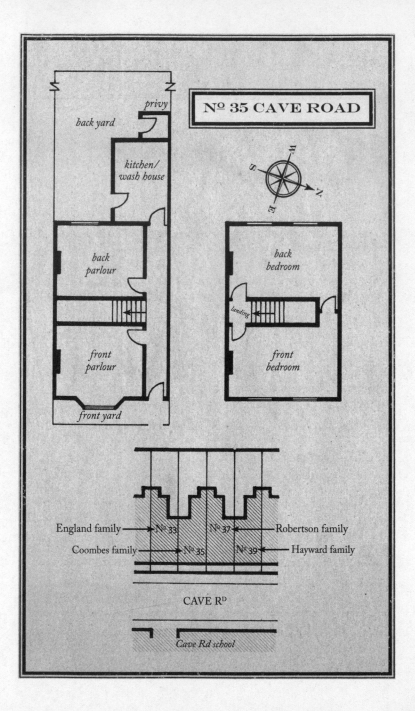

N° 35 CAVE ROAD

back yard

privy

kitchen/
wash house

back
parlour

front
parlour

front yard

back
bedroom

landing

front
bedroom

England family → N° 33

Coombes family → N° 35

N° 37 ← Robertson family

N° 39 ← Hayward family

CAVE R^D

Cave Rd school

A NOTE ON MONEY

In 1895, a British pound (£1) comprised 20 shillings (20/-) or 240 pence (240d). £1 could then buy the equivalent of goods that in 2014 cost roughly £100 ($150), and 1/- could buy goods that in 2014 cost about £5 (or $7.50). These comparisons, based on the Retail Price Index, are explained on the website measuringworth.com.

In *Life and Labour of the People: Volume I* (1889), the social reformer Charles Booth detailed the expenditure of several East London families. Over five weeks, a couple and their two sons with an annual income of about £70, slightly higher than that of the Coombes household, spent as follows:

Meat 19/1d	Sugar 3/5d
Potatoes 2/4d	Milk 5/-
Vegetables 1/1d	Tea 5/3d
Fish 2/8d	Coffee, cocoa &c 2/11d
Bacon &c 1/2d	Pepper, salt &c 5d
Eggs 1/-	Beer and tobacco 4/10d
Cheese 4/10d	Fire and light 9/-
Suet 1/2d	Rent 22/6d
Butter and dripping 5/10d	Washing and cleaning 3/4d
Bread 7/3d	Clothes &c 22/9d
Flour 1/11d	Education, medicine &c 1/-
Rice, oatmeal &c 8d	Insurance &c 2/11d
Fruit, jam &c 6d	

Total over five weeks: 133/1d (approximately £6 13/-)

The average prices of some of these items:

Meat 7d per lb	Cheese 8d per lb
Potatoes 1/2d per lb	Milk 4d per quart
Eggs 1d each	Coffee 1/- per lb

PROLOGUE

In June 1930 an eleven-year-old boy walked four miles along a dirt track in New South Wales, south-eastern Australia, to report a crime. He went into a police station in a village in the bush and told the officer on duty that he had been beaten with a brush hook. The boy showed the constable the evidence: his right arm and leg were heavily grazed and bruised; his nose, his left cheek and his right eye were dark with cuts and swellings. The policeman put the child in his car and set out to investigate. The incident was reported in the local press, but to protect the identity of the child neither his name nor that of his attacker was given.

PART I

TEN DAYS IN JULY

THE THREE OF US

Early in the morning of Monday 8 July 1895, Robert and Nathaniel Coombes dressed themselves, collected the family's rent book from a room downstairs, and went out to the back yard. It was just after 6 a.m. and already bright and warm.

Robert was thirteen and Nattie twelve. Their father had gone to sea on Friday, as chief steward on a steamship bound for New York, leaving the brothers and their mother, Emily, at home together. They lived in a small, new, yellow-brick terraced house at 35 Cave Road, Plaistow, a poor but respectable working-class district in West Ham, the biggest borough in the docklands of East London.

In an attempt to attract the attention of their neighbour in number 37, Robert picked up a handful of stones and threw them at the roof of the washhouse next door.

At 6.15 a.m. James Robertson heard the stones clattering on the washhouse roof and came out. Mr Robertson saw the two Coombes boys in their yard: Robert, dark-haired, with blue eyes, thick eyebrows and sun-tanned skin, and the paler, smaller Nattie. He knew them as sharp-witted lads. Robert produced a gold sovereign, worth twenty shillings (or £1), and asked Mr Robertson if he could change it for them. Mr Robertson said that he had no silver but offered to change the coin for two half-sovereigns. He fetched the two gold coins from his house. Robert then asked him if he would pay the rent on 35 Cave Road on their behalf as no one would be at home when the landlady called by later that morning. Mr Robertson agreed, and Robert gave him back one of the half-sovereigns along with the family's rent book. Robert explained that he and Nattie were going to watch the cricket at Lord's, in north London. Mr Robertson asked if their Ma was going with them.

'No,' said Robert. 'We had a telegram late last night from Liverpool and she is going there. We've had a rich uncle die in Africa, and Auntie wants to see Ma.' Emily Coombes sometimes travelled to the north-west of England to visit her well-to-do older sister and her mother.

Mr Robertson asked whether she had gone already.

'No,' said Robert. 'She is going directly. She has had a faint.' (Or 'She has had a fit' – when asked to recall the conversation, Mr Robertson could not be sure.)

'How long ago was that?' enquired Mr Robertson.

Robert pulled a gold watch from his pocket and consulted it. 'About an hour and a half ago,' he said.

Mr Robertson asked who was with their Ma. Robert jerked his thumb behind him, in the direction of the house. 'Mrs. . .'

'Mrs England?' suggested Mr Robertson. Amelia England was the Coombes family's neighbour on the other side, and a close friend of Emily Coombes.

'No,' said Robert. He did not explain further but added: 'Perhaps Ma will see Mrs Robertson before she goes.'

The boys set out for Lord's.

Robert and Nattie were among more than 12,000 people to travel to St John's Wood that Monday to watch the Gentlemen v Players match, the fixture of the season at the most famous cricket ground in England. The streets near Lord's were lined with lawns and villas, and on the day of a big match they were packed with people, the men in top hats, bowlers, flat caps or straw boaters, the few women in dresses with bell skirts and high necks, their hats perched on pinned-up hair and their parasols tilted at the sun. A handful of police constables in domed helmets and flared jackets moved among the crowd.

The great draw that day was the legendary cricketer W. G. Grace, who, at forty-six, was enjoying an astonishing renaissance. He had just become the first player ever to score a thousand runs in the opening month of a season and was, according to the *Illustrated London News*, the most popular man in the British Isles. He would be batting for the Gentlemen, a team composed of well-born men who played for pleasure rather than profit. Their opponents, the Players, were professional cricketers, most of them of working-class stock. In theory, the match pitted those who were paid to play against those who were not, though many of the Gentlemen were known to benefit handsomely from tours, gifts and testimonials. Grace was foremost among cricket's 'shamateurs'.

Robert and Nattie paid a few pennies apiece to gain admittance to the ground and made for the low, roped-off stands to either side of the pitch. The more affluent spectators took their places in the tiered pavilion reserved for members of the Marylebone Cricket Club.

It was a clear, hot day, tempered by soft breezes. Just after noon the bell rang and the Gentlemen strode out from the pavilion in their whites to take their places as fielders on the huge swathe of green. The Players' first batting pair emerged from their shabbier dressing room through a side entrance by the stands, which were partly covered with a white awning and backed by a belt of trees.

The Players had won the toss and elected to bat. They expected to score well on a pitch hardened by three months of drought, but the wicket proved far more volatile than anticipated, and their batsmen performed disappointingly. By 4.40 p.m. they were all out for 231.

Twenty minutes later, W. G. Grace and Andrew Stoddart opened the innings for the Gentlemen. Grace lumbered onto the field in his whites, a tiny red and yellow cap on his big, bearded head. It was thirty years almost to the day since he had played in his first Gentlemen v Players match at Lord's. His partner, Stoddy, was another cricketing hero: a graceful, spirited batsman, with a magnificent moustache, he had led the English side to victory in the last test series in Australia, and had been honoured with a wax statue at Madame Tussaud's museum in Baker Street.

Despite some excellent bowling from the Players, Grace and Stoddart were still at the crease two hours later, having notched up 137 runs between them. The stumps were pulled at 7 p.m. The two batsmen would continue their innings the next day.

The Coombes boys left St John's Wood at dusk and got back to West Ham after dark. At about 9 p.m., Robert called on Mr Robertson. He went to the front door of number 37 while Nattie waited outside the gate.

'I have come back for the change,' said Robert. 'Is the house all right?'

'I expect so,' Mr Robertson replied. 'I haven't seen anything.' He gave Robert the rent book and three shillings in change – the rent for each house in Cave Road was seven shillings a week, about average for the area but a sum that would secure only a large room in the centre of London.

Once inside their house, the boys did not go to the bedrooms upstairs. Instead, they bedded down in the back parlour – Robert took the sofa and Nattie the armchair. They fell asleep in their clothes.

The next morning Robert and Nattie set out for Lord's again. Their mother's friend Amelia England, who lived at number 33, saw them in the street and asked where they were going. Robert replied that they were visiting an aunt in St John's Wood. He added that their mother was out of town but he had just received a letter from her, in which she had enclosed some money. 'Very likely she will be home tomorrow evening,' he said.

The crowd was even bigger at Lord's on Tuesday and the weather just as fine. For half an hour before play commenced, the fans streamed out of the trains, cabs and omnibuses.

The Gentlemen resumed their innings at 11.30 a.m. Within fifteen minutes Stoddart was bowled out for 71, but Grace kept going. As he neared his hundred the crowd grew excited and when he made the century a storm of applause was raised by the spectators and the players alike. It was Grace's seventh century of the season in a first-class game. His achievement that morning was all the greater because the bowling had been exceptional.

At 1.40 p.m., Grace's innings ended with a catch at the wicket. Eight of his ten team mates had also been dismissed by the time they broke for lunch at two and, despite Grace's century, the Gentlemen had only 252 runs for nine wickets.

The Coombes brothers had brought provisions to the match. They ate their food in the shade of a shed in the grounds.

When play continued after lunch, the Gentlemen were all out in ten minutes, having scored only seven more runs. The Players came on for a second innings and by the time the stumps were pulled at 7 p.m. they had scored 269 runs and lost just six wickets. They were well ahead.

Robert and Nattie made their way back again to East London, but instead of going straight home they headed for the new Theatre Royal in Stratford, two miles north-west of Cave Road. The play they watched that evening, *Light Ahead*, told the story of a man framed for murder by a shipyard employee who had turned forger, bigamist and killer. The theatrical newspaper *The Era* observed that the show would appeal to 'the pit and gallery', a working-class audience such as that found in Stratford, but pronounced it 'a straggling, uneven piece' that 'proceeds on its course for a considerable time with no light ahead whatever as to how it is to turn and in what manner it will end'. The highlights of the production were a specially constructed lifeboat, which was hoisted onto the stage for the finale; a 'winning and womanly' heroine; and an audacious villain, whose gleeful malignancy excited the admiration even of the *Era*'s critic.

In the back parlour of 35 Cave Road, where Robert and Nattie again slept that night, Robert kept his collection of 'penny dreadfuls' – or 'penny bloods'. These were melodramatic adventures in the same vein as *Light Ahead*, published weekly as magazines. They were set all over the world: on the high seas, in the crime-ridden streets of London and New York, the jungles of Africa, on the plains of the Wild West and the islands of the Far East. Some took place in a fantastical future of electrical stagecoaches and flying machines, others in a blood-soaked past of noble crusaders and haunted knights.

Among Robert's most recent purchases was *Jack Wright and the Fortune Hunters of the Red Sea*, part of an American series loosely inspired by the novels of Jules Verne. Jack is an orphan inventor – a 'manly-looking boy' with a 'fine, athletic figure'– who travels the globe in ingenious vessels of his own making, fighting rogues and tracking down treasure. In his Red Sea adventure, published in the first week of July, Jack sails across the Atlantic from America to Africa. His submarine, the *Meteor*, is a slender pod of plate glass and steel, its compact cabins washed with silvery light, flashing with instruments, gleaming with levers, wires and electro-magnets. After much danger and derring-do – storms of rain and sand, the rescue of a drowning maiden, fights with Arab pearl divers and Yankee bank robbers – he reaches his quarry: a cache of treasure at the bottom of the Red Sea, guarded by a twenty-foot-long winged lizard. To vanquish the dragon and lay claim to the loot, Jack dons a submarine suit and dives through a blood-red sea to the creature's cave. Once he is inside the grotto, a hunk of coral rolls over the entrance. 'He was entombed alive!'

The giant lizard springs at Jack and sinks its double row of curved black teeth into the boy's flesh. Jack wriggles free, aims his pistol and shoots, but the creature only briefly recoils. 'The beast was floating high over his head near the ceiling, squirming its long, slender body like a snake, and glaring down at him with its enormous, fiery eyes.' It darts towards him again, 'its huge red mouth gaping'.

'If it reaches me,' thinks Jack, 'I have no doubt that it will tear me to pieces, goaded as it is to the height of its fury.' When the creature surges forward and curls its body around his, Jack drops his pistol and draws a dagger. 'Plunging it into the beast's head, he buried the blade up to the hilt, and a convulsive throe of pain seemed to dart through it, and it sank to the ground.' The monster lets go of Jack as it falls. Upon seeing the 'repulsive object' stretched out dead in front of him, the boy breathes a sigh of relief and rises to his feet. 'Cruel, savage, spiteful!' he mutters. 'I never before encountered a beast so fearless and bloodthirsty.' The rubies and sapphires on the seabed are now his for the taking. Jack gathers them up, and digs his way out of the cave to freedom.

On Wednesday, another fiercely hot day, Robert took a key from the top of the clock on the mantelpiece in the back parlour and went upstairs with his brother. He unlocked the door to his mother's room, at the front of the house, and both boys went in to raise the window blinds, which had been down since Sunday night.

The boys' funds were running low and neither of them had a job. Nattie was playing truant from Cave Road school, a hulking three-storey block for 1,500 students built opposite their house the previous summer. Robert had left the school in May, having completed his eighth and last year of state-funded education. He had then found work in a shipyard by the docks, but after a fortnight had jacked it in. The brothers decided to head for the docks now to look for a man called John Fox, who a few years earlier had been an assistant steward to their father. Fox made his home on the ships lying at anchor: he slept in the galleys and ran errands for the officers and crew. Robert thought that he might help them to raise some money.

The horse-drawn trams and buses to the nearest dock gate ran south-west along the Barking Road, the thoroughfare at the end of Robert and Nattie's street. The route was busy with shops: grocers, butchers, fried-fish sellers, tailors, hatters, post offices, a bicycle seller, a marine supplier, a cheesemonger, chemists, coal merchants, confectioners, bakers. The closest church was just past the tobacconist at 500 Barking Road, the Coombes family's doctor at number 480, the police station at 386. At number 110 was a new public hall and free library, which in February had become the first building in West Ham to be equipped with electricity.

A mile and a half down the Barking Road, the boys passed the crowded lanes of Canning Town, a darker, more desperate district than their own. The casual labourers from these rickety terraces pressed at the dock gates each morning, hungry for work. Over the previous two decades the docks, factories and railways had drawn a multitude of people to West Ham, swelling the population from 12,000 in 1870 to close to 200,000 by 1895. 'London over the Border', as it was known, was the industrial hub of the empire and a new metropolis of the poor. This was both the city and the city's shadow, its furthest dirty reach.

The streets by the Thames teemed with British and Irish labourers, and with sailors from all over the world – Malays, Lascars, Swedes, Chinamen. 'There is no seaport in the country,' said the novelist Walter Besant, 'which is so charged with the atmosphere of ocean and the suggestion of things far off.' The noise was tremendous: the clatter of trains and trams, the blasts of ship horns, the grinding of chains, the whine of winches, the thunder and crash of the machines at the Thames Ironworks Shipbuilding Company, where Robert had briefly worked in June.

Robert and Nattie were admitted to the Royal Victoria Dock through a giant gate by the hydraulic coal cranes. John Fox was usually to be found on one of the vessels owned by the National Line, for which the boys' father worked, so Robert and Nattie went first to the National's steamer *Spain*. The ship stank of animal flesh, urine and excrement, the main trade of the National Line vessels being the carriage of live cattle from New York to London. Robert asked an officer on the *Spain* whether Fox was on board.

'I don't know,' said Charles Pearson, chief officer of the National steamship *Queen*. 'Go and look. Whose boy are you?'

Robert replied that he was Mr Coombes's son. Pearson knew the older Robert Coombes, having sailed with him on the SS *Holland* out of Liverpool. He asked Robert who wanted Fox.

'The man at the gate,' said Robert.

Pearson turned to Nattie: 'I suppose you are one of Mr Coombes's boys too?' Nattie said that he was.

The brothers went aft in search of Fox. As they could not find him, they decided to try the SS *America*, the only other National Line vessel then moored in London.

The *America* was in the Royal Albert Dock, which lay immediately east of the Royal Victoria, but the scale of the docks was such that it took the boys more than two hours to tramp round one and then the other, past the metal sheds and the pungent tobacco warehouses and the skeletal cranes, round the dockers loading and unloading the cargos. The river alongside was low and sluggish, glittering in the sun.

Many noxious industries that were banned from the centre of London had established themselves on this stretch of the Thames, and a haze of coal dust and smoke hung over the docks. The sour, urinous scent of the Bryant & May match works mingled with the musty caramel of the Tate and the Lyle sugar refineries; with the smells of rotting cow carcasses in the John Knight soap factory; of simmering oranges and strawberries in James Keiller's marmalade and jam works; of boiling bones and offal in Odam's chemical manure works; of bird-droppings at the Guano Works; and with the acrid, stinging chemical vapours of the factories making rubber, caustic soda, sulphuric acid, telegraph wire, dyes, creosote, disinfectant, cables, explosives, poisons and varnish. For weeks there had been no rain to rinse the air.

The boys could not find Fox on the *America*, so they went back to the Victoria Dock to try the *Spain* again. This time Nattie waited outside the gate while Robert approached the dock constable on duty.

'I want to go to the National Line steamer lying just alongside there to see John Fox,' Robert told William Gradley. 'I have an important message to deliver to him, having come from Plaistow.'

Gradley let him through.

'I shall not be long,' said Robert.

At last Robert found Fox on the *Spain*. A short man of forty-five, with a thin moustache and a straggly beard, Fox was wearing a dark, threadbare suit and a peaked sailor's cap. Robert asked him to come to stay with them in Cave Road: their mother had gone suddenly to Liverpool to visit her family, he said, and had left word that she wanted Fox to look after the boys and the house. Robert told Fox that when Emily Coombes returned she would pay him half a crown for each day that he spent at Cave Road – half a crown was 2/6d (an eighth of £1), a decent daily rate for unskilled work. Fox agreed to come. The pair crossed the bridge out of the docks.

'Good night, Bradley,' called Fox to Gradley as they went out through the dock gate; though he had known the dock constable for six years, Fox still hadn't learnt his name.

They joined Nattie and made the journey back to Plaistow.

In the back parlour of 35 Cave Road, Robert reached behind the door and lifted down a dark grey tweed suit belonging to his father.

'Here you are, John,' he said. 'Here's a pair of father's trousers for you. They don't fit him.'

Fox went to the kitchen behind the parlour to put on the suit. He left his old clothes on a stool by the copper cauldron that heated the household's water.

Robert told Fox that his mother had suggested that they pawn the family's watches to raise some money until her return. He asked whether Fox would pledge them on their behalf – pawnbrokers would not take pledges from children.

'I will try if I can,' said Fox.

The boys handed him their watches – Robert's gold and Nattie's silver – and the three went out to Limehouse. They travelled three miles west, crossing the iron bridge over the black waters of Bow Creek, the mouth of the River Lea and the repository of West Ham's untreated sewage.

Limehouse was a Thames-side neighbourhood in the older part of East London, frequented by sailors. Robert and Nattie had lived here until they were nine and eight years old, latterly in a large house in Three Colt Street that their grandparents had owned. In the past few years the district had grown even noisier and more louche. It was a hive of brothels, pubs, Chinese laundries and opium dens.

John Fox visited two pawnbrokers, one for each watch. At George Fish's shop in the Commercial Road the boys waited outside while Fox went in to pledge the American-made gold-plated watch. The manager, William White, had difficulty with the catch, but once Fox had shown him how to open it he offered a ten-shilling loan against the watch's value. He issued a square pasteboard ticket bearing a description of the pawned item, attached a duplicate to the watch and entered in his ledger the name and address that Fox gave him: Robert Coombes, 35 Cave Road. He did not question Fox's identity – this was a transient part of London, where most customers were strangers, and in any case it was common practice for hired 'moppets' to pawn goods on behalf of respectable people who did not wish to advertise their financial troubles. White deducted the halfpenny ticket fee from the loan and gave Fox the remainder. The watch could be redeemed by returning the money with 25 per cent interest within the next three months.

A few doors along, at Ashbridge & Co., Fox tried to get twelve shillings for the silver watch but accepted ten.

Fox handed Robert the pawn tickets and the proceeds – just under twenty shillings, or £1.

'Let us share it between the three of us now,' said Robert.

Robert and Nattie had missed the final day of the Gentlemen v Players fixture at Lord's. The evening papers carried reports of the match (the Players had won by a slender thirty-two runs) as well as the results of the latest games in the nineteenth Wimbledon lawn tennis championships, and the news that the polling dates for a general election had been set. The very unpopular Liberal prime minister, the Earl of Rosebery, had resigned in June, and Parliament had since been dissolved. The polling for a new government would take place over three weeks, starting on 13 July. The date set for the voters of West Ham South and West Ham North to elect their Members of Parliament was the next Monday, 15 July.

At Cave Road on Wednesday evening, Robert fetched a blanket from the back bedroom upstairs, and he, Fox and Nattie went to bed in the back parlour. Fox lay on the floor, as he had done before when staying overnight.

Robert asked Fox if he knew the way to India. Fox said that he did.

In the Jack Wright stories, the young hero takes two comrades on his adventures around the world: Fritz Schneider, a short Dutchman, and Timothy Topstay, a wooden-legged, glass-eyed, tobacco-chewing, whiskery old sailor who has served on merchant ships with Jack's father. John Fox, the former shipmate of Robert and Nattie's father, was now hunkered down with the boys in the back parlour like Tim Topstay hunkered down with Jack and Fritz in the sealed cabin of Jack's electrical submarine.

ALL I KNOW IS THAT WE ARE RICH

Flush with their pawnshop funds, Robert, Nattie and John Fox walked the next morning to William Richards's coffee house, at the junction of Cave Road and the Barking Road. The boys were carrying bamboo fishing rods, having decided to take a trip to the seaside after breakfast. Fox was wearing his new suit. All three entered the coffee house but Nattie stopped in the lobby and, despite Robert's entreaties, refused to come any further.

Mr Richards's place was one of dozens of coffee shops in West Ham, serving coffee and tea, slices of bread and butter, eggs, bacon, chops and steaks. The windows of a coffee shop, described by *Punch* magazine as 'the *restaurant* of poor respectability', were usually decorated with gold lettering, while the interior gleamed with polished wood and brass. The customers – labourers, hansom cab drivers, the lower grade of clerk – sat on benches in wooden stalls, where they could peruse the day's papers as they dined. Mr Richards greeted Robert and Fox, remarking that Fox was looking smart. Fox smiled. He and Robert ordered and ate their breakfast, and then Robert paid the bill with a shilling (12d, or a twentieth of £1) and offered the coffee-house keeper a chunk of cake tobacco. Mr Richards said he did not smoke but Robert left the tobacco on the table anyway. He and Fox collected Nattie from the lobby, crossed the road to a fruiterers, and set out on their excursion to Southend-on-Sea.

The nearest seaside town to London, Southend lay at the mouth of the Thames forty miles east of West Ham. In the eighteenth century the highwayman (and penny dreadful hero) Dick Turpin had smuggled goods to Plaistow from Southend. The town was now a favourite destination for the London working classes: they steamed down to the coast by train or boat on Sunday school excursions, works outings and bank holiday beanos. A record 35,000 people had travelled by rail to Southend for the Whit bank holiday in June. The train from central London, which cost 2/6d for the round trip, called at Plaistow and West Ham stations, while the *London Belle* steamship sailed from Woolwich, across the river from the Victoria and Albert docks, at 10.15 each morning.

John Fox, Robert and Nattie reached Southend at about noon. The sun was hot and the sky blue. They walked through the Pier Hill fairground, which boasted a steam-powered 'razzle-dazzle' (an aerial platform that tilted as it turned), a merry-go-round, swing boats, coconut shies, and stalls selling shrimps, oysters and cockles. The famous iron pier, completed five years earlier, stretched a mile and a half out to sea. Just inside its stuccoed entrance was a pavilion, at which Little Elsie the Skirt Dancer would twirl her silk robes at that evening's show, and an electric train that carried visitors to the pier head. At low tide a vast bed of mud stretched beneath the promenade decking; at high tide the water lapped at the pier's pillars, and yachts danced close by on the waves. The boys cast their fishing lines into the sea.

Robert told Fox they would all three of them soon sail away to some place.

'What place?' asked Fox.

'Some island,' said Robert.

Almost exactly twelve months earlier, Robert had visited Southend to see the most notorious murderer of recent years.

Robert was a pupil at Stock Street school in Plaistow when he read of the killing of Florence Dennis, a twenty-three-year-old dressmaker whose body had been found pressed into the mud by a brook just outside Southend on 24 June 1894. She had been shot through the head and had fallen to the ground still clasping her straw hat in one hand; the post mortem revealed that she was eight months pregnant. James Canham Read, a thirty-seven-year-old employee of the Royal Albert Dock, was immediately identified as the chief suspect: he had been seen twice with Florence in Southend that weekend.

Read, who had lived in East London for nearly twenty years, was known around the docks as a responsible and educated family man. He earned more than £150 a year as a cashier and was entrusted with paying out some £2,000 a day to the Albert Dock's labourers and to the lightermen who ferried goods by barge from the ships to the quays. A slim, fastidious figure with a dark moustache, he was fond of reading, and had set up a library when he worked in the Victoria Dock. He lived with his wife and eight children in Jamaica Street, Stepney, just west of Limehouse.

On the day that Florence Dennis's body was discovered Read went on the run, taking with him more than £100 from his office at the dock. Crowds gathered outside his house in Jamaica Street and hollered abuse at his family. The local and national papers reported avidly on the hunt for the fugitive.

After a fortnight, the police tracked Read down to a village south-west of London, where he was living under a false name with yet another woman. He had been leading a triple life, and it seemed that he had killed Florence Dennis because she had threatened to expose him and so to collapse the walls between his several selves. The 'lower-middle-class Lothario', as *The Times* described him, was taken by train to Southend to be arraigned.

The news of Read's arrest spread fast. By the time he and his police guards reached Southend in the evening of 7 July, scores of people were waiting beside the railway. They ran after the cab that drove Read to the police station.

When Robert learned of Read's arrest, he slipped away from his house and set off for Southend. He had two shillings for the train fare, which was enough to take him only as far as Grays, a village on the Thames twenty miles east of London. He walked the remaining twenty miles to Southend, stopping to catch some sleep under a hedge by the roadside.

At 11 a.m. on Monday 9 July, Read appeared before a magistrate in the courthouse by the police station, just off the main road between Southend railway station and the pier. Hundreds of people pressed in to the court or stood outside looking up at the windows, hooting and whistling.

Read wore a light tweed suit and a white straw hat. He affected a nonchalant air, approaching the dock with a quick and elastic step and then calmly denying the murder charge. The magistrate remanded him for trial at Chelmsford, Essex.

When Read was tried for murder in November, he again displayed uncanny control of his emotions – his 'command of himself' was 'simply marvellous', said the *Pall Mall Gazette*. He continued to protest his innocence, and his brother Harry provided an alibi, but the circumstantial evidence against him was very strong. James Canham Read was found guilty of murder on 15 November. He walked jauntily out of the courthouse, stopping to shake hands with people who had assembled outside, and stepped gaily up the steps of the prison van.

Few doubted Read's guilt, observed the *Evening News*, but his 'nerve', his 'cool, yet daring' demeanour and his 'keen and bright intelligence' won the admiration of many: the crowd seemed to feel 'an inclination to cheer him'. Harry Read followed him out of the court – he was 'obviously shaken', said the paper, 'but behaved with wonderful fortitude, showing of what stuff these two remarkable brothers are made'. A peculiar heroism had attached itself to the pair. On 4 December 1894, James Canham Read was hanged. In his will, he left nothing to his wife or children but instead bequeathed everything to the brother who had tried to protect him. Harry drowned in the Regent's Canal in East London the next year, apparently in a drunken accident.

James Canham Read was refined, calculating, ruthless, with a compulsion to possess and control women even if it meant killing them. In his smooth composure, he resembled both the villains and the heroes in the penny dreadfuls that Robert liked to read. The killer in *The Bogus Broker's Right Bower*, a New York crime story in Robert's collection, had 'a coolness somewhat remarkable even in a murderer'. The detective on his track is 'the coolest and best prepared ferret', 'a fox with nerves of steel'. Mora, the villainess, is the chilliest of all: 'Everything depends on coolness and holding on with bull dog tenacity,' she says. 'I am still Mora, the Cool.' Mora acts with icy precision even as her gypsy blood boils. Her coolness is a capacity, the ability to have two faces and to hide one from the world.

In the five days after their trip to Southend, the Coombes brothers amused themselves by playing cricket with John Fox in the back yard, and cards at the parlour table. They visited the Balaam Street recreation ground, a park near their house that had opened the previous summer. It contained a pond on which children could sail toy boats, a raised stand on which a brass band performed each week, lawns and ornamental flower gardens. The boys of Plaistow also played in the streets, as they had before the park opened, sometimes in small gangs known as 'clicks'. Robert would take his bat out for a game of cricket, wedging a stump between the stones on the pavement opposite the house. Football was popular with the local boys, as were games of knocking down ginger (rapping on people's doors and then running away), pitch and toss (a gambling game), leapfrog, and 'robbers and thieves'. Nattie continued to skip school.

Though Plaistow was a crowded working-class suburb, it was bordered by fields and marshland. Just over the wall at the end of the Coombes family's yard was a large market garden. From the front of the house on a clear day, you could see across the marshes and the river to the hills of Kent. The German writer H. A. Volckers had strolled up to the neighbourhood from the docks one summer Sunday in 1886, approaching through the fields directly south of Cave Road. 'The country was all level, with ditches of water running through,' he reported, 'and on each side was the smooth roads; fields, containing fine grass; sleek, fat cows, calves, and horses feeding on them; acres of land with onions, young turnips, lettuce, rhubarb, &c.' In Plaistow, Volckers passed a crowd listening to members of the Peculiar People sect sing 'Jerusalem, my happy home' and another group following a Salvation Army drum and flute band down the street. Many middle-class visitors to West Ham recoiled at the repeating streets, the level, dingy, narrow vistas, the shabby men and women herding themselves into trams like cattle; but on this sunny afternoon, the German traveller was struck by the rosy cheeks of the children, and the abundance of carnations, roses and geraniums filling the pots on the windowsills of the neat little houses.

Fox and the boys occasionally ate out, but they usually dined off food prepared by Robert. As the eldest son in a family without daughters, Robert had learned to be handy about the house; he was not only accustomed to 'boys' jobs' (fetching coal, laying the fire, emptying the privy in the yard) but also to washing, cooking and cleaning. The ground floor of 35 Cave Road was supplied with gas and running water, and the kitchen was equipped with a coal-powered iron range. Robert took deliveries from the tradesmen who called at the house, asking them to leave the usual quantities and paying them for the goods; he baked sausage rolls and jam tarts with a batch of flour that his mother had ordered; he washed his clothes and hung them to dry on a line over the fireplace. He and Nattie also had to feed the family's cats and an American mocking bird named Bill.

Each evening, Fox smoked his pipe and Robert smoked cigarettes. There was no age restriction on who could purchase tobacco, despite public concern about the number of boy smokers, and it was possible to buy a box of five 'fags' for a penny; rolling tobacco was cheaper still.

The trio continued to use the back parlour as their bed-room, though on the night after their trip to Southend, Robert suggested to Fox that he sleep in the back room upstairs. Robert and Nattie went up with him and, while Fox was pre-paring the bed, Robert unlocked the door to their mother's bedroom and went in for a couple of minutes. Nattie waited outside. The boys then went down to their usual berths in the back parlour.

Robert set about devising fresh money-raising schemes. On Saturday he wrote a letter for Fox to take to the National Line offices at the Albert Dock. Fox delivered the letter to John Hewson, the company's chief cashier, at about noon. Hewson, who was sixty-four, lived in the relatively well-to-do West Ham district of Forest Gate, north of Plaistow. He was responsible for paying Robert's father's wages, and was able to hand out cash advances. A distinguished-looking man with a long nose and a white beard, Hewson was known to be tender-hearted. When an overladen National Line vessel disappeared on its way from New York to London in 1889, with seventy-four seamen aboard, the distraught wives of the missing men turned up at the company offices in the City, pleading for an advance on their husbands' wages. They were treated harshly by everyone except Hewson. 'He was kind and said he was sorry for us,' one woman told an MP inquiring into the case: 'he was troubled for us; the rest were angry with us for coming to the office.'

In his office at the Albert Dock, Hewson read Robert's letter.

'Dear Sir,' it ran. 'Will you please advance the sum of four pounds as my mother is very ill with heart disease and will have to pay a heavy docters bill. Will you plese bring it your-self or give it to John Fox. I remain, Yours truly, R Coombes.'

Despite his good nature, Hewson was suspicious. Robert had once before obtained money from him under false pre-tences. He handed the letter back to Fox, saying he would not believe it unless he were provided with a doctor's cer-tificate. Fox pocketed the letter and went back to Cave Road with the news.

On learning that this plan had failed, Robert asked Fox to pawn his mandolin. Robert was as fond of playing music as he was of reading, and the mandolin was a treasured posses-sion. Between eight and nine o'clock in the evening, Fox took the instrument to another pawnbroker, this one much closer to home: Richard Bourne's shop, opposite the railway station on Plaistow High Street. When the broker observed that there was no key to fasten the mandolin's case, Fox said that the case would close securely without being locked. Bourne advanced him five shillings. This time Fox gave the name Nathaniel Coombes, along with the address 35 Cave Road.

The boys and Fox spent much of Sunday in the back yard. The weather had cooled off a little but was still bright and dry, with more than nine hours of sunshine. Fox, wearing Mr Coombes's jacket, trousers and waistcoat, played his harmonica, breaking off to chat with James Robertson of number 37 over the garden fence. Robert and Nattie shot at each other with toy bows and arrows. They grew so noisy that Fox warned them that if they didn't pipe down he would report them to their mother when she got back.

Cowboy and Indian games were popular among English boys. Robert's penny dreadful collection included a reprint of an American 'dime novel' about Buffalo Bill, as the famous bison hunter and showman William F. Cody was known. For six months in 1892, when Robert was ten, Cody had staged a Wild West extravaganza at Earl's Court in London, with a herd of horses and a troupe of Red Indians. According to the stories, the young Buffalo Billy was marked out by pluck, endurance, nerve, a restless urge for adventure. He was loyal and honourable – he tended to his wounded comrades, gave his widowed mother the money he earned by driving cattle – but could be ruthless in a crisis. On one occasion he got into a fight with a boy who had set him up for a humiliating whipping at school. Since the bigger boy was getting the better of him, Billy drew a pocket knife, opened the blade with his teeth, drove it into his enemy's side, and left him for dead.

Over the weekend, the election campaigning in West Ham South gathered pace. The incumbent Member of Parliament, James Keir Hardie of the Independent Labour Party, led a parade through the streets on Saturday, with marching bands and banners. At an evening meeting at the public hall in the Barking Road, the socialist playwright George Bernard Shaw gave a speech in support of Keir Hardie, and an organ belted out rousing tunes. 'Glory, glory hallelujah,' the people sang, 'Keir Hardie's marching on.'

The constituency had recently acquired a reputation for radicalism. In a famous strike of 1889, the dockers of West Ham had succeeded in securing a minimum rate of 6d an hour, and when Keir Hardie was elected MP in 1892 West Ham South had become the first Independent Labour seat in the country. A long-haired, wild-eyed Scottish miner, Hardie told his followers that he would use the state 'to lift the weary load which is crushing the heart and life, and beauty and joy out of the common people'. He was able, according to a supporter, to make the workers 'feel that there is sunshine somewhere if they could but come at it'. But a rise in unemployment in 1894 had been worsened by a harsh winter of fogs, ice and snow, when parts of the Thames froze over and many of the yards were forced to close. In 1895 some 10,000 men in West Ham were without work, and the district was poorer than ever. Many blamed Lord Rosebery's Liberal government, which Keir Hardie's party had supported, for failing to relieve the people's plight.

There were more radical elements in West Ham even than Keir Hardie. Earlier in July a local anarchist called Edward Leggatt had been prosecuted for travelling second class on the railway while carrying a third-class ticket. 'I only recognise one class,' proclaimed Leggatt, 'namely, the working class, who produce all the wealth of the world, and are therefore the only useful class, and the only class entitled to ride.' Given the choice of a fine or fourteen days in prison, Leggatt said: 'I'll do the fourteen days – long live Anarchy, and to hell with the Government!' Some anarchists took more lethal action: in 1894 an activist had accidentally blown himself up while trying to bomb the Greenwich Observatory, across the river from West Ham.

At 8 a.m. on Monday 15 July the polls opened in the twin constituencies of West Ham South and West Ham North and the men of the borough began to turn out to elect their MPs – an Act of 1884 had extended the vote to all men who lived in a property worth £10 or more. A donkey traipsed up and down Balaam Street bearing placards that urged voters to support Major George Banes, the Tory candidate, while a bricklayer brandished a hod and shovel adorned with portraits of Keir Hardie. The right-wing *Evening News*, encouraging its readers to drive the Liberals and radicals out of London, appealed directly to the labourers of Canning Town: 'West Ham Workers – Attention! the late Liberal government refused to place any of the recent naval contracts at the Thames Iron Works, Canning Town, although there was exceptional distress there through slack trade.' The local publicans also supported the Conservatives, who had promised not to interfere with the licensing laws. Some of the owners of the 'boozing shops' near the docks were charging a penny for three shots of whisky and a threepenny cigar, then bundling their customers into vehicles provided by the Tories to ferry voters to the polling stations.

While Nattie went to play in the Balaam Street park, Robert made his way to the Albert Dock to try to persuade John Hewson to give him some money. He took with him an old doctor's certificate, from which he had torn off the date in the top corner – 20 March 1895 – in the hope that Hewson would accept it as new. The sharper villains in Robert's penny dreadfuls were adept at forging and altering documents: 'I am an extra good penman, you know,' boasts the Irish master criminal Captain Murphy in Robert's novelette *Joe Phoenix's Unknown*, 'and by means of a little dextrous use of chemicals it will be easy for me to take out the original numbers of the bonds, or shares, and put in others.'

Robert placed the certificate on Hewson's desk and waited as he read it: 'I certify that Mrs Emily Coombes of 35 Cave Rd is under my care,' read Hewson. 'She is suffering from an internal complaint and still remains in a very weak state. JJ Griffin MD.'

Hewson told Robert that he would come later to Cave Road to visit Mrs Coombes.

'Will you bring the money with you?' asked Robert.

'I'll see,' said Hewson. He put the letter in his file.

Robert again looked in on his mother's room that day, then locked the door and gave Nattie the key. 'Keep the key,' he said. Nattie put the key in the back parlour. Robert told Nattie that he was going to write a letter to their father. He sat at the table, with a blotting pad, paper, pen and ink, and proceeded to do so. 'Dear Pa,' Robert wrote,

> I am very sorry to iform you that me ma has hert her hands. You no that sore on her finger it has spread out all over her hands and is unable to write to you. Just before I had writen in this letter a bill from Mr Greenaways come and Ma had to pay it. Mr Griffin also had charged a heavy doctors bill. Ma said will you please send her home a dollar or two. We are all very well and Ma's hand Improving. Ma was offered four pounds for bill the mocking bird. I enclose the bill and hopeing you are very well. I remain, Your loving son, R Coombes.

Robert folded the letter and put it in an envelope with a £1 8/6d bill from the Limehouse tailor Isaac Greenaway & Sons. The tailor's bill, dated 10 July, detailed the costs of repairing a jacket, fitting the same jacket with a fur collar, and purchasing a waistcoat and a pair of fancy Scotch grey trousers.

Robert also wrote a letter to the *Evening News*, the best-selling evening paper in London. Its edition of 15 November 1894, which carried the first reports of James Canham Read's conviction for murder, had sold close to 400,000 copies – a world record, the paper claimed. The *Evening News* was pitched at the respectable and conservative working classes who populated the Plaistow end of West Ham South, while poorer, more dissident types prevailed in Canning Town and the other riverside districts.

'Sir,' wrote Robert to the editor, 'Will you please be kind enough to place my advertisement in the *Evening News* for 1 week. I send the money in stamps.' The newspaper's classified section promised that an advertisement could be placed for the price of a telegram – that is, sixpence for twelve words and half a penny for each additional word. Robert's notice read: 'Wanted £30 for 6 months will pay £6 a month by instalments. Write to RC 35 Cave Rd Barking Rd Plaistow E.'

Robert had modelled the wording on similar ads that had appeared in the paper's columns: '£2 wanted privately for 2 months at 10 per cent interest', announced 'F' of Kensington on 4 July. Robert was asking for a bigger loan and a longer period to pay it back, and in return was offering a generous interest rate of 20 per cent. He addressed the letter to the newspaper's offices near Fleet Street.

At about six o'clock in the evening of 15 July, Robert and Nattie's aunt Emily called round to see her sister-in-law. Emily was a dark-haired woman of thirty-eight, whose husband, Nathaniel, was a younger brother of Robert and Nattie's father. He worked as a greengrocer, as his father had before him, but in the depression of the early 1890s was struggling to make ends meet. The couple lived with their seventeen-year-old daughter a mile north-east of Cave Road, in another of the terraces that had been built on the marshland in the past two decades, as regular as if they had been punched out on a production line.

Emily brought with her a friend called Mary Jane Burrage, who was also a friend of her sister-in-law. Mrs Burrage, a thick-set woman of forty-five, was married to the chief butcher on the SS *Ionic*, a White Star liner that ferried sheep to

England from New Zealand. Like Robert and Nattie's father, George Burrage had sailed with the National ships out of the Liverpool docks until moving to West Ham with his family in the 1880s to work on vessels based in East London.

When Aunt Emily knocked at 35 Cave Road, John Fox came to the door and opened it a few inches. Emily had never seen Fox before. She noticed that he was wearing her brother-in-law's best churchgoing suit, which she had herself brushed and put away after its purchase six weeks earlier. She nudged her foot across the threshold and asked for Mrs Coombes. Fox told her that she was not in. He kept the door almost closed, as if to stop Emily seeing into the house.

'Where is she?' asked Emily.

'She is out,' replied Fox.

Emily pressed him: 'I am her sister-in-law and I want to know where she has gone to.'

Fox replied that Mrs Coombes had gone to her sister's in Liverpool, for a holiday.

Emily observed that it was funny that her sister-in-law had not mentioned this to her, at which Fox pushed the door shut. She and Mrs Burrage were turning away to leave when they saw Robert and Nattie running towards them. The boys had been playing in the park. Nattie stopped at the gate but Robert came forward to greet his aunt. Emily asked him where his Ma was.

'She has gone to Liverpool, auntie,' he replied. 'A rich aunt has died and left us a lot of money and all that I know is that we are rich.' Then Robert started back towards the recreation ground.

Aunt Emily remarked to Mrs Burrage that it was unkind of her sister-in-law to go away without mentioning it to her. Robert reappeared with some other boys and called to Nattie, who ran after him. Aunt Emily and Mrs Burrage gave up and made their way home.

That evening, a girl from Cave Road called on Aunt Emily at her house in Boleyn Road, East Ham. The girl said that she had been sent by her mother, who had noticed an unpleasant smell at number 35 and did not think that all was right.

There was no running water when Robert and Nattie got home from the park. At 5 p.m. the East London Water Company had shut off West Ham's supply without warning; the reserves were so low that the company had decided to open its taps for only two and a half hours a day. East London slowly became suffused with the smell of unflushed drains.

As the polling deadline of 8 p.m. approached, boisterous crowds assembled near the public hall at the southern end of the Barking Road, hooting and cheering the last men to cast their votes for West Ham South's MP. In the course of the evening the crowd moved north to Stratford to hear the borough's results, along roads lit by gas lamps, past the glowing lanterns of the pubs and the wild flares of the oil lamps on the costermongers' stalls. By 11 p.m. about 20,000 people had congregated outside the ornate town hall on Stratford Broadway, bringing the traffic to a standstill. When a tram tried to drive through, the crowd scattered, some people running into the front line of constables who had been sent to keep order. The policemen retaliated with punches, while the mounted patrols rode their horses into the mass of men and women. Rather than fight back, the residents of West Ham launched into a rendition of 'Rule Britannia', singing out that 'Britons never, never, never shall be slaves'.

At midnight, the candidates for West Ham South and West Ham North appeared on the balcony of the town hall for the reading of the results. It was announced that the Tory contender for West Ham South, Major Banes, had secured 4,750 votes to Labour's 3,975: he had beaten Keir Hardie, the dockers' champion. The Liberal incumbent for West Ham North had also been ousted from his seat by the Conservative challenger.

Keir Hardie made his way back to Canning Town to thank his supporters, thousands of whom had gathered outside the Labour Party's central committee room in the Barking Road. 'Tomorrow,' he told them, 'when the news reaches a hundred thousand workmen's homes, there will be a feeling as if something has gone out of their lives.' Yet he urged his supporters not to lose heart: they would win through one day. 'Good night, lads!' he said. Many of the men in the street broke down in tears.

The local publicans celebrated the Tory win with a triumphant display of fireworks and coloured lights.

3

I WILL TELL YOU THE TRUTH

As the milkman left his delivery on the doorstep of 35 Cave Road early in the morning of Wednesday 17 July, he noticed a particularly horrid smell emanating from the building. He informed the neighbours, who again sent word to the boys' aunt in Boleyn Road.

Aunt Emily turned up at 35 Cave Road at 9 a.m. No one answered when she knocked, so she collected Mary Jane Burrage from her home in New City Road, on the other side of the Barking Road, and at 10 a.m. they once more tried Emily Coombes's front door. Since there was still no reply, the two women decided to call on Robert and Nattie's grandmother in Bow, west of Plaistow, to see if she knew what was going on.

The seventy-four-year-old Mary Coombes lived on the edge of Bow Cemetery in a two-up, two-down terraced house almost identical to the homes of her elder sons in Plaistow. She shared the house with her unmarried son, Frederick, and her widowed daughter, Ann. She also owned several

properties in Limehouse that had been left to her by her husband upon his death in 1882. Aunt Emily asked her if she
knew the whereabouts of her other daughter-in-law Emily,
whom they had 'lost'. The older Mrs Coombes said that she
had no idea where she was. Emily assured her that they would
find the missing woman that day.

Mary Jane Burrage sent a telegram to Mary Macy, the older
sister of Robert and Nattie's mother, and that same morning
received in reply a telegram from Liverpool stating that Emily
was not there. Robert and Nattie's uncle Nathaniel tried the
Cave Road house himself, then went to look for the boys in
the recreation ground. He could not find them.

At 1.20 p.m., Aunt Emily and Mary Jane Burrage banged
again at the door of 35 Cave Road. Mrs Burrage had brought
along her youngest son, James, a boy of Robert's age. At first
there was no reply, but at their second knock Robert opened
the door. Emily pushed past him, followed by the Burrages, and
marched through to the back of the house. Robert, Nattie and
Fox had been playing cards – Nattie scrambled them up when he
saw his aunt. He rose to his feet but Fox stayed in his chair, smoking a pipe. A strong smell of tobacco permeated the room.

Emily asked Robert where his Ma was.

'She is with Mrs Cooper,' Robert said. 'I will take you to
see her.'

'No,' said Emily. 'Your Ma is in this house, and I won't go
away until a policeman comes.'

'All right,' said Robert.

On hearing his aunt's warning, Nattie climbed out of the
back parlour window and ran for the market gardens beyond
the yard.

Emily asked Robert whether she could go into his mother's
room.

'No,' he said. 'It is locked.'

She asked him where the key was, and he replied that he did not know.

'All right,' she said. 'I will burst open the door.'

Mrs Burrage said to Robert: 'Your mother is lying dead in that room upstairs.'

'No, she isn't, Mrs Burrage,' said Robert. 'She's in Liverpool.'

'I don't believe it,' said Mrs Burrage.

She and Aunt Emily went upstairs, but when they tried to force the door found that it would not give. They sent someone to fetch a spare key from the landlady. The key was brought, and Aunt Emily opened the door to the bedroom. There she saw the form of a woman, lying on the bed, the face covered by a sheet and a pillow. Overcome by the smell of rotting flesh, she drew back and sent Mary Jane Burrage and her son to find a policeman.

Now that the bedroom door was open, the stench spread swiftly through the house. At 1.30 p.m. Harriet Hayward, of 39 Cave Road, approached the front door and bent to peer through the frosted glass panels to see if she could spy the boys in the passage. She was startled by the smell issuing from the letter box. The day was becoming intensely hot. A black cloud of blowflies hovered at the upstairs windows. Mrs Hayward hurried away to fetch Mrs Robertson from number 37. 'Come and have a smell,' she urged her.

The Burrages found Constable Robert Twort in Greengate Street, a block away from Cave Road. A single man of twenty-four, Twort lived as well as worked at the Barking Road police depot. He was dressed in a high-collared dark navy woollen tunic with his number on the collar (686K), high-waisted fishtail trousers and a domed helmet. He carried a truncheon, a pen and notebook and a whistle. Twort went straight to the house with the Burrages. Aunt Emily showed him upstairs.

In the front bedroom, PC Twort turned down the sheet and lifted the pillow to reveal a woman's body, severely decomposed and swarming with maggots. He saw a knife on the bed and a truncheon on the floor. He sent word to the police station, asking for an inspector and the divisional surgeon to come to the house at once.

Aunt Emily approached the bed and looked at her sister-in-law's body, but the face was so disfigured that she could not recognise her. She returned to the back parlour, where Robert was standing by the window. Fox was sitting on a chair between the door and the dresser.

'You are a bad, wicked boy,' she told Robert. 'You knew your Ma was dead in the room and you ought to have told me.'

'Auntie,' he replied. 'Come to me and I will tell you the truth and tell you all about it.'

His aunt went towards him.

'Ma gave Nattie a hiding on Saturday for stealing some food,' said Robert, 'and she said, "I will give you one too." Nattie said: "I will stab her. No, I can't do it, Bob, but will you do it? When I cough twice, you do it." I did do it.'

Emily asked him if his mother was awake at the time.

'Yes,' he said. 'She was lying with a hand over her face.'

'Did your Ma cry?'

'She did not cry nor speak. I covered her up and afterwards went away to Lord's cricket ground.'

Emily asked at what time he had killed his mother.

'About a quarter to four on the Monday morning,' said Robert, 'a week ago. I slept with Ma that night and I kicked about a great deal, and she punched me. Nattie was in his room. I did it by myself.'

She asked how he had killed her.

'I got out of bed and I stabbed her,' said Robert. 'Nattie was in the back room, and coughed twice, and that was when I done it, when Nattie coughed. I did it with a knife, and it is on the bed.'

Mrs Hayward of 39 Cave Road had by now come in to number 35, taken a quick look at the corpse on the bed upstairs and then joined the party in the back parlour. She addressed John Fox.

'What, you John!' Mrs Hayward said. 'You have been here all this time. Didn't you know what was going on?'

'No, missus,' he replied. 'I know nothing about it. The boys fetched me from the ship.'

Robert said: 'No, Mrs Hayward. John knows nothing about it. I did it.'

'You bad boy,' said Harriet Hayward.

Aunt Emily asked him the whereabouts of his father's gold watch.

'I have pawned it,' said Robert. 'I got Fox to do it. I'll give you the ticket.' He took the pawn tickets from a bookshelf on the parlour wall and was about to hand them to her when Twort came into the room. On discovering a murder, a policeman was meant to keep close watch on the body until relieved by another officer, but Twort had found the smell so overpowering that he had remained upstairs for only five minutes.

Aunt Emily told the constable that her nephew had been making a confession to her. Twort cautioned Robert and then asked him to repeat what he had told his aunt. As Robert spoke, Twort took notes in his book.

'I did it,' Robert began. 'My brother Nattie got a hiding for stealing some food, and Ma was going to give me one. So Nattie said that he would stab her, but as he could not do it himself he asked me to do it. He said, "When I cough twice, you do it." He coughed twice, and I did it. I am sorry that I did it. I did it with a knife, which I left on the bed. I covered her up and left her.'

Twort asked where Nattie was. 'I think he has gone to Woolwich,' said Robert, 'as we were going there this afternoon.' Woolwich was across the Thames from the Victoria and Albert docks, a short ride on a free ferry.

Twort turned to John Fox and asked what he was doing in the house. Fox said that he had been there since Wednesday. He added: 'I do not know nothing what has taken place.'

At 2 p.m., Police Sergeant Henry Baulch, a married man of thirty, also from the Barking Road station, knocked at the door of 35 Cave Road. Mrs Hayward let him in as she left the house. Aunt Emily and Twort met him in the passage and took him through to the back parlour.

Robert repeated his confession to the sergeant: 'My brother, Nattie, said he would kill mother, as she had given him a hiding for stealing food. He then asked me to do it. Nattie then said, "When I cough twice, you stab mother with the knife", which I did. We then went to a cricket match at Lord's and have slept in the house ever since.' Robert gave Baulch four pawnbrokers' duplicates: those for the watches and the mandolin, and another for an item that his mother had pawned before her death.

'I took the property,' Robert told him, 'and gave it to Fox to pledge.'

'Yes,' Fox said, 'Robert gave it to me and I pawned it.' Twort told Fox that he must accompany him to the station. He led him away.

Baulch stayed in the house with Robert until the police surgeon, Alfred Kennedy, showed up at about 3 p.m. When Dr Kennedy went upstairs to examine the body, Baulch took Robert to the police station at 386 Barking Road.

Meanwhile, other constables were hunting for Nattie. At five o'clock he was found on Tunmarsh Lane, a route to the Plaistow marshes only minutes from his home. PC George Hardy asked him: 'Is your name Coombes?'

'Yes,' said Nattie. 'I didn't kill my mother. It was my brother who did it when I was in bed.'

'You will have to come with me to the station,' said Hardy.

At the police station, Detective Inspector George Mellish charged Robert Allen Coombes and Nathaniel George Coombes with murder, and John Fox with being an accessory after the fact. Fox was very nervous, jerking his head, looking round him wildly. The boys were calm and said nothing. They were all locked in cells.

Mellish, forty-five, was a member of Scotland Yard's Criminal Investigation Department, and had worked for fifteen years for the K division, which covered West Ham and Limehouse. He lived north of Plaistow with his wife and eight children. At 5.15 p.m., he left the police station with Inspector George Gilbert, of the Barking Road branch, to survey the crime scene at 35 Cave Road.

The inspectors examined the corpse of Emily Harrison Coombes. Her body was on the left-hand side of the bed and inclined slightly to the left. She was dressed in a chemise, a petticoat, drawers and stockings – on the night of her death she had gone to bed in her underwear rather than a nightdress. There were two gaping wounds near her heart, each about an inch and a half deep. These were infested by maggots, and maggots had also destroyed her thighs, calves and genitals, her eyes and her nose. Her chemise and bedclothes were stained with dried blood. A blood-soaked 'diaper' – a cloth of fine white fabric with a raised diamond pattern – was lying on the left-hand side of the bed, near the washstand. The maggots had wriggled across the bedclothes and dropped on to the floor.

The police discovered a bloodied wedding ring and two purses on the bed. The leather purse was empty. The white purse, a seaside souvenir constructed from two shells joined by a hinge, contained four threepenny pieces and two foreign coins. Elsewhere in the bedroom were an empty jewel case and a quantity of loose jewellery: a gold bracelet, a brooch, shirt studs, two more wedding rings, a pair of silver earrings. The chest of drawers had been ransacked and its contents strewn on the floor. On top of the chest was a pawnbroker's ticket and a locked cash box with a smashed base.

In the back parlour downstairs the police found Robert's collection of penny dreadfuls, which they gathered up as evidence. They also discovered the key to Emily Coombes's bedroom, tucked under a sofa cushion, and the torn-off date of the medical certificate that Robert had shown John Hewson. From the scullery they took a boy's flannelette nightshirt, which had been hanging on a line over the fireplace, as well as two full-size blue serge jackets, a pair of serge trousers and a waistcoat.

On a table they found three unsent letters on a blotting pad, two by Robert (to his father and to the *Evening News*) and one by his mother, written to her husband on the day before she died. They found the rent book – paid up to 8 July, but missing the 15 July payment – as well as an IOU for £5 and a post office savings book with a balance of £35. Robert's father had left £10 in cash to tide the family over during his five-to-six-week absence, of which the boys had spent about £7 in ten days.

There was a knife on the bed in the front bedroom, as Robert had said. Mellish and Gilbert saw the truncheon on the bedroom floor, as well as an empty revolver in the front parlour and a new hatchet in the back bedroom. They thought that the truncheon might have been kept as protection against intruders, or as a stick to pound washing. The presence of the gun was unexplained – perhaps it was a souvenir brought back from America by Robert and Nattie's father, like the silver watch and the mocking bird. The hatchet was probably used to chop wood; the police inspectors thought that this one might also have hacked open the cash box in the bedroom.

Inspectors Mellish and Gilbert summoned an undertaker to transfer Emily Coombes's corpse to a coffin shell and transport it to the public mortuary on the Barking Road.

PART II

THE CITY OF THE DAMNED

4

THE MACHINE AND THE ABYSS

Robert, Nattie and John Fox stayed overnight in the Barking Road police cells and on Thursday morning were taken to the magistrates' court in Stratford for a preliminary hearing. The courthouse in West Ham Lane had been built eleven years earlier to designs by the architect also responsible for the Stratford town hall, which was next door, and the Barking Road public hall and library. It was a three-storey yellow-brick building, Italianate in style and adorned with Portland stone carvings of the Royal Arms. There was no separate court for young defendants. Though both Robert and Nattie were children – defined by the Children's Act of 1889 as a boy under fourteen or a girl under sixteen – they were considered criminally responsible if they could tell right from wrong, and would be tried in the same way as adults.

A huge crowd had assembled outside the courthouse. The *Sun*, a Liberal halfpenny paper, observed that the excitement generated by the recent election in West Ham 'had given place to an excitement of a very different kind'. The court opened when the district's stipendiary magistrate, Ernest Baggallay, reached Stratford from his home in Kensington, an affluent neighbourhood near the centre of London. 'West Ham Police-Court depends for its opening on whether Mr Baggallay has caught his train or not,' said the radical evening paper the *Star*. 'To-day it was half-past eleven before he arrived to deal with public business.' The police cleared him a path through the crowd.

Baggallay had accepted the position of salaried magistrate for West Ham eight years earlier, after surrendering his seat as Conservative MP for Brixton, south London. He was a slender, moustachioed man of forty-five, neatly turned out, who leant forward pertly in his seat as he heard the cases brought before him. He was sometimes dismissive of witnesses. In Canning Town police court that week, he had listened to two women testify against a neighbour accused of having neglected and beaten three of his children. One woman told the court that the children had come to her starving, saying that their father was giving them no food; the other said that she had heard the father knocking them against the wall. Baggallay was impatient with their testimony. 'Let us have the doctor's evidence,' he suggested. 'These women do so exaggerate.' The doctor confirmed that he had treated members of the defendant's family for bruises and black eyes. An engine driver then testified to having heard the children screaming and begging for mercy. Even after this, Baggallay declined to find against the accused. Despite the passage of the Children's Act, which made it possible to prosecute a parent for neglect or cruelty and even to remove a child from his or her family, many magistrates were reluctant to intervene in such matters. Corporal punishment was commonplace, and the popular presumption remained that a parent's authority over a child was close to sacrosanct.

Fox, Nattie and Robert were led into the courtroom together. Fox slouched towards the dock in Mr Coombes's grey suit, which looked several sizes too large for him. Robert walked in coolly and stood upright in white flannel trousers, brown boots and a blue tennis jacket braided with gold. Nattie also held himself erect, but was so small that he could barely see over the dock's top rail. He wore knickerbockers and a light tweed jacket. Both boys stood with their hands clasped behind their backs, as they had been taught to do at school. Their father was not present: the older Robert Coombes was halfway across the Atlantic, unaware that his wife was dead and his sons were in court for her murder.

The law barred defendants from testifying, but since Fox, Robert and Nattie had no legal representation they were entitled to question the witnesses that Baggallay called. The first was Alfred Kennedy, forty-eight, the police surgeon who had visited Cave Road on Wednesday. He had run a practice since the 1870s in Balaam Street, and he served as surgeon for the K division of the Metropolitan Police. After the doctor's evidence about the condition of the corpse, Baggallay turned to Fox and asked: 'Fox, do you wish to ask the witness any questions?'

Fox stammered softly, 'All I know is . . .' and tailed off.

'Well,' said Baggallay, 'you need not make a statement; nothing is said about you by the witness. The same applies to you boys. The witness simply refers to what he found.' Alfred Kennedy then left the courtroom for the mortuary, where he was due to conduct the post-mortem on Emily Coombes's body.

Aunt Emily gave her evidence. She said that she had last visited her sister-in-law on Saturday 6 July, and had arranged to see her again two days later. On Monday, she said, she knocked several times at the door of 35 Cave Road but received no reply – this was the first day on which Robert and Nattie were at Lord's. She related how she had tried the house again the following Monday, when Fox opened the door to her, and how she finally forced her way in on Wednesday, with Mary Jane Burrage, and discovered the crime. When she described how Robert had confessed to her, she broke down in tears, and she sobbed through the rest of her testimony.

Baggallay asked Fox, 'Do you wish to ask any questions, Fox?'

'You found me in the parlour,' Fox said to her.

'Yes,' said Baggallay. 'She says so.'

'That was the only place I was,' said Fox.

Aunt Emily was led weeping from the court.

James Robertson took the witness stand and told the court that he had changed a sovereign for Robert on Monday 8 July and that his wife had then paid the rent for 35 Cave Road.

PC Twort gave evidence about the arrest of the boys. Fox asked him: 'Did I tell you I was sleeping in the parlour?'

'Yes,' said Twort.

'Did I say it was done two and a half days before I came there?'

'No,' replied Twort. 'You said nothing about it.'

Fox did not get a chance to question PS Baulch, as the sergeant fainted in the witness box while describing his visit to Cave Road on Wednesday. He was carried out of the court. Two or three women in the public gallery had already collapsed during the hearing and been removed from the room.

At the conclusion of the evidence, Detective Inspector Mellish asked for the boys and Fox to be remanded in gaol while the investigation continued. He suggested that Robert be examined by the prison's medical officer. Baggallay said he hardly knew what to do with boys of their age – he had never sent lads so young to prison, but he could see no alternative. He remanded them and Fox to Holloway gaol.

As such a big crowd had assembled outside the court house, Baggallay asked the police to avoid walking Fox and the brothers through the streets in handcuffs, but instead to find a cab to take them to the railway station. Mellish said that he would arrange a conveyance. The boys were both seen laughing as the police hustled them into a horse-drawn cab in West Ham Lane.

The *Stratford Express* approved of how Ernest Baggallay had protected the boys from being paraded through the district on their way to the station. The magistrate had saved them from becoming a piece of street theatre, shielding them from the 'vulgar gaze', the 'vulgar derision or – still more stinging – vulgar sympathy' of the public.

At 4.30 that afternoon a street vendor in Northern Road, Plaistow, was selling copies of the *Evening News*, the right-wing halfpenny paper in which Robert had planned to advertise for a loan. The edition of Thursday 18 July carried reports that the Tories had routed the Liberals and radicals throughout the metropolis in the early stages of the general election: 'Bravo, London!' the headline ran. 'A glorious victory!' The vendor was calling out to passersby that the issue contained reports of the Coombes hearing. A disgruntled customer notified a passing police constable from the Barking Road station that he had found no mention of the case in his copy of the paper. The constable warned the newspaper salesman to stop defrauding the public, at which the vendor punched the policeman in the eye, knocking him down, and then kicked him repeatedly as he lay on the ground.

Holloway gaol, which lay seven miles west of Stratford, was the city's main remand prison and the largest such institution in the country. An average of seventy men and boys were admitted each day to be held within its walls until called for trial. The gaol was constructed in the 1850s on the panopticon principle, with a hub radiating out to six wings. From the entrance on Parkhurst Road, it looked like a castle, its central arched gateway flanked by crenellated turrets and statues of stone griffins clutching leg irons and keys. 'May God preserve the City of London,' read the foundation stone in the prison wall, 'and make this place a terror to evil-doers.'

Robert was familiar with stories of crime and punishment. As well as having seen James Canham Read appear before the magistrates in Southend, he had read many penny dreadfuls that featured Cockney villains. In *Joe Phoenix's Unknown; or, Crushing the Crook Combination*, the East End criminals dream up 'dodges' to acquire 'a tidy bit of swag'. They then 'cover their tracks', 'lie low' and if unlucky enough to be caught by 'bobbies' or 'peelers' are put in 'bracelets' and brought before the 'beak'. They will try to 'brazen the thing out' but may end up 'doing time' in 'stone jug'. On no account will they 'peach' or 'split on their pals'.

The police rang the bell at the Holloway entrance. A grate opened in the heavy oak door, an eye peered out, and the iron bolts were drawn back to admit the new prisoners. They were directed to the left, where the 350 men being held on remand were housed in five wings, supervised by forty warders. A single wing to the right accommodated sixty-five female convicts.

New arrivals were taken across a courtyard to the inner entrance of the prison, and into a long passage with reception cells on either side. They waited until summoned by a warder, who informed them of the prison's rules, then told them to strip to the waist in order to be weighed and measured. A warder cropped the prisoners' hair, sent them to bathe, bundled up and stored their clothes, and issued them with dark grey uniforms.

Robert, Nattie and John Fox were led through the central hall, beneath a glass roof in a massive iron frame, to individual cells in the three-storey blocks. Each cell measured thirteen by seven foot and was nine foot high, with an asphalt floor, whitewashed walls and a small window. Pinned to one wall were the prison regulations, a copy of the prison timetable and a card detailing the prisoner's name, number and age. The cells also contained hymn books and copies of the Prayerbook and the Bible. The boys and John Fox took to their pallet beds for the night.

The inquest into Emily Harrison Coombes's death opened the next day – Friday 19 July – at the Liverpool Arms, a large public house at the southern end of the Barking Road. The coroner was Charles Carne Lewis, sixty-two, who had succeeded his father as coroner for Essex in 1882. The most notorious death he had investigated to date was that of Florence Dennis, the young woman who had been murdered by James Canham Read in Southend the previous summer. His most recent case, which had concluded the day before the Emily Coombes inquest, was an inquiry into a series of deaths at the East Ham sewage works. On 1 July an employee at the

sewage pumping station had become dizzy with fumes as he
climbed down a ladder into a well; he lost his balance and fell
in. One of his workmates descended the ladder to try to help,
but collapsed and fell into the pit as the sewer gases overtook
him; three more men attempted rescues, and every one fainted
and fell. All five drowned in the filth at the bottom of the well.
Their deaths were attributed in part to the putrid conditions
created by the drought.

Lewis took his place at the head of a big dining table in a
bright, square room in the Liverpool Arms. The room was
furnished with bronze urns and large-leafed plants, which
were reflected in a long gilt-framed mirror on the mantelpiece.
The walls were covered with rich paper and hung with oil
paintings. Next to Lewis sat his clerk, surrounded by parch-
ments and legal volumes, passages of which were marked off
with strips of blue paper. The jury of twelve men sat round
the table; their foreman was Joseph Horlock, a forty-nine-
year-old master builder who lived opposite the pub. Detective
Inspector Mellish and Inspector Gilbert were present on
behalf of the police.

The coroner's inquest and the magistrate's hearing were to
run concurrently: the chief task of the coroner's court was to
establish how Emily Coombes had died, and that of the magistrates' court to decide who, if anyone, should be charged
with causing her death. Yet there was room for overlap and
even conflict in their deliberations. If a coroner's jury found
that the cause of death was murder, they could name suspects
and order their arrest.

A crowd of about 500 people had assembled outside the
Liverpool Arms, and when a closed cab drew up just after
11 a.m. they made a rush at its doors. The police managed
to hold back the mob, allowing John Fox and two Holloway

warders to enter the pub. Robert and Nattie had been spared the ordeal of attending the inquest because of their youth. Fox was given a seat in the coroner's court, where he sat for a few moments, his head leaning against the wall, before Lewis announced that he did not intend to examine him and did not consider it advisable that he be present. A member of the jury asked whether Fox should at least be allowed to hear the evidence, and Lewis replied that this was exactly what he did not want. The warders took Fox away. Several hundred people chased the cab that carried him off.

Lewis swore in the jury and called Alfred Kennedy, who had now completed the post-mortem on Emily Coombes's body.

'The whole of the brain has been consumed by vermin,' Dr Kennedy told the coroner and jury, 'and the right lung nearly destroyed by maggots. Through the base of the heart, which is partly eaten away, there is a clear stab, and one also through the extreme right side. There is a notch on the spine corresponding with this wound.'

The doctor said that Emily Coombes's bedding and underclothes had been stained with dry blood, which indicated that she had been alive when she was stabbed. 'There is no doubt,' he said, 'that death was instantaneous.'

The jurors were invited to leave the pub for the mortuary on the other side of the Barking Road. They had to make their way through a crowd to enter the building. Emily Coombes's body was in a double coffin, designed to contain the smell of a corpse and to slow its decomposition. The internal shell, which held the body, was usually filled with melted pitch and sealed shut. The upper part of the shell was fitted with plate glass so that mourners (or, in this case, jurors) could see the face of the dead person. Emily Coombes's features had been mutilated by maggots. The jurors completed their inspection as quickly as they could.

When the coroner and jury returned to the pub, Lewis called Robert and Nattie's Aunt Emily to give evidence. She was dressed in deep mourning, with a broad-brimmed black hat sitting horizontally on her high bun of dark hair. Her voice broke as she described the 'offensive smell' that assailed her as she entered 35 Cave Road on Wednesday, to find her nephews playing cards and Fox puffing on his pipe. She repeated Robert's confession to her, quoting him as saying: 'I kicked about and Ma pushed me. I then got out of bed and stabbed her.'

The coroner pointed out that Robert's account of the murder was confusing. 'I don't quite see,' said Lewis, 'how this part of the story tallies with the other part, in which he said the blow was to be struck after Nathaniel's signal from an adjoining room. It will probably, however, be cleared up later.'

The foreman of the jury asked Aunt Emily if she had not thought it strange that her sister-in-law seemed to have vanished.

'All through I thought it was strange,' said Emily, 'but Mrs Coombes had some funny ways. She would not write for weeks at times.'

After hearing two further witnesses, Lewis adjourned the inquest. It would reconvene in ten days, on 29 July.

Now that the post-mortem and the viewing of Emily Coombes's corpse were complete, arrangements were swiftly made to inter the body. Emily had paid a couple of pence a week to a burial insurance scheme, as was common practice among working-class people who wished to spare their families the financial burden of an unexpected death. The undertaker,

Richard Wortley of 269 Barking Road, was instructed to keep the costs of her funeral low so that her husband could retain some of the pay-out. In the morning of Saturday 20 July, Wortley transferred Emily Coombes's body to a plain wooden coffin, screwed down the lid and conveyed it by hearse and carriage to the Tower Hamlets and East London Cemetery, three miles west. Bow Cemetery, as it was known locally, had since its establishment in 1841 been the chief burial ground for the poor of East London. A third-class interment here cost about fifteen shillings. By 1895 the cemetery contained more than a quarter of a million bodies, most of them in shared public graves, and had become neglected and overgrown. Many of the headstones had fallen down and were half-covered by weeds and grass.

At 1 p.m. Emily's body was lowered into a long trench of public graves in a section of the cemetery adjacent to Lockhart Street, where Robert and Nattie's grandmother Mary Coombes lived. Since the police had kept the details of the funeral a secret, only two or three members of the family were present. Robert and Nattie were not invited to attend. The mourners cast earth on to the coffin and the priest – a Reverend Yates – stood over the grave and read the words of committal.

That day four policemen, led by Inspector Gilbert and Detective-Sergeant Don, went to 35 Cave Road to burn the filthy bedding from the front bedroom. Despite the disinfectants with which the room had been doused three days earlier, both Gilbert and Don reported that the stench was almost unbearable. After their visit, they left a constable at the gate to make sure that sightseers were kept out.

Ever since the discovery of Emily Coombes's body, local men and women had been visiting Cave Road to see the house and to discuss the case with whoever was passing. West Ham was so full of people, and the people so avid for entertainment, that spontaneous gatherings were commonplace. A few weeks earlier a fourteen-year-old boy had climbed a tree in The Grove, near Stratford Broadway, and started dropping twigs and bits of bark on to the hats of people walking below. He refused to budge when the police ordered him down, and it was reported that nearly 3,000 people turned up to watch the constables remove him from the tree with the aid of a fire ladder. The inhabitants of West Ham looked for their drama, whether comedy or tragedy, in the streets.

The penny paper *Lloyd's Weekly*, which had a circulation of more than 750,000, sent an artist and a reporter to Cave Road. The artist sketched the house: the arched doorway and bay window on the ground floor, the two open windows of Emily Coombes's bedroom above, the low fence and the metal gate bounding the front yard. The journalist interviewed the locals who had gathered nearby. He was told that Robert and Nattie had a very bad reputation, and that their mother had been too lenient with them, 'always allowing them to have their own way'. Robert was said to have been a constant source of trouble to the school officials: he had frequently been late and had often played truant. Three years earlier, the reporter heard, the brothers had run away to Liverpool to visit an aunt, using money stolen from their mother's cashbox. The police had been informed but when the boys were found their mother interceded and managed to hush up the affair. Over the past ten days, the *Lloyd's* man was told, Robert and Nattie had led a 'fast' life in the West End of London, riding about in cabs and watching shows at the theatre.

One neighbour said that Robert was a talented mandolin player. 'This love of music,' the *Lloyd's* reporter observed, 'is not infrequent among the bad folk of criminal history.'

Several other journalists turned up to interview the bystanders. The *Forest Gate Gazette* was informed that Robert had treated his friends to lavish quantities of ginger beer and ice cream in the days after his mother's death. The *News of the World* heard that Fox was a 'semi-lunatic' and a religious fanatic – the paper ran its report under the headline:

HORROR ON HORROR'S HEAD
THE MOST DREADFUL MURDER OF THE CENTURY
TWO PLAISTOW BOYS SLAY THEIR MOTHER
AND PLAY CARDS BENEATH THE CORPSE WITH A MANIAC

The *West Ham Herald* was told – also incorrectly – that Nattie had continued to go to school after the killing, and had been found once or twice with tears streaming down his cheeks. When his playmates asked him what was wrong, he said: 'I am crying about Mother.' Nattie was said to have told a friend that he wanted to kill himself. The *Herald* reported that Aunt Emily arrived at 3.30 p.m. on 17 July to find Nattie alone in the house, sobbing as he informed her that his mother was lying dead in her bedroom.

Several of the stories relayed by the newspapermen depicted Nattie as vulnerable, powerless, distraught, and Robert as the insouciant mastermind who took pleasure in the plunder of his mother's house. These accounts suggested that one boy, at least, had traces of conscience, even if the other was thoroughly bad.

An editorial in Saturday's edition of the *Stratford Express*, which had the highest circulation of any West Ham paper, described the murder at Plaistow as 'the most horrible, the most awful and revolting crime that we have ever been called upon to record. In the wildest dreams of fiction, nothing has ever been depicted which equals in loathsomeness this story of sons playing at cards in a room which the dead body of their murdered mother filled with the stench of corruption.' The 'Plaistow Horror', it said, 'is a story which must depress all who are longing for the improvement of mankind. It will pain public feeling to an extent which has rarely been equalled. It seems to plunge us back at once into the Dark Ages.'

The newspaper was alluding to the popular belief that the human race was in crisis. 'We stand now in the midst of a severe mental epidemic, a sort of black death of degeneration and hysteria,' wrote the Hungarian author Max Nordau in *Degeneration*, a work of 1892 published in English early in 1895. As evidence, Nordau pointed to the prevalence of madness and criminality among the poor, as well as the publication of decadent literature by such artists as Henrik Ibsen and Oscar Wilde. 'The day is over,' he warned, 'the night draws on.' Nordau's tract was much discussed in the British press. Its feverish tone was mocked in some quarters, and its apocalyptic ideas treated with scepticism by many, but its pessimism was commonplace. 'A wave of unrest is passing over the world,' warned the British author Hugh E. M. Stutfield in the summer of 1895: 'Revolt is the order of the day. . . ours may be an age of progress, but it is progress which, if left unchecked, will land us in the hospital or the lunatic asylum.'

Darwin's theory of evolution was widely accepted by the end of the nineteenth century, but with it had come the possibility that the human organism could develop backwards as well as forwards. The atrophy of the species was attributed to the speed and pressure of modern life – telegrams, railways, big business, a craving for instant pleasure – and to an increasingly urban, industrial environment. 'The close confines and foul air of our cities are shortening the life of the individual, and raising up a puny and ill-developed race,' wrote James Cantlie in *Degeneration amongst Londoners*. 'It is beyond prophecy to guess even what the rising generation will grow into, what this Empire will become after they have got charge of it.' In *The Time Machine*, published in 1895, H. G. Wells imagined a future in which the workers had degenerated into pale, ape-like Morlocks living in darkness underground, toiling on machines to make goods for the frail, decaying Eloi on the Earth's surface.

The far east of London was the ultimate industrial wilderness. Where the German visitor to Plaistow in 1886 had seen brass bands and fat-cheeked children, most journalists and novelists saw only pinched, degraded lives. An *Illustrated London News* reporter described West Ham's lines of 'little hideous slate-roofed houses of stucco and pale brick. Row follows row, all dreary, all mean.' The French novelist Emile Zola said that he had never seen such miles of soulless brick and mortar. The English writer Ford Madox Hueffer (later known as Ford Madox Ford) described West Ham as a featureless fog, 'a vast cloud beneath a cloud as vast', while Walter Besant saw it as a 'sea of the working class': 'its history is mostly a blank, making no more mark than the breezes of yesterday have made on the waves and waters of the ocean'. It was a city without a centre, said Besant, 'a city without art or literature, but filled with the appliances of science'. To a passing visitor, he wrote, it seemed a 'joyless' region, 'the City of dreadful Monotony', 'a vast city without a heart'.

Many onlookers detected an atavistic horror beneath the blank uniformity of East London. 'As there is a darkest Africa, is there not also a darkest England?' asked William

Booth, the Methodist preacher who founded the Salvation Army. 'The stony streets of London, if they could but speak, would tell of tragedies as awful, of ruin as complete, of ravishments as horrible, as if we were in Central Africa; only the ghastly devastation is covered, corpselike, with the artificialities and hypocrisies of modern civilisation.' The technologically advanced environment seemed, perversely, to be propelling people back to their bestial origins, the factories and machines turning out morons and monsters. The landscape was both futuristic and primeval. Every resident of the district, wrote Hueffer, was 'conscious of having, as it were at his back, the very green and very black stretches of the Essex marshes'. The American novelist Jack London characterised East Londoners as a 'people of the machine and the Abyss'.

In *The Nether World*, a novel of 1889, George Gissing described a railway journey east out of the city. From the train carriage, the passengers see the 'pest-stricken' suburbs sweltering in sunshine that 'served only to reveal the intimacies of abomination'. The train passes 'above streets swarming with a nameless populace', stops at stations 'which it crushes the heart to think should be the destination of any mortal'. At last the train leaves 'the city of the damned', carrying its passengers 'beyond the utmost limits of dread'.

A KISS GOODBYE

On the Thursday after the arrest of the Coombes boys and John Fox, the *Star* newspaper managed to secure an interview with Mary Jane Burrage, who had been present at the discovery of Emily Coombes's body. Mrs Burrage told the reporter that she had been an intimate friend of the murdered woman, whom she used to see almost every day. Emily, she said, was a bright, happy person, an exemplary wife and mother, and a careful housewife. As for Robert and Nattie, 'no boys were ever better brought up, but they were dark, sullen lads, with never a smile for anybody'. They were 'deceitful and dishonest in small things', she said, and when they told her that their mother had gone to Liverpool for a funeral she had known instantly that it was 'all lies': 'I knew she would never go away without telling me, and I knew she would not leave the boys in the house alone.'

'The neighbours laughed and sneered at me when I first said she was dead,' said Mrs Burrage, 'but now they see.'

Mary Jane Burrage was exhausted by her ordeal, said the *Star*. She recalled the horror of finding the corpse – 'the thing on the bed', as she described her friend's body. 'The smell!' she exclaimed, reeling at the memory. 'The flies were everywhere.' On the right side of Emily's face, she said that she had seen a clot of blood, apparently from a wound to the temple, and afterwards had watched the doctor remove the clot to reveal a writhing cluster of maggots.

Mrs Burrage reported that the boys' grandmother in Bow was 'nearly mad with shock'.

The *Star* correspondent asked if Fox had rented a room in the house.

'No,' she said. 'Old John was not a lodger – Mrs Coombes never had any lodgers, she was not that kind of woman.' Mrs Burrage was at pains to impress on the reporter that both she and her friend were respectable housewives who did not need to bring in extra cash.

Mrs Burrage claimed that Fox had never been to the house in Emily Coombes's lifetime, unless perhaps to do a job for Mr Coombes. In this, as in other matters, she expressed with certainty things that she did not know for sure. Family, friends and neighbours were to testify that John Fox had been a frequent visitor to Cave Road before the murder, whether to chop wood for Emily Coombes or to look after the boys; he had even helped the family move in to the house in 1892. Mrs Burrage went on to assert that Fox was thirty-six (he was forty-five) and to cast doubt on his honesty, saying that he was adept at faking simple-mindedness, or 'playing silly'.

The reporter asked her to comment on certain rumours about the boys and their mother.

'It is not true that they were kept without pocket money,' she replied, 'and it is a lie to say that Mrs Coombes drank – as great a lie as ever was told. You can see that by her beautiful house.' For Mrs Burrage, the condition of the house was proof of her friend's virtue and sobriety. She told the reporter that 35 Cave Road was prettily furnished and well kept, replete with lovely and interesting objects, some of them valuable, which Mr Coombes had brought back from his travels.

Mrs Burrage said that she dreaded to think how he would take the news.

Throughout the murder and the arrests, through the first hearings before the magistrate and the coroner, Robert and Nattie's father had been sailing to New York on the SS *France*, oblivious to the catastrophe that had befallen his family in Plaistow.

Robert Coombes senior was a slight man of fifty-one, with a receding chin, sandy sideburns and a moustache. The eldest son of a prosperous potato merchant and greengrocer, he was born in 1844 in Southwark, on the south bank of the Thames, but his family moved north of the river to Limehouse when he was a boy. He was a butcher by the age of fifteen and by twenty-five a master pork butcher in Notting Hill, West London, employing three men and three boys including his younger brother Frederick. In 1873, though, he was declared bankrupt. Thanks to an Act of 1869, bankrupts were no longer automatically imprisoned. Coombes instead had his assets seized and distributed among his creditors. Having lost his business, his home and its contents, he went north to Liverpool and became a ship's steward for the National Steamship Company Limited, a fleet established in 1863 to ferry emigrants across the Atlantic.

It was in Liverpool that he met Emily Allen, whose father was a captain on emigrant ships to Australia. Emily was born in the town of Karachi, then part of India, and bore the middle name 'Harrison' in honour of a captain who had rescued her pregnant mother from a shipwreck on the river Indus. She was dark and attractive, with thick eyebrows and a firm jaw.

The two were married in 1878. Robert Coombes was thirty-three (though he gave his age as twenty-six on the marriage certificate) and Emily was twenty. They were said to be a loving couple. After the opening of the Royal Albert Dock in 1880, they moved from Liverpool to East London, where much of the National Line's business was being transferred, and where he briefly ran his father's greengrocery business. Robert, their first son, was born in Mile End Old Town on 6 January 1882 and Nathaniel in Limehouse on 20 February 1883. The family spent a year in Liverpool in 1890 and on their return to London rented a house at 24 Liddon Road, Plaistow, before moving half a mile north-east in 1892 to Cave Road. The people of East London were in constant flux, observed the social reformer Charles Booth: they shifted from one part of it to another 'like fish in a river'.

Coombes served chiefly on the National Line vessels *England* and *France*, both of them iron-hulled steamships built in the 1860s, with single funnels (white with a black band circling the top) and three masts. Though the company's steamers were large, they were neither as luxurious nor as fast as the Cunard or White Star liners. A National ship took a fortnight to reach New York from London, whereas rivals could make the crossing in six or seven days. By 1895 the company had abandoned the passenger trade and converted all of its ships to carry cattle. It was cheaper to transport live animals than to slaughter them first and keep the meat chilled on the crossing.

As a chief steward, Coombes drew on his experience as a butcher and a greengrocer. He bought the provisions for a voyage before setting sail and was in charge of the stores and the kitchen while at sea. Each crew member was apportioned rations of coffee, tea, water, sugar, bread, beef, pork and peas. They were prepared and served, under Coombes's supervision, by a baker, a butcher, one or two cooks and a couple of assistant stewards. On a passenger liner, the steward could be a grand figure with dozens of staff, like the manager of a large hotel; on the cattle ships, he had a lowlier role. The sailors tended to look down on him and his men as 'flunkeys'.

Coombes was paid a basic £7 for each five- or six-week round trip, which was supplemented by about £2 in tips and over-time – this was considerably more than most of the seamen, who received £4 per trip, though less than the master, the engineers and the ship's mates. He undertook about seven voyages a year, giving him a total salary of about £65. According to a measure of affluence devised by Charles Booth in his massive survey *Inquiry into Life and Labour in London* (1889–1903), this placed Coombes above the poverty line, in category 'E', 'fairly comfortable'. He and his wife aspired to the respectable, relatively well-to-do life to which they had been raised – with good clothes for churchgoing, musical instruments for the children, literary magazines, an exotic bird in a cage – but they did not own property and employ servants as their parents had done. Their income was stretched to the limit: when Coombes was at sea Emily sometimes wrote to ask him to send home extra funds, and she occasionally pawned their possessions. The family's gold and silver watches, bracelets and rings were symbols of status but also insurance against an uncertain future, objects that could be easily pledged or sold.

Because he was a bankrupt, Coombes could not build up his own business as his father had done, and his job was not secure. A ship's crew was discharged after each voyage and although he had so far been regularly re-employed by the company, there was no guarantee of work. The National Line was barely in profit: the market for American beef was declining, and the company's difficulties had been exacerbated by the loss of two uninsured ships in 1889 and 1890. Five further ships were scrapped or abandoned in 1894 and early 1895, leaving just six in the fleet. There was talk of winding up the company altogether, or at least selling off the rest of the older vessels, which included both the *England* and the *France*.

On 20 July, the day of Emily Coombes's burial, the *France* was approaching the lighthouse at Sandy Hook, a spit of land near New York at which the Atlantic steamers were met by the pilot boats that would guide them into the harbour.

George Waldie, the captain of one of the Sandy Hook pilot boats, was sent to deliver the news of Emily's murder to her husband. Waldie, forty-eight, had emigrated to America from Scotland as a young man. On Saturday afternoon he took out Pilot Boat 13 to meet the *France*. He drew alongside and boarded, bearing a newspaper that carried a report of the murder in Plaistow. He delivered the paper to the ship's captain, who called Coombes into his cabin and handed it to him. Captain Hadley reported that Coombes read the account of his wife's death and his sons' arrest 'in a dazed sort of way' and was afterwards unable to speak. He was 'prostrated with grief and horror'.

When the *France* sailed in to the National Line's berth on Pier 39 of the North River at noon the next day, a friend of Coombes boarded the ship and handed him a cable from one of his relatives that urged him to return immediately to London. The friend invited him to stay with him first at his home in Newark, New Jersey, which lay ten miles west of the

North River piers. Coombes agreed. Before he left the *France*,
though, he gave interviews to several newspapermen.

Coombes looked pale and bewildered. He described 'in a
mechanical way', said the man from the *New York Times*,
'what he knew of the characteristics of his inhuman offspring', Robert.

'I knew the boy was queer,' he said, 'but I never dreamed
of this. It is terrible, terrible. I loved my wife devotedly, and
to think. . .'

At this point, the journalist wrote, Coombes paused and
looked straight into the mist gathering down the bay.

'My elder boy had an abnormally developed brain,' he continued. 'I was so informed by my family physician, who told
me that Robert must be carefully watched. There was always
something peculiar about him.

'When Robert was very young he began to act queerly. As
he grew older he showed unusual intelligence for one of his
years. He was a phenomenon in some respects and yet there
were traits developed in him which indicated the existence of
some mental failure. Local doctors could not diagnosticate his
trouble. He was at times the embodiment of all that is lovable
in a child, and then would come over him a spell that would
frighten us. For instance, if he read of a ghastly murder, his
whole mind would seem to be absorbed in it. Nothing could
divert him from it. In these spells he would neglect the companionship of his playmates. After the spell passed he would
be a child again, as innocent and unsophisticated as anyone
of his age.

'One time there was a murder near London. A man called
Read had committed a brutal crime. The papers were filled
with the particulars. My boy read about it and ran away from
home. He travelled miles to get a look at the murderer.

'According to the diagnosis of several physicians whom I called into the case, the boy was afflicted with a preponderance of brain matter. They said he had too much brain tissue for the size of the skull, and that in consequence the brain matter was crushed in too tight a space, and that accounted for the boy's eccentricities, and also explained his periods of phenomenal mental brightness. I do not pretend to know what their theory was, but they told me that if he lived to be fourteen years old the brain trouble would disappear. But he did improve as the years went by, and I had come to believe that the doctors were right, and that he would eventually be of sound mind.

'He kissed me on the docks in London two weeks ago Thursday,' said Coombes, 'and then to think he went back and killed his mother!'

Coombes was quick to clear Nattie of any part in the crime, and eager to implicate John Fox. 'The younger boy was not to blame,' he said. 'He acted entirely on the command of the older boy. He was only eleven years old, and if the older boy told him it was all right he would believe it.' Nattie was in fact twelve.

'The half-witted man, John Fox, who is associated with the boys in this terrible crime, is responsible for it, I believe,' said Coombes. 'He was formerly employed on the National Line of steamers, but had become so irresponsible that he was not permitted to go to sea again. He frequently loitered around my premises doing chores and running errands. Latterly I have forbidden him to come to my house.'

Captain Hadley, who had been master of the *France* for more than ten years, endorsed Coombes's suspicions. Fox, he told the *New York Times* reporter, used to sail with him but had become so useless that he was not allowed to come on board the steamer. On one occasion he was found 'lurking' in a dark gangway with a long knife, lying in wait for a shipmate against whom he bore a grudge. Captain Hadley said Fox was what he called a 'softy'. The captain spoke highly of the Coombes boys, both of whom he said that he knew well; Mrs Coombes, he said, had been particularly proud of the intelligence of her elder son. Hadley expressed his belief that Fox was to blame for the crime.

A reporter from the *Pittsburgh Commercial Gazette* noted that Mr Coombes was evidently under great mental strain. Coombes told him that he had lived on the best of terms with his wife and sons. 'My wife had always been a good and kind mother to her children, and I am at a loss to understand how they could attempt this dreadful crime. I am positive that John Fox had some hand in the deed. It is evident that both boys have been influenced by him.'

The reporters spoke to other members of the crew. Those who knew the family described the chief steward's wife as 'extremely handsome' and his sons as good-looking. They said that they had noticed nothing queer about Robert, but agreed that he had considerable influence over his younger brother.

A *New York Tribune* reporter who spoke to Coombes in his cabin found him a self-possessed and 'intelligent-looking' man. Coombes elaborated on Robert's diagnosis. 'The physicians who examined him said that when he arrived at the age of fourteen his skull would have become large enough for his abnormally developed brain.' He explained that he had had no inkling that Robert might be violent. 'While peculiar, he never did anything to lead us to believe that he might become dangerous. He appeared to be developing a morbid sentiment, which at times gave us uneasiness. If he happened to read of a ghastly or horrible murder, his whole mind appeared to become taken up by it, and nothing could divert him. During these morbid spells he would read all the literature of that character that he could obtain. When the spell wore off he would become natural again and play with his companions as innocently as any child.' Coombes recalled once more how on his last day in London, 'Robert came down to the dock to see me off, and kissed me good-by.'

It would have been costly for Coombes to rush back to London rather than complete his round trip on the *France*. He told the reporters that he would stay in New York until the next Saturday, and return with his ship as planned.

In Holloway Road, north London, half a mile from Holloway prison, a widowed cooper (or barrel-maker) read a newspaper report about the murder of Emily Coombes and wondered whether the man who had been charged as an accessory to the crime was the same John Fox who had once been apprenticed to him. He visited Fox in gaol.

'I found him to be my apprentice of many years ago,' wrote the seventy-one-year-old John Lawrence in a letter to the *West Ham Herald*. 'I feel it my bounden duty to do all I can on behalf of the poor fellow in the very serious and dreadful position that he has unwittingly placed himself in.'

THIS IS THE KNIFE

Fox, Robert and Nattie waited in Holloway gaol for a week. At six o'clock each morning, they were woken by the sound of keys grinding in locks as the warders opened the cell doors. At 7.30 they were given breakfast (a saucerful of porridge) and at ten taken to the exercise court, a large high-walled yard around which they walked in single file. They were returned to their cells after an hour. At midday they had dinner – meat or soup or 'stirabout' (corn and oatmeal) served in a tin pot – and at five a tea of bread and gruel or cocoa. Smoking was prohibited. Apart from the daily exercise hour and two chapel services on Sunday, they remained alone in their separate cells. The doors were locked for the night at seven.

Those prisoners charged with murder or attempted suicide – on average two new admissions a day – were placed under the observation of George Walker, the Holloway medical officer, so that he could report to the Treasury on their mental condition. Dr Walker interviewed Robert, Nattie and John Fox soon after their admission. In the prison register, he listed Robert's occupation as 'errand boy', his level of education as 'imperfect' and his mental state as 'unsound'. He observed that Fox seemed very slow-witted.

In the afternoon of Sunday 21 July two violent thunderstorms broke over London, unleashing the heaviest fall of rain in eight months. The streets and buildings were pelted with hailstones. After the downpour, noted the *London Standard,* the city looked 'a fortnight younger', its parks and gardens refreshed, its birds singing out in relief. The *Evening News* reported that an inch of water had fallen into the Lea, the river that divided West Ham from the rest of London, ending the longest drought in a hundred years.

Robert, Nattie and John Fox were recalled to the West Ham magistrates' court on Thursday 25 July. A magistrates' court could not try capital crimes, but the hearing before Baggallay would determine whether the prisoners were to be committed for trial at the Central Criminal Court at the Old Bailey. The boys and Fox were taken by three police constables from Holloway to Stratford, where they were met by Detective Inspector Mellish. It was a grey, warm morning, the air close and still. The prisoners alighted at the courthouse to find about a thousand people gathered on West Ham Lane in the hope of catching sight of them.

Robert and Nattie had no legal representation, but a friend of Fox – probably his former master John Lawrence – had engaged a Stratford solicitor, Charles Crank Sharman, to defend him. Sharman met his client at the courthouse that morning.

Charlie Sharman, forty-five, was a flamboyant, charismatic figure in the West Ham courts, known for sporting exotic flowers in his buttonhole and for mounting bold and often successful defences. In 1894 he secured the acquittal of a Walthamstow church verger, who had been charged with assaulting a seven-year-old girl, by arguing that it was 'highly unlikely' that he would risk his position by committing such an act. Sharman had been almost undone as a lawyer four years earlier, when a former clerk wrote a letter accusing him of attempted sexual assault. Sharman retaliated by prosecuting the clerk for blackmail and his case was supported in the West Ham court by Baggallay – a fellow Conservative Party activist, and therefore a political ally as well as a colleague. But when the case reached the Old Bailey in May, the court heard evidence that Sharman had a history of indecent assaults on men and women; the jury not only acquitted the clerk on the charge of blackmail but said that they believed him to have been justified in sending his letter. The disgrace to Sharman should have been devastating – the penalty for a homosexual assault was life imprisonment – but he was practising again in the East London courts by the end of the month. A call in the press to have him struck off the rolls went ignored, and though he resigned his post as Conservative agent for the constituency of West Ham North, by 1895 he had been reappointed even to this.

Sharman had spent the summer of 1895 working as election agent for Ernest Gray, the Tory candidate in West Ham North, and his efforts paid off when, on 15 July, Gray took the seat from the Liberal incumbent. Since Gray had been absent through illness during the campaign, Sharman claimed the credit for the win. He seemed to be riding high when he took on John Fox's defence, thoroughly restored to his position of influence in the district.

Ernest Baggallay reached the courthouse before 10 a.m., much earlier than he had done on the previous Thursday. The reporters and the public pushed in to find their seats as soon as the court opened. When the usher called 'Silence!' they rose to their feet and Baggallay entered to take his place on the bench. He began by dealing with the charges against the men and women who had been arrested the previous day and held overnight at police stations in West Ham. The Coombes brothers and John Fox were called at 11.15 a.m.

The court was hushed as Fox, Nattie and Robert walked in. They climbed the steps to a raised platform in the middle of the room, enclosed on three sides by iron rails and guarded on the fourth by a burly police constable. Fox looked even scruffier than before. He was no longer wearing Mr Coombes's Sunday best, and instead had put on a greasy, ragged blue serge suit – it was 'the sort of thing one expects to see on engine cleaners and stokers', said the reporter from the *Star*. The *Evening News* correspondent described Fox as 'a short squat man, clad in loose, wrinkled garments that hang flabbily from his sloping shoulders. He is limp and dingy looking, his hair tumbled, and a weedy growth of dark moustache and beard showing against the soiled pallor of his face.'

Robert, by contrast, was a picture of composure and wellbeing. He was 'a slim, active-looking lad of average height, healthy, and browned with open air and sunshine', reported the *Evening News*: 'such a boy as we see in scores on any playground of the people on a summer's afternoon, wearing a dark blue tennis coat, piped with silk cord, white flannel trousers, turned up at the end, and brown leather shoes. He is cleaner than most boys of his class, his turn-down collar white, his sunburnt face well washed, his close cropped dark hair brushed off his forehead.' To wear a shirt with a collar was a mark of respectability – the labouring classes usually went collarless – and the cricket flannels and tennis blazer also smacked of social aspiration: whereas football was a predominantly working-class game, both cricket and lawn tennis were preferred by the middle and upper classes.

The *Evening News* reporter allowed himself a brief meditation on how Robert's mother might have troubled herself over the burst of hair lifting off his forehead: 'There is no curl in the bunch of it that rises stiffly from his brow,' he wrote; 'it is such obstinate hair as mothers labour at in the hope to coax it into a neat parting, and one thinks that a dead hand has often wrestled with its stubbornness when the church bells were ringing on a Sunday morning.'

Nattie was wearing pale breeches, dark stockings, and a jacket with a white sailor collar. Though there was only a year between the brothers, he was dressed in the clothes of a schoolboy and Robert in those of a young man. Robert seemed quite the Cockney dandy, a worldly Dodger to Nattie's wide-eyed Oliver Twist.

Guy Stephenson, aged thirty-three, the son of the Director of Public Prosecutions and a barrister who practised at the Old Bailey, was first to address the court. As the junior lawyer in the legal team that would prosecute the case if it were tried, he was preparing the case for the Crown. He had performed a similar role in the trial of the murderer James Canham Read the previous year.

'After very careful consideration,' said Stephenson, 'I wish to ask Your Worship to discharge the younger boy. I then intend putting Nathaniel Coombes into the witness box and asking him to tell us the whole story. He has not been approached, and would be merely asked to tell his story.'

'Do you propose to offer any further evidence against the lad Nathaniel?' said Baggallay. 'At present I must say I see no evidence against him at all.' Either the magistrate had not understood Stephenson's request, or he was trying to claim the idea of dismissing Nattie as his own, because he asked him exactly the question that had just been put to him: 'Would it not be as well if he should at once be discharged?'

'If you please, Your Worship,' said Stephenson.

'Then he may be discharged,' said Baggallay. 'Let him stand down and go into that room till he is called for.'

A police sergeant took Nattie to an anteroom. He was now to be a witness against his brother.

Baggallay called the first witness, Police Sergeant Charles Orpwood of the Barking Road station, who had measured up 35 Cave Road. The sergeant produced a plan of the house and described its layout to the court. On the ground floor, Orpwood explained, were a passage, or hallway, a front parlour and a back parlour, each parlour measuring eleven foot by nine foot nine inches. Upstairs were two bedrooms, each fourteen foot wide and nine foot deep, with a communicating door. The staircase between the two floors had fourteen steps, and cut across the house, dividing the front and back parts. The house was narrow, with a total width of fifteen feet. The back yard, which contained a washhouse (elsewere described as the kitchen) and a privy, was about fifteen foot long.

Next to be called were Mary Ann Brecht, who ran a general store at 273 Barking Road (two doors up from the undertaker who had arranged Emily Coombes's funeral), and John Brecht, fourteen, the youngest of her five sons. The *Sun* characterised the Brechts' store as a 'kind of old curiosity shop'. Mrs Brecht had sold Robert the knife found next to his mother's body.

John appeared first. He said that he had been alone in his mother's store when Robert Coombes had come in about three weeks earlier and pointed to a dagger among a set of knives displayed on a card in the window. 'Johnny,' he had said, 'how much do you want for that knife in the window?' John said that the knife cost sixpence. Robert said: 'I will come tomorrow and see Mrs Brecht about it, and ask what will be the lowest you will take.' John told the court that he remembered Robert as a fellow pupil at the North Street board school in Plaistow.

Since Robert still had no solicitor to represent him, Baggallay gave him a chance to put his own questions to the witnesses: 'Do you wish to ask any questions, Robert Coombes?'

'Yes, sir,' said Robert. 'I never went to North Street school, and I never knew his name.' Robert had attended three West Ham schools, but North Street was not among them. This was irrelevant to the case: Robert was not disputing that he had been to the shop and enquired about the knife. By correcting John Brecht, he was acting like a schoolboy eager to score a point. He seemed to have little sense of what was at stake for him in this hearing.

Baggallay addressed the witness. 'Have you seen the prisoner before?'

'Yes,' said John Brecht.

'Where?' asked Baggallay.

'I have seen him in the Broadway,' said John, abandoning his claim that they had been schoolmates, 'near my mother's other shop.' This was Plaistow Broadway, where Mrs Brecht had a second store, just north of Cave Road.

Mary Ann Brecht, fifty-two, the daughter of a dairyman and the wife of a house painter, was next to testify. She said that Robert had entered her shop in the Barking Road on Wednesday 3 July or Thursday 4 July and asked her: 'How much do you want for that knife in the window?' 'Which one?' she said. He pointed to the knife and she told him it was sixpence. 'Is that the lowest you will take for it?' asked Robert. 'Yes,' she replied; 'it is very cheap.' Robert accepted the price and Mary Ann Brecht fetched the knife for him, asking if he wanted it wrapped up. 'Yes please,' he said. Mrs Brecht wrapped the knife and handed it to him. He gave her a six-penny piece and she, relenting, gave him a penny in change. 'It will make your mother a fine breadknife,' she said. 'Oh yes,' said Robert as he left.

The police produced the blood-stained knife in evidence. It was a sailor's sheath knife with a curved, beak-like point, which had been made to look like a dagger by a cross-guard of brass between the four-and-a-half-inch blade and the black handle. The *News of the World* observed that it was nothing like a kitchen implement, but rather 'a terrible dagger', 'the kind of knife one sometimes sees in the possession of a Malay sailor or a swarthy coolie hanging about the docks'. In assuring Robert that it would make his mother a good breadknife, Mrs Brecht may have been trying to assuage her unease about selling him just the kind of sharp, showy weapon that a boy might like to brandish.

The court heard evidence from the pawnbrokers with whom Fox had pledged goods. William White of George Fish's pawnshop in the Commercial Road remembered taking a gold-plated American watch from a short, dark man who gave the name Robert Coombes. He showed the watch to the court. Henry Goldsworthy of Ashbridge & Co produced a silver watch, which he said had been pledged by a short, dark man wearing a sailor's peaked cap. Richard Bourne, who ran the pawnbrokers by Plaistow station, showed the court Robert's mandolin.

Aunt Emily, who had given evidence the previous week, was called back to answer questions about the pawned goods now laid out in the courtroom. The mandolin was Robert's, she confirmed. The gold watch was his father's, but his mother used to wear it when her husband was at sea. The silver watch was bought for Robert, she said, though she was not sure whether it had been given to him. She knew that he used to wear the watch when his father was away.

Stephenson asked her how old Robert was.

'He is thirteen years of age,' Emily said.

Baggallay interrupted to point out that they had a better authority for Robert's age. 'You have the certificate,' he said to Stephenson. 'Put it in.'

Stephenson handed over a copy of Robert's birth certificate, which Detective Inspector Mellish had obtained from the Registry for Births, Marriages and Deaths at Somerset House the previous day.

Baggallay looked at the certificate. 'He was thirteen last January,' he observed. 'It is not important as a matter of evidence, but it is important as a matter of fact.'

Rosina Robertson of 37 Cave Road came forward to testify. Mrs Robertson, twenty-eight, was the wife of James, the painter and decorator who had changed Robert's sovereign on 8 July. The couple had three boys, aged between one and six, and had recently moved to Plaistow from Canning Town. She and her husband had last seen Emily Coombes standing at her front door on the Saturday evening before her death, she said, and had stopped to chat to her for a few minutes.

'On the evening before the discovery of the body,' she said, 'at about ten o'clock or a quarter past, I heard voices in the front bedroom of number 35.'

She was asked if they were men's or boys' voices.

'I could not say,' she replied. 'I called my husband's attention to them.'

She said that she had seen a swarm of flies at the two upper front windows of number 35, and had noticed that the blinds of the room were raised on Wednesday 10 July. She first saw Fox at the house on the same day.

Charlie Sharman, on behalf of John Fox, questioned Mrs Robertson about the voices she had heard on the night before the body was discovered.

'I was in bed at the time I heard the voices,' she said – her bedroom was adjacent to Mrs Coombes's bedroom next door. 'The voices sounded as if they were in the front room, or on the little landing, I could not say which. The landing was at the top of the stairs.'

Sharman asked Mrs Robertson exactly when the blinds had been raised and when she first saw Fox.

'The blinds were up on Wednesday morning. It was not until the evening that I saw Fox.'

Baggallay asked her how she came to notice him.

'I was on the look,' said Mrs Robertson, 'like everyone else was.'

John Hewson, the National Line cashier, told the court how Robert visited his office with the medical certificate attesting to Emily Coombes's illness. Hewson said he had noticed that the top had been torn off the certificate, and he was not inclined to trust the boy in any case. A year or two earlier Robert had called on him and said: 'My mother is very ill in bed – will you let me have £2?' On that occasion, Hewson had given him the money and then discovered his story to be false.

Stephenson asked him: 'And two days later did the mother come and see you? What did she say?'

'No, no,' interrupted Baggallay, 'we can't have that. It is a fact that the boy called, and that he got the money.'

Constable Twort testified that Robert's letter to Hewson had been found in Fox's jacket after his arrest.

Inspector Gilbert produced the letters that he had found at 35 Cave Road. Baggallay glanced through them, and read out to the court Robert's letter to the *Evening News* and then the letter that he had written to his father, in which he claimed that his Ma's hand was hurt.

Robert was calm throughout, occasionally letting a slight smile pass over his lips but otherwise betraying no emotion. The reporter from the *Evening News* noticed that he was none the less keenly aware of the journalists in the room. 'Of all the people in this Court none seems so cool and unconcerned as this boy,' he wrote. 'He stands easily in the dock, his hands crossed on the rail in front of him, his eyes sometimes following the movements of the witnesses, but more often straying to the right, where the busy pens of the reporters are at work on their table.'

As each witness prepared to leave the box the magistrate asked Robert: 'Have you any questions to put?' and Robert replied briskly: 'No, sir.'

'Even when evidence of the most fatal kind is being given against him he does not lose his indifferent air,' noted the *Evening News*, 'or the unconcerned smartness of his negative reply. He might be a confident pupil, sure of his answers to the teacher, so little does the tragedy in which he is the central figure move him.'

Fox, on the other hand, seemed scared out of his wits. His face, said the reporter, was 'almost blank in its expression of stupidity, straining to follow the thread of evidence. He keeps his hands clenched behind his back, the fingers ceaselessly shifting their grasp of each other in the effort to fix and retain a steady grip.'

Nattie, too, looked terrified. Having been brought back into the courtroom to await his turn in the witness stand, he sat on a bench leaning against the shoulder of a 'motherly woman'. He struck the *Evening News* reporter as 'a poor little puny fellow. . . with a white face and eyes that bear traces of recent tears'. Though he had now been discharged from custody, 'his little pale face is more full of fright and concern than that of the lad who stands in the dock'.

After Inspector Gilbert's evidence, Nattie was called to the stand. He seemed very anxious, and unprepared for his role as a witness. As a defendant, he would not have been called on to testify at all.

Nattie answered some simple questions from Stephenson, giving his address and the names of the schools he had attended. His last day at Cave Road school, Nattie said, was 'on the Friday before this was done'.

'You say "before this was done",' said Stephenson. 'Now I want you to tell us all you know about it.' Nattie spoke a few indistinct words and then started to sob. He took out a handkerchief.

Baggallay intervened, and began to question the boy more gently, taking him step by step through the events surrounding the murder.

'You went to school last on Friday?' asked the magistrate.

'Yes,' said Nattie.

'That was the day your father went to sea?'

'I could not tell.'

Nattie's father had left home on the Thursday and had spent the night on board the *France* before sailing for New York on Friday.

'Which room did you sleep in?' tried Baggallay.

'The other room.'

'Was that the room at the back?'

'Yes.'

'Which room did Robert sleep in?'

'He slept with mother.'

'In the front room?'

'Yes.'

Baggallay indicated the knife. 'Did you know he bought that knife?'

'The next day after he showed it me.'

'Which day did he show it you?'

'The next day after he bought it.'

Nattie said that Robert had been cleaning knives when he showed him the dagger, saying, 'I've got a little one here.'

'And what did he tell you about it?'

'He said, "This is the knife I've got and intend to do it with."' At these words, the spectators gasped and murmured. Coupled with the testimony of the Brechts, it seemed the starkest proof of premeditation.

'Did he say what he was going to do?' asked Baggallay.

'He said he was going to keep it.'

'Did he say what for?'

'No.'

'When did you first know your mother was dead?'

'The day it was done.'

'How did you know?'

'He came and told me.'

'Where were you when he came and told you?'

'In bed.'

'In the back room?'

'Yes.'

'What morning was that?'

'It was Monday.'

'What time?'

'Between 4 and 5.'

'Was it daylight?'

'Yes.'

'Do you remember what he said when he told you that?'

'He said, "I done it", and I said, "You ain't done it".'

'Why did you say, "You ain't done it"? Had he said anything about it? Had you said anything about it?'

'Yes I had, and said, "Are you going to do it?"'

'To do what? Had you talked to him about it?'

Nattie did not reply. He covered his face with his hands.

'Did you talk to him before?' asked Baggallay. 'When did you talk to him about it?' The magistrate and the boy were circling round the murder – or 'it', as both referred to it – Nattie evasively, Baggallay so as neither to lead nor distress the child.

'I think it was the week before.'

'Was that before he bought the knife?'

'Yes, sir.'

At this point Nattie began to cry again.

'Now, what did you say to him?' continued the magistrate. 'Did you ask him to do it?'

'Please, sir. I said, "Are you going to do it?"'

Here Stephenson, the prosecutor, interjected: 'Was he the first to speak about doing it, or were you?'

Nattie continued to avoid the question. 'He said he had bought a knife, and was going home to do it. It was not this knife here. It was one like what we use for dinner. He said, "There is a knife just by the Barking Road that will do it."'

It seemed that Robert had bought two knives: an ordinary

kitchen knife, which he had told Nattie about when they were
both out of the house one day; and then the dagger-like knife
from Mrs Brecht's shop, which he showed his brother back at
Cave Road.

None of the lawyers pressed Nattie on whether it was he
who had urged Robert to kill their mother on the weekend of
her death.

Baggallay asked: 'When your brother came in to the room,
as you say, early in the morning and told you, what did you do
after that?'

'He said, "Come and look if you don't believe me."' Again
gasps of horror ran round the courtroom.

'Did you go and look?'

'Yes; but I never went close to the bed. I went into the room
and looked and heard a groan, and then I went back to bed
again.'

If Nattie had heard his mother groaning in her bed, Dr
Kennedy had been wrong to tell the coroner that Emily
Coombes's death was instantaneous.

'Did you go at all after that and look at your mother?'

'About twice.'

'How many days afterwards?'

'I think it was on the Wednesday and Thursday.'

'On that morning did you two boys go out?'

'Yes; we went to Lord's Cricket Ground.'

'Had you any money?'

'Yes.'

'Where did you get it from?'

'She had some in her dress.'

'Who had?'

'My mother.'

'Did you take it?'

'No; Robert got it out. I saw him take it. He brought the dress into my room and there took the money out.' This was the dress that Emily had taken off the previous night, before going to bed in her underclothes.

'Did you see the money box? Who broke that open?'

'That was broke open a long time ago.' Nattie did not specify that it was he and Robert who had smashed it open, before running away to Liverpool together a year or two earlier.

'When did John Fox come to the house?'

'He came on the Wednesday afternoon.'

'Now, when you went upstairs on the Wednesday and Thursday did you go alone?'

'No, my brother went up with me.'

'Anyone else?'

'John Fox went up to make the bed.'

'Did he go into the front room?'

'No.'

'Was anything said between you and Fox about your mother?'

'No.'

'Did he ask about your mother?'

'He asked my brother where she had gone, and he said she had gone to Liverpool.'

'Did he ask any more questions?'

'No, sir.'

Stephenson asked Nattie when the unpleasant smell in the front bedroom had first become apparent.

'There was a bad smell in the house when I opened the door. That was going on for a long time before my aunt came, but Fox did not say anything about it.'

Baggallay asked Nattie if he had seen Robert write the letters to his father and to the *Evening News*. Nattie said that he had.

Sharman then submitted questions on Fox's behalf. These were put to Nattie by Baggallay, since he had established a rapport with the boy. In reply, Nattie confirmed that the two boys went together to fetch Fox and that they did not tell him that their mother was dead.

Nattie was dismissed, and Guy Stephenson said that this closed his case.

Sharman addressed the magistrate. 'I submit that there is no evidence to show that Fox knew of the terrible crime that had been committed,' he said. 'To be convicted, it would be necessary that he should be proved to have full knowledge of the crime; but there is not a tittle of evidence that he did. On the contrary, the little lad said that nothing was said about it, and that Fox was told the mother had gone to Liverpool. He was fetched for the purpose of minding them, and there the matter seems to rest, with the exception of the pawning of the goods. This was done at the instance of Robert, who said his mother gave him permission to do so.' Sharman added that two of the three articles that Fox pawned had belonged to Robert rather than his parents. Fox could not have believed that there was anything illicit about pledging these.

Baggallay pointed out that the visits to the pawnbrokers were not the only indication that Fox had colluded with the boys: he had also taken the letter to Hewson asking for money on 13 July. Sharman replied that it was by no means clear that Fox was aware of the contents of the letter.

For the Crown, Stephenson argued that though many of Sharman's remarks were pertinent, it would be better to address them to a jury. Fox and Robert, he insisted, should both be tried.

'Yes,' said Baggallay, 'under the circumstances I do not see how I can do other than commit both for trial.' Sharman asked for bail for Fox, and Baggallay said he would accept two sureties in £100 each pending trial at the next sessions of the Central Criminal Court.

Nattie left the court in the care of his mother's family. Robert was taken back to Holloway gaol. He was laughing as he got into the cab.

Over the weekend, the national press reported on the case. The *Illustrated Police Budget* remarked that Robert Coombes was the embodiment of the 'New Boy'. Like the New Woman, the paper said, the New Boy is 'a terror — partly created by the School Board. He is bossy and cheeky, he smokes, drinks, and as a fact goes in for other vices as soon as possible.' In 1895 the phenomenon of the New Woman — an asser-tive firebrand, smoking cigarettes and riding bicycles in her 'rational' dress of knickerbockers and stockings — was being picked over and parodied in the press. Here was a child to match, even to surpass, the subversive woman: a working-class upstart with so little respect for his elders that he thought nothing of killing them.

The *Daily Chronicle* reported that the French neurologist Désiré-Magloire Bourneville was taking an interest in the Coombes case. Dr Bourneville was head of psychiatry at the Bicêtre Asylum, near Paris, where he specialised in treating delinquent and mentally deficient adolescents. Bourneville held the view that both Coombes boys were responsible for the murder, and had been motivated by an atavistic impulse. His interpretation was based on the theories of the Italian scientist Cesare Lombroso, a believer in racial degeneration who argued that criminals and lunatics were throwbacks to a lower stage of evolution. Bourneville said that he would like to have data by which he could trace the hereditary characteristics that had led to Robert and Nattie's crime: 'germs of perversity, alcoholic mischief, or other more delicate imprints'.

And yet, Bourneville admitted to reporters, the premeditation of the 'Plaistow boy-murderers', their calm levity after the killing and their cunning explanation of their mother's absence did not indicate primitive mental development. This was a peculiarly puzzling case, he said, likely to baffle every modern group of criminologists.

The *Evening News* did its best to describe Robert's physiognomy in terms that conformed to the stigmata of degeneration identified by scientists such as Lombroso and Bourneville. 'The boy is large-headed,' noted that paper's reporter, 'his skull projecting at the back, his ears big and noticeably standing out. His forehead is straight, but low, and his nose and mouth protuberant, the chin receding, the cheekbones high, and the line from eye to mouth disproportionately long. His eyes are dark, deep-set, and shifty, and the bumps behind his ears highly developed.' The characteristics listed by Lombroso as traits of atavism included a low, sloping forehead, large and prominent ears, deep-set eyes and an insensitivity to pity or pain. Yet in the newspaper illustrators' images Robert did not resemble the pale, buckled urban criminal of the criminologists' textbooks: he looked robust, alert, a prime specimen of a boy. Perhaps his twisted, atavistic self was concealed from view, as the wicked Mr Hyde was concealed within the upright Dr Jekyll in Robert Louis Stevenson's novella of 1886.

A group of doctors based in Nancy, in the north-east of France, were also said to be following the case. Instead of ascribing mental disturbance to hereditary impairments, the Nancy school, led by Hippolyte Bernheim, believed that the mind could be warped by disturbing experiences and cured by hypnotic suggestion. When Sigmund Freud studied briefly under Bernheim at Nancy in 1889, he gained 'the profoundest impression of the possibility that there could be powerful mental processes which nevertheless remained hidden from the consciousness of man'.

Nattie was taken to temporary accommodation in East London by his mother's relatives, who had travelled down by boat from Liverpool. The 'motherly woman' on whom he had leant in the courtroom was probably his mother's older sister Mary Macy, who lived in Toxteth Park with her widowed mother, Tryphena. Mary was forty-three and had five children, the eldest of them a man of twenty-three and the youngest a boy of Nattie's age. She was also guardian to the ten-year-old son of her other sister, Isabella, who had died in 1888 at the age of twenty-five. Nattie knew his Aunt Mary well, since the whole family had lived near her in Toxteth a few years earlier.

The family gave a reporter from the *East London Advertiser* permission to interview Nattie. The boy told the journalist that his brother had been passionately fond of penny dreadfuls, and it was through reading one of these that the idea became fixed in his mind of going to India in search of 'romance and riches'.

Of the identifiable penny dreadfuls in Robert's collection, only one had an Indian component: *Cockney Bob's Big Bluff; or, the Thugs Terror* features a trio of Indians caught up in a New York detective adventure. The villain is the Rajah Jaipur, who possesses a man-eating tiger; his enemy is Ongo Phal, a snake-charmer with a lethal python; and the heroine of the story is the beautiful Rana, who is first seen sleeping on a couch, clad in 'loose garments which fell about her exquisite figure in a manner that betrayed its perfect contour'. Ongo warns Rana: 'White men come! Lose not a jiff! Get out big hurry!' Yet Rana falls in love with a white man called Harold, and when the Rajah attacks her beloved she feels Harold's pain as if it were her own, their shared suffering tinged with eroticism: his every groan 'cut her to the heart, like the sharp thrusts of a keen knife wielded by a strong hand'.

Nattie said that in June, Robert had pleaded with his mother to be allowed to go to India, but she refused to countenance the idea and insisted that he stay at the ironworks. It was this dispute, said Nattie, that first put the idea into Robert's head of murdering her: Robert hoped that if he killed her while his father was at sea, he would be able to help himself to her jewellery and the money that had been left for their upkeep.

Emily Coombes was at all times devoted to her sons, Nattie claimed, and in fact spoilt them with her kindness. In this interview, conducted under the supervision of his murdered mother's family, Nattie portrayed Emily Coombes as loving and generous. He did not explain why he had colluded with Robert's plan to kill her, and nor did he acknowledge the act that prompted the murder: the thrashing that she had given her younger son.

CHRONICLES OF DISORDER

The inquest into Emily Coombes's death reopened at the Liverpool Arms on Monday 29 July. Mellish and Gilbert again watched on behalf of the police. Nattie, who was due to testify, was brought in by one of his uncles. He sat stolidly through the questioning of the other witnesses.

Much of the evidence repeated that which had been heard before Baggallay on Thursday, but Charles Carne Lewis called a few extra witnesses and adopted a different line of questioning. Despite the fact that the magistrates' court had discharged Nattie, Lewis was particularly probing about his role in the crime.

First, Lewis had a few further questions for Robert and Nattie's aunt Emily. She looked very worn, according to the *Leytonstone Express*, when she came in to the court. In answer to the coroner, she testified that she had never seen anything in either of the boys to indicate that they 'did not know what they were about'.

'They were rude boys,' she said. 'I thought them impertinent.'

'To you?' asked the coroner.

'No, sir, to their mother.' In fact, said Aunt Emily, she believed that her sister-in-law had been generally 'too fond of the children and too weak with them'.

'You mean you think the mother spoilt them, being so fond of them?'

'Yes.'

'So as a sort of natural return they were very rude to her?'

'Yes.'

Her sister-in-law, she said, had been 'very proud and fond of Robert'.

One of the jurymen asked if it was within the scope of the inquiry to ask what kind of reading the lads indulged in.

'The last book Robert had to read while his mother was alive was *The Last Shot*,' said Emily.

Detective Inspector Mellish said that the books found in the house would be produced.

Joseph Horlock, the foreman of the jury, asked Emily whether Nattie had overheard her exchange with Robert on the Monday before their mother's body was discovered.

She said that he had: 'When I asked Robert where his mother was, Nathaniel must have heard what he said in reply.' This confirmed, if confirmation were needed, that Nattie was privy to his brother's lies about their mother's whereabouts.

Asked about Nattie's reactions on the day that the body was found, she said: 'Directly I remarked, "Your mother is in the house", Nathaniel made a dash and jumped out of the window.'

A jury member asked: 'He was sensible enough to know that something was the matter?'

'Yes,' Aunt Emily replied.

Mary Jane Burrage then gave evidence for the first time. A 'pale and sedate-looking person of middle age', as the *Sun* described her, she told the court that she was an intimate friend of Robert and Nattie's mother, whom she had known for three years. She had last visited her on the Saturday evening before her death. The Coombes brothers were 'very intelligent but also very rude boys', she said. 'They knew well what they were about.' Mrs Burrage confirmed that Emily Coombes had taken pride in Robert's academic achievements. She said that she had been very kind to her sons in every way and had been exasperated by their behaviour.

Nattie was a particular problem, Mrs Burrage said. 'She complained to me many times of Nathaniel being such a bad boy he would not obey her. Nathaniel has been present and heard her say so. I used to try to console her by saying he would improve as he grew older.' Emily Coombes had described Nattie as being very cruel to her, said Mrs Burrage. 'He "cheeked" her so habitually that she often declared she didn't know what to do with him. When told to do anything, he openly defied her, and at dinner would snatch things off the table and help himself in spite of her remonstrance.' Nattie, said Mrs Burrage 'was addicted to pilfering food'. It was a theft of this kind for which he had been beaten shortly before his mother's murder.

Mrs Burrage's evidence cast a new light on the relationships within the family. According to her, Emily not only favoured Robert but was in constant conflict with Nattie. She saw him as the child most liable to antagonise and undermine her.

Rosina Robertson of 37 Cave Road testified that the Coombes brothers were 'very sharp boys' who 'appeared to know thoroughly well what they were about'.

Harriet Hayward of number 39 agreed. 'They always appeared to be sharp and intelligent lads,' she said. 'They appeared to know right from wrong.' Mrs Hayward, thirty-three, had been married for eleven years to John Hayward, a carpenter, with whom she had several children. She had known the Coombes family since they moved to Cave Road early in 1892, and she told the coroner that she had seen John Fox calling at their house for the past three years. He had often been left in charge of the boys when their mother went out.

'Is he a bright kind of fellow?' asked Lewis.

'Mrs Coombes used to say he was a very trustworthy man,' replied Harriet Hayward.

'You are a woman of the world,' said the coroner. 'You know what I mean. Did he seem to be a bright kind of fellow, or a simple one?'

'A simple one,' she conceded.

In reply to a question from a juror, Mrs Hayward said she had never heard that Fox had been banned from the house. On the contrary, she said, John Fox and Mr Coombes 'seemed always to be on friendly terms, and Mrs Coombes seemed also to treat him well'.

The Brechts appeared again, and supplied a few more details about the knife that they had sold Robert. One of a lot of 140 sample knives that Mary Ann Brecht's husband had bought second-hand, it was made of Sheffield steel, marked 'Shenton & Co', and had been damaged by water when doused during a fire. Mrs Brecht said she knew Robert well, having often seen him playing in the street outside her shop.

When John Hewson gave his evidence about the medical certificate that Robert had brought to the docks, the boy's ingenuity and nerve provoked 'grim laughter' in the room. The atmosphere of the coroner's court in the Liverpool Arms was more informal and less dramatic than that of the police court in Stratford, more conducive to dark humour than to gasps and faints.

The coroner, unlike the magistrate, allowed Hewson to describe what happened after Robert tricked him out of £2 in 1894. Two days later, said Hewson, Mrs Coombes had come to him at the docks and asked if he had seen the boys. She was very distressed. 'I told her what I had done,' said Hewson. 'She said there was not the slightest occasion for her to send to me for money. She then said she had not seen them, for two days.' A day or two after that Hewson heard that a detective had found the brothers in Liverpool.

Inspector Gilbert, as Mellish had promised, produced the gaudily coloured penny dreadfuls taken from the back parlour. Among the works that he laid on the coroner's table were *The Witch of Fermoyle*, *The Mesmerist Detective*, *Under a Floating Island*, *Cockney Bob's Big Bluff*, *Buffalo Bill*, *A Fortune for £5* and *The Bogus Broker's Right Bower*.

Nattie was called to give evidence after lunch. He wore a brown tweed suit with a band of black crape around the left arm. This was the first time that either of the boys had been seen with any item of mourning dress. The coroner reminded Nattie that he need not say anything that might incriminate himself. He was at first self-composed ('calm almost to the degree of indifference', said the *Sun*) as he stood at the coroner's table, though his voice was very soft. The jurymen leaned forward to catch his replies as he answered some preliminary questions, and asked him to speak up. When the subject turned to his mother's murder, he became upset.

A long time before his mother thrashed him that weekend, Nattie said, 'something was said' about her – when pressed as to what, he burst into tears, sobbing so desperately that it was difficult to get anything out of him.

Nattie slowly grew calmer, and pulled a black-edged mourning handkerchief from his pocket to wipe his face. Lewis asked him what he thought Robert had meant when he told him he was going to buy a knife to 'do it' with. In spite of Nattie's distress, the coroner dealt with him more directly than the magistrate had done the previous week.

'I did not know what he meant.'

'But you have already told me that you thought he was going to kill your mother,' said Lewis.

'Please, sir,' said Nattie, starting to cry again, 'I thought he was going to kill Ma. He said he was going to do it whenever he could.'

The coroner asked why Robert had killed her.

'Because he wanted some money to go to some places in India.'

'But couldn't he go without killing your mother?'

'He wanted her money. I was to go with him and John Fox was to take us both. He said he knew his way there.'

'Who put India into your brother's head?'

Nattie gave no answer. Over the weekend he had told the reporter from the *East London Advertiser* that it was the penny dreadfuls that had inspired Robert's dreams of India, but his brother might also have heard stories of the exotic Far East from his history and geography teachers at school, from his father's seafaring friends, or even from his mother, who was born in India. The subcontinent was the glory of the British Empire, and the newspapers in the first week of July had been full of the wonders of 'India in London', the big summer show at Earl's Court, which boasted snake-charmers, elephants, a six-legged sacred cow, swaying punkahs, stalls

selling goat curry, and barges offering rides past palaces and
flower gardens.

Lewis turned to the question of what Robert had done after
showing Nattie their mother's body, a matter that the magistrate had not addressed. Nattie said: 'He stayed in mother's
bed all the same.'

'What?' asked Lewis incredulously. 'After he murdered
her?'

Nattie confirmed that Robert had gone back to bed with
their mother.

'How do you know this if you were in bed?' asked Lewis.

'He said he was going back to bed,' said Nattie. Robert
emerged from their mother's room five minutes later, he
explained, and came to the back bedroom.

Robert's return to his mother's bed struck the coroner with
horror. It had an edge of erotic creepiness. More directly, it
suggested a further act of violence. Robert had thought he had
killed his mother but Emily Coombes had not been quite dead.
When Nattie entered her room, she seemed to be stirring back
into life, groaning into wakefulness, and Robert seems to have
had to attack her again, whether with another thrust of the
knife – two wounds were found in her heart – or by stifling her
with the pillow that was found covering her face. The murder
had been far less clean and swift, far more disturbing to both
victim and perpetrator, than Dr Kennedy had indicated.

Nattie said that Robert emerged from their mother's bedroom with her dress, from the pocket of which he pulled a
purse. He had shaken out its coins on Nattie's bed.

'How much money was there?' asked the coroner.

'I don't know. He counted it, but did not tell me.'

The purse was evidence of conquest, proof of a transfer of
power. By killing his mother, Robert had freed himself from

her clutches and released the treasures that she had hoarded in her lair.

The police showed the court a purse that they had retrieved from the house, but Nattie said that it was not the right one – the purse Robert had brought to his room had elastic round it. Inspector Gilbert produced another purse, which had been found on Fox when he was searched at the station, and Nattie identified it as the one that Robert had taken from their mother's dress.

'Now,' said Lewis, 'tell us about the arrangement as to coughing outside the bedroom door.'

'My brother proposed it, and said I was to cough twice, but I did not do so.' On the day that they were discovered, Robert had claimed that it was Nattie who suggested the cough signal; and that Nattie had coughed as promised. He had repeated this three times – to his aunt and to two police officers. Nattie had not been asked about this contradiction in the magistrates' court, and nor did the coroner pursue it any further. Nattie's simple denial seemed to satisfy him. In any case, as Lewis had noted, Robert had also said that his mother's punch had prompted him to stab her.

'Did Fox go up to your mother's room?' Lewis asked.

'No, sir.'

'Why was the key taken out of the door?'

'Robert took it down so as no one should get in.'

'Do you know why he did that?'

'No, sir.'

'Was it not because your mother was there?'

'Yes, sir.'

'Do you know why the key was afterwards put under the couch in the front room? Who put it there?'

'I did, on the Tuesday before we were found out. Before that it was on the clock.'

Robert had bought the knife, Nattie said, while their father was still in London.

'When he bought it he hid it in the dustbin in the yard, and he left it there till Father went away. He brought it into the house on the Saturday, and put it up the chimney in my back room. He took it out on the Sunday night, and said he was going to put it under the pillow. He also said he was going to try to do it that night.'

On the Sunday, said Nattie, he and Robert and their mother had breakfast, dinner and tea together. He had gone to sleep in the back bedroom at 8.45 that night.

And on the day that they were discovered, the coroner asked, 'You jumped out of the window?'

'Yes, and that was all of it. We got found out, and was took to the police station.'

The carelessness of Nattie's reply provoked some laughter from the jury – he might have been admitting to a prank or a petty theft. The boy laughed too.

Lewis told the jury that he thought a further adjournment was necessary, to give the police time to trace Fox's movements in the days after the murder. The inquest would resume on Thursday. Sergeant Erry, the coroner's officer, agreed to take care of Nattie in the meantime.

During the first adjournment of the inquest into Emily Coombes's death, Charles Lewis had investigated the deaths from diphtheria of several children whose parents were Peculiar People, members of a Wesleyan sect formed in Essex in 1838. In accordance with their interpretation of a passage in St James's Epistle, the parents had not called a doctor when their children fell ill, and instead tried to cure them through prayer and the anointment of oil.

The Children's Act of 1889 enabled the state to prosecute a parent for the ill-treatment or culpable neglect of a child, and an amendment of 1894 specified that failure to obtain medical help could be an offence. Yet all that the coroner's court was able to do in the Peculiar People cases was give a verdict of death from natural causes – it was hard to prove that a death from diphtheria could have been prevented or even delayed by medical intervention. Lewis announced that he was 'sick and tired' of having these cases reported to him when he was powerless to act, and demanded that the law be tightened up. When a Peculiar father explained to him, 'I stand up for the Lord', Lewis returned: 'You can lie [down] and die, if you like, but it is cowardly, most cowardly, to allow helpless children to do so.'

On Wednesday 31 July, during the second adjournment of Emily Coombes's inquest, the coroner dealt with the death of yet another Peculiar child who had not been attended by a doctor. Lewis berated the parents, saying that he was sure that they would have called in help if their pig or donkey had fallen ill. The parents did not disagree. They simply pointed out that the Bible said nothing about animals.

A few new witnesses were heard on Thursday 1 August, the final day of the Coombes inquest: two dock constables and a marine engineer who had seen Fox in the week after the murder; the keeper of the coffee house at the end of Cave Road; and the headmaster of Robert and Nattie's school. The sightings of Fox at the docks proved confusing, two witnesses claiming they had noticed him wearing a smart suit on days before it could have been given to him by Robert. The coffee-house keeper, William Richards, also seemed muddled about dates, insisting that the trio came to his shop with fishing rods on Tuesday, which was the day before Fox had been collected from the *Spain*. He added that Fox and Robert had been in the habit of visiting his shop together for the past two years; usually Fox arrived first and waited for the boy. Richards claimed that he had often tried to hear what they said to one another but had been unable to do so. The headmaster of the Cave Road school testified to the intelligence of both brothers, and noted that Robert had been very attentive during his scripture lessons.

Nattie, who had been held in police custody since Monday, was then briefly examined again. He was not this time given a seat. He stood up to answer the questions.

'When was the first talk about going to India?' asked Lewis. 'Was that before your mother was killed?'

'Yes, sir.'

Joseph Horlock, the foreman of the jury, asked: 'What day was it that you first talked about the coughing signal and killing your mother?'

'It was on the Sunday,' said Nattie.

'Did you ever ask your brother not to kill your mother?' asked Lewis.

'Yes, once I asked him not to do it.'

'When was that?'

'I don't know.'

'Was it before the Saturday? Before your father went away?'

'It was before he came home.' The boys' father had returned from his previous voyage on the SS *France* on Monday 24 June, the day before Robert gave in his notice at the Thames Iron Works. This suggested that the brothers had discussed the murder plan in the fortnight that Robert was employed at the iron yard.

'Did you ask him not to kill her before the knife was put up the chimney in your bedroom?'

'No, I said nothing to him.'

Detective Inspector Mellish showed the jury the suit that Fox had been wearing when arrested. Inspector Gilbert produced the boy's nightshirt that had been found hanging on a line in the kitchen. It was lightly spattered with blood.

Lewis addressed the twelve members of the jury before inviting them to reach a verdict. 'This case is one of the most revolting, heartless and unnatural ever presented to a jury,' he said. He told them that their chief responsibility was to establish the cause of death, a matter on which Dr Kennedy had been very clear. 'Not only was there one stab, which went through the heart,' said Lewis, 'but two, and the knife produced was found on the bed.'

Yet, he reminded the jurymen, they also had the power to name the suspected perpetrator or perpetrators of Emily Coombes's murder and to commit him or them for trial. They would almost certainly name Robert, since he had made a confession; the question was whether they would also commit Fox or Nattie. Lewis acknowledged that the Treasury had withdrawn the case against Nattie, but told the jury that this should not prevent them from naming him if they thought he was implicated in the crime: 'If the jury should be of opinion that he had knowledge of what was going to be done, and the purpose of it, he would be an accessory before the fact, and as such be liable with the principal.' If Nattie knew why the knife had been bought, Lewis explained, he was – according to the law – guilty along with the person who made the purchase.

He clarified the definition of an 'accessory before the fact': this was someone who, even if he was not present at the crime, had 'procured, counselled, commanded or abetted' another person to commit the felony. However, said Lewis, 'he could not be an accessory if he had countermanded anything that had been said'. Lewis's keen questioning of Nattie on the matter of whether and when he had discouraged Robert from killing their mother was intended to untangle this issue: only if Nattie had tried to stop Robert after the purchase of the knife would he be in the clear.

The Coombes brothers were young, the coroner observed, but 'the law says that between seven years and fourteen years an infant is liable, and can be charged with felony if the jury is thoroughly well-satisfied that he has the capacity to understand good from evil. Therefore if you are of opinion that one or both of these boys thoroughly understands right from wrong, then they are amenable to the law.'

The jury did not need to deal with the possibility that John Fox was an 'accessory after the fact', Lewis said, and should commit him for trial only if they believed that he had been involved in the murder plot. His conduct after the killing fell outside the jurisdiction of the inquest, which dealt with just the death and not its aftermath.

The jury retired, and after an hour and ten minutes delivered the verdict towards which the coroner had been guiding them: 'Wilful Murder against Robert Allen Coombes, and as an accessory before the fact against Nathaniel, inasmuch as he conspired with his brother Robert to murder his mother, and he never did anything to prevent his brother carrying out the dreadful deed.'

The foreman, Iorlock, commended the police on the manner in which they had conducted the case and offered the jury's condolences to the husband and relatives of Emily Coombes. The jurors signed a document attesting to their verdict, and

Lewis sent a certificate to the registrar at Somerset House, giving the cause of Emily Coombes's death as 'wilful murder'.

The coroner issued a warrant for the re-arrest of Nathaniel George Coombes. Nattie was taken back into custody and delivered to Holloway by Detective Sergeant Don. He was to remain in gaol, with his brother and John Fox, until the September sessions of the Central Criminal Court at the Old Bailey.

Horlock added a rider to the jury's verdict: 'We consider that the Legislature should take some steps to put a stop to the inflammable and shocking literature that is sold, which in our opinion leads to many a dreadful crime being carried out.'

'There can't be any difference of opinion about that,' said Lewis.

In the mid-1890s the prevalence of penny dreadfuls (as they were known in the press) or penny bloods (as they were known to shopkeepers and schoolboys) was a subject of great public concern. 'Tons of this trash is vomited forth from Fleet Street every day,' observed the *Motherwell Times* in 1895, 'and inwardly digested by those whose mental pabulum is on a level with the stuff for which it craves.' More than a million boys' periodicals were being sold a week, most of them to working-class lads who had been taught to read in the state-funded board schools set up over the previous two decades. An Act of Parliament of 1870 had given local authorities the power to enforce school attendance, and successive Acts made elementary education compulsory (in 1880) and then free (in 1891). Between 1870 and 1885, the number of children at elementary school trebled, and by 1892 four and a half million children were being educated in the board schools. The new wave of literate boys sought out penny fiction as a diversion from the rote-learning and drill of the school curriculum, and then from the repetitive tasks of the mechanised industries to which many of them progressed. Since cheap magazines were traded on street corners, in playgrounds and factory yards, each issue could have many readers. Penny fiction was Britain's first taste of mass-produced popular culture for the young, and was often held responsible for the decay of literature and of morality.

The bloods sold for a halfpenny, a penny or tuppence, depending on the length of the story, while proper novels for boys – whether *Robinson Crusoe* or *The Prisoner of Zenda*, the romances of Walter Scott or the adventures of Jules Verne – cost two or three shillings each. Most of Robert's novelettes were sixty-four-page pamphlets priced at tuppence, their titles picked out in scarlet and yellow on vividly illustrated covers. At eight and a half inches tall and six inches wide, they were small enough to slip inside a jacket pocket, or between the leaves of a textbook or a prayerbook. They were sold by newsagents, tobacconists, confectioners and chandlers.

A week after Robert and Nattie's arrest, a *St James's Gazette* journalist was assigned to analyse the contents of every cheap boys' weekly that he could lay his hands on. He read thirty-six different titles, some of which he said had a circulation of more than 300,000, and he reported on the results over several issues of the newspaper. The task was 'repulsive and depressing', he said; the writing 'brutalised my whole consciousness', reviving 'the fundamental instinct of savagery inherent in us all. It disgusts, but it attracts; as one reads on the disgust lessens and the attraction increases.' The Coombes boys, he concluded, 'with their intelligence scientifically developed at the expense of the ratepayers, had been wound up to regard

murder as a highly superior kind of "lark" by a sedulous study
of the worst kind of gory fiction and cut-throat newspaper'.

In fact, most of the books in Robert's collection, though
slapdash and hackneyed in style, were not particularly gory.
Earlier in the century, penny pamphlets had contained monstrous, Gothic tales – they were dubbed 'dreadfuls' because
they elicited terror – but they now consisted chiefly of detective mysteries, Westerns, futuristic fantasies, tales of pirates,
highwaymen, hunters and explorers. The adventure yarns
were strikingly manly productions, heavily influenced by
Henry Rider Haggard's *King Solomon's Mines* (1885), whose
hero boasts that 'there is not a petticoat in the whole history',
and Robert Louis Stevenson's *Treasure Island* (1883), which
according to Arthur Conan Doyle marked the beginning of
the 'modern masculine novel'.

Many of the stories that Robert read were English re-issues
of New York dime novels, among them the Jack Wright submarine tale; the Buffalo Bill adventure; a fable about the
medieval crusades; and a mystery featuring Joe Phoenix, a
hard-boiled Manhattan detective with an astonishing capacity for impersonation and disguise. These stories had their
share of alluring women (with full, red lips, lithe figures,
bright golden hair floating behind them) and of exciting violence. The brave warrior in *The Secret of Castle Coucy; or, a
Legend of the Great Crusade* leaps on his French foe with an
axe, 'and with one tremendous thrust sent the spike between
the two blades of the axe right into Gaston's breast, piercing
mail-shirt and cuirass, and casting the proud knight to the
earth, gasping for breath, and uttering groans of irrepressible
agony'. The detective hero of *Cockney Bob's Big Bluff* feels
'a tingling, burning, electric thrill all over his person' when
he comes upon a crook. 'The strange and subtle power he

possessed was becoming aroused. In his soul there was a mad tumult of fury.'

The novelist James Joyce, who was born in the same year as Robert Coombes, wrote in his short story 'An Encounter' about the cheap adventure tales circulated secretly in Dublin schools. Joyce's narrator recalls how he used to be enthralled by Wild West stories and American detective fiction featuring 'unkempt fierce and beautiful girls'. The boy's teacher reprimanded his pupils for reading such rubbish, but as soon as 'the restraining influence of the school was at a distance', the narrator recalls, 'I began to hunger again for wild sensations, for the escape which these chronicles of disorder alone seemed to offer me.' Though he and his friends played at Indians in the streets near his house, he longed for 'real adventures to happen to myself. But real adventures, I reflected, do not happen to people who remain at home. They must be sought abroad.' The boy and a friend skipped school one day to visit the city quays, lured by the big ships and the wide sea. As they rested in a field after watching the commotion at the docks, they were approached by a well-spoken man in a shabby suit who talked to them of literature – Walter Scott and Edward Bulwer Lytton – and of the pleasure of administering warm whippings to boys. Unsettled by their encounter, a real adventure that they had not anticipated, the boys hurried home in time for tea.

The dreadfuls had their defenders. In an article of 1888, Robert Louis Stevenson recalled with rapture how he had been 'mastered' by penny fiction as a boy: 'I do not know that I ever enjoyed reading more.' Yet most commentators were alarmed by the rise of escapist stories for the young. Every month, it seemed, the newspapers reported on children led astray by such yarns. In 1889 two schoolboys aged eleven and thirteen absconded from West Ham with a pistol, an old dagger and a terrier dog, and their parents informed the magistrates that the boys' minds had been turned by reading penny dreadfuls. In 1892 two Dundee runaways aged twelve and fourteen were apprehended in Newport, Wales, in possession of a revolver, a hundred ball cartridges, a travelling rug and a handwritten document: 'Directions for skedaddle: Steal the money; go to the station, and get to Glasgow. Get boat for America. On arriving there, go to the Black Hills and dig for gold, build huts, and kill buffalo; live there and make a fortune.' In 1893 a Yorkshire boy of fifteen stole £25 from his employer, a ship's chandler, and then took the train to London with the intention of sailing for Australia. When he was caught his father said he had found hidden in the boy's room a novelette entitled *The Adventures of the Brave Boy and the Bushrangers*.

Inquest juries frequently linked suicide to cheap literature. When a twelve-year-old servant boy hanged himself in Brighton in 1892, the jury delivered a verdict of 'suicide during temporary insanity, induced by reading trashy novels'. When a twenty-one-year-old farm labourer in Warwickshire shot himself in the head in 1894, the coroner suggested that the fifty penny dreadfuls found in his room had had 'an unhinging and mesmeric effect' upon his mind. The jury was inclined to agree: 'Deceased committed suicide whilst in an unsound condition of mind, probably produced by reading novelistic literature of a sensational character.'

Occasionally, penny dreadfuls were associated with murder. In 1888 two eighteen-year-olds were charged with killing the timekeeper at a sawmill in Tunbridge Wells, Kent. According to the *Daily News*, the 'natural depravity' of the lads had 'found a strong stimulus in the penny dreadfuls of one sort or another which were found in their lodgings'. One of the accused men, though, said that he had attacked the timekeeper because he had docked his pay by more than two shillings – the timekeeper was 'a master's man', the lad said, and not a friend to the workers. The suspect wrote a letter to a local newspaper and signed it 'Another Whitechapel Murderer', an allusion to the ongoing murder spree by 'Jack the Ripper' in East London. When the case came to trial, the jury was faced with a tangle of possible causes for the crime, as they would be in the Coombes case: social discontent, financial need or greed, innate depravity, fantasies of violence inspired by fictional or real-life stories. The men were found guilty, and the judge ignored the jury's recommendation to mercy on account of their age; both were hanged.

Some cheap periodicals for boys tried to dissociate themselves from the dreadfuls. 'No more penny dreadfuls!' proclaimed the new *Halfpenny Marvel*, founded by the publishing magnate Alfred Harmsworth in 1893. 'These healthy stories of mystery adventure, etc, will kill them.' The next year Harmsworth produced another halfpenny paper, the jingoistic *Union Jack*, copies of which were found in the back parlour of 35 Cave Road: 'Parents need not fear when they see their children reading the "Union Jack",' the editor announced. 'There will be nothing of the "dreadful" type in our stories. No tales of boys rifling their employers' cashboxes and making off to foreign lands, or such-like highly immoral fiction products.'

Since 1884, when the vote had been extended to most British men, the press had often pointed out that children raised on penny dreadfuls would grow up to elect the rulers of the nation. Such pamphlets were 'the poison which is threatening to destroy the manhood of the democracy', announced the *Pall Mall Gazette* in 1886. The *Quarterly Review* went a step further, warning its readers in 1890 that 'the class we have made our masters' might be transformed by these publications into 'agents for the overthrow of society'. The penny bloods gave a frightening intimation of the uses to which the labourers of Britain could put their literacy and newly won power: these fantasies of wealth and adventure might foster ambition, restlessness, defiance, a spirit of insurgency. There was no knowing the consequences of enlarging the minds and dreams of the lower orders.

8

HERE GOES NOTHING

In Holloway gaol on Monday 5 August, Robert became
highly agitated. The warders informed George Walker, the
prison's medical officer, that the boy was singing, whistling
and being impertinent. Dr Walker asked that he be brought
to him in his office. Robert took a seat at the table and told
Walker that he had pains in his head. The doctor asked him
if he heard voices. Robert replied that he heard voices saying, 'Kill her, kill her', and, 'Kill her, kill her, and run away!'
Walker questioned him about how the voices spoke to him.
Robert said that they seemed to whisper into his ear.

During this interview, Robert explained to Dr Walker that
he had decided to kill his mother because he was afraid that if
he did not do so she would kill Nattie. She had thrown knives
at his younger brother, Robert said, and had threatened to
knock out his brains with a hatchet.

It was common for a parent to use physical force to discipline a child – in many households, a cane or a strap hung
by the fireplace for this purpose – but Robert was describing
assaults that were dangerous and uncontrolled. If his account

was true, Emily Coombes was not only doting, indulgent, affectionate to her children, but also given to bursts of anger and violent reproof. She switched between surrendering her authority and enforcing it with abandon. Nattie's complicity in the murder plot made clear that both boys could feel hatred for her. She frightened her sons.

On Saturday, Robert was frenzied again, to such an extent that he was moved to a padded room in the infirmary for several hours – most prisons were equipped with such cells, cushioned with horse-hair and leather, to contain epileptic, insane or suicidal inmates. The afternoon was humid, but the night was broken by an hour and a half of thunder and lightning, and then the rain came down in torrents. On Sunday, Robert was calmer, and he was returned to his normal quarters.

One of the more gruesome stories in Robert's collection of penny bloods featured a wild-eyed loon. In *The Rock Rider; or, the Spirit of the Sierra*, an American cavalry officer called Beckford loses his wits after his wife is killed and his daughter abducted by a posse of Red Indians. For many years afterwards he lives in a cave in the mountains of the Mid-West. From time to time he hears voices in his head telling him, 'Ride! Ride! Blood comes!', at which he snaps 'into the white heat of fury all at once' and becomes 'the maniac all over'. Blazing with hatred, Captain Beckford strikes out on his mule to slaughter Indians, carrying a shield over which he has stretched the mummified face of his wife, as menacing as the Gorgon Medusa: it is 'pinched and white, with wide-open, staring eyes, and teeth revealed by parted lips'.

Beckford kills and decapitates Indians. He hoards their heads in a cave in the mountains, which is watched over by his negro sidekick, Cato. ''Tis thy place to guard the Cavern of

Death,' Beckford tells Cato; ''tis mine to bring in the victims, for I am the avenger of innocent blood.' Cato is terrified by the cave. 'Don't make me go in dar, sah!' he pleads. 'De heads dey groan, and de devil he be at work at dem.'

The whites and the Indians in *The Rock Rider* are fighting over the land of the Mid-West, an erotic landscape of clefts, craters and recesses, wild vines and jutting mountains, hollows and pools. Much as they defend the terrain they have conquered, the white men are determined to preserve the purity of their women, whom they would rather destroy than see taken and defiled by the 'red niggers'. Towards the end of the story, a dashing Frenchman rescues Beckford's kidnapped daughter, Blanche, from an Indian camp in a 'haunted gorge'. He is dressed in gleaming thigh-high boots with silver spurs, white corduroy trousers, a slashed and braided velvet jacket. Blanche wears a short, tight tunic. 'Sooner than give you back alive,' the French dandy promises her, 'I will blow out your brains with my own hands.' By the deranged chivalric code of the penny dreadfuls, to kill a woman could be the means of saving her honour. A murder pre-empted – and mimicked – a rape.

Robert and Nattie's father spent a week in New York while the *France* was prepared for the return trip. It took several days for the dockhands to fuel the steamer, carrying coal alongside by barge and hoisting it up to the deck in buckets. At the company office near the pier, Coombes hired fifteen itinerant workers to look after the cargo of cattle on the journey back to England. These 'cowboys of the sea' would be given free passage both ways across the Atlantic, with 11 shillings to cover their board and lodging in the ten days or so that the ship was docked in London.

Several hundred head of cattle, captured on the plains of the American West and carried to New York by train, were herded up a narrow gangplank and into pens between decks. When the ship cast off on Saturday 27 July, the cows stumbled and slipped in their pens until they learned to sway with the roll of the ship. At night, some of the cattlemen patrolled the vessel with lanterns. Others rose at five to feed and water the animals. They sluiced the decks, pitched manure into the ocean, fetched hay, desalinated buckets of sea water for the cows to drink.

The *France* sailed in to the Thames Estuary on Saturday 10 August, the day that Robert became wild in Holloway. The cattle bellowed with excitement, sensing that land was near.

From the mouth of the Thames, wrote Joseph Conrad, London appeared in the distance as 'a brooding gloom in sunshine, a lurid glare under the stars'. The river was busy with craft – barges, skips, yachts, tugs, lighters, steamers – and as the ship sailed into the city, the factories and warehouses reared up on either side. 'The river runs as between high walls,' wrote Ford Madox Hueffer, 'shining with a more metallic glitter under smoke and the shadow of groves of masts, crane-arms, chains, cordage.'

On Sunday the *France* docked at Deptford, on the south bank of the Thames. The cows were released from their pens and driven by the cattlemen down a gangway to the pier and then into a shed to be slaughtered. Coombes headed to Holloway to see his sons.

That morning at Westminster Abbey, Canon Basil Wilberforce delivered a sermon in which he contrasted the villainy of the West Ham 'boy-murderers' with the heroism of the East Ham sewage workers, who had given their lives in their efforts to save one another. Yet he urged compassion for the Coombes brothers. Like the French alienists, he attributed the murder to a physiological flaw that affected both boys: the Plaistow matricide, said Wilberforce, was clearly the result of hereditary madness. He asked the congregation not to think of the brothers as 'children of the devil' but instead to remember that they possessed a 'deep inmost God nature, which is ever present in man, however much it might be concealed'.

The master cooper John Lawrence was raising money by subscription to hire a barrister for John Fox in the forthcoming trial. Lawrence explained in his letter to the *West Ham Herald* why he had such faith in Fox's innocence. During the years of his apprenticeship, Lawrence wrote, he had found Fox 'at all times to be very truthful, honest, civil, and industrious; in fact, all that an employer would desire, both morally and physically. But his mental capacity was far inferior to any of the children who were his chosen and only associates.' Fox had sometimes caused him 'great annoyance', said Lawrence, but he had none the less 'always been to me an object of pity'.

John William Fox was born to an unmarried, illiterate woman in a dingy courtyard opposite the Leadenhall poultry market in the City of London in April 1850. His mother was unable to support him, so when John was nine the City's Board of Guardians sent him to its industrial school in West London. The 800 children at the school were housed in large dormitories; they spent half of their time at schoolwork and half labouring on the estate. Fox was due to be transferred at the age of sixteen to the City of London workhouse, where he would continue to be maintained at the rate-payers' expense, but the Board managed to find him a position as an apprentice instead. He was indentured to John Lawrence in the summer of 1866, his parish providing £50 to contribute to his board and lodging over the next seven years. Fox remained with Lawrence for the full term of the apprenticeship, living with him and his wife and daughter in their house in the Holloway Road.

In the 1870s, Fox left the Lawrences and moved east to West Ham. There was plenty of work in the district for coopers, who made and repaired barrels for the docks, the breweries and the sugar refineries, but he began to take jobs on the ships. Fox became a servant to captains (he was paid just over £1 for each voyage) and then an assistant steward with the National Line, working for a time under Robert and Nattie's father. He performed menial duties, cleaning and cooking for the officers and crew, and earned about £3 per voyage, less than half of the amount paid to the chief steward and £1 less than the ordinary sailors. Between trips, he lodged in a carpenter's house in Canning Town.

In the summer of 1890 Fox was one of ninety-five men aboard the *Egypt*, the largest of the National Line steamships, as it crossed the Atlantic from New York to Liverpool with a cargo of cattle and cotton. On 17 July a fire broke out in the ship's hold. All the men on board worked furiously to douse the burning cotton bales with hoses and jets of steam, while the 600 cows tied up on the decks hollered in pain as the flames licked at them. Eventually, the master told his men to abandon ship.

The sailors were lowered into the water in six lifeboats. They rowed away and after a quarter of a mile stopped to look back. They saw the mainsail fall blazing into the ship's heart. Some of the cows broke free of their halters and leapt away from the flames into the sea, then struggled to swim clear of the burning vessel. The oarsmen rowed hard to avoid being capsized by the terrified, thrashing creatures.

A passing ship saw the distress signal set off by the *Egypt*'s boatswain and sailed to the rescue of the men in the lifeboats. Once the sailors had been lifted to safety, the captain's wife tended to their burns. For hours afterwards, the men occasionally spotted a cow beating its legs against the water until it gave up the fight and surrendered to the sea.

The rescued sailors were conscious of their luck. Six months earlier the National Line steamship *Erin*, on which Fox had also once served, had vanished in the middle of the Atlantic with 527 head of cattle and seventy-four men. The two disasters wiped out the National Line's reserve funds.

John Fox had been badly burnt in the fight to put out the *Egypt*'s fire. He was so shaken by his experience that he developed a stutter, and a horror of the open sea. He did not serve on a ship again.

In August 1895 John Lawrence visited his former apprentice in prison and forwarded a transcript of their conversation to the *Evening News*.

'How came you to be in the house with the boys Coombes for days after they killed their mother?' asked Lawrence in the interview, published on 13 August.

'They came and fetched me from the ship,' said Fox.

'How came you to be wearing their father's clothes?'

'Robert Coombes said they were a misfit,' said Fox, 'and his mother told him to give them to me.'

Lawrence asked him what share of the money from the pawnbrokers Robert had given to him.

'He did not give me any share at all,' said Fox. 'He gave me nothing.'

'But surely, if you gave him all the money, he gave you some back?'

'No. Not a penny.'

'Is it true that you went with a letter to Mr Hewson containing an application for money?'

'Yes; Robert told me to take it and I did.'

'Did he read the note to you, or give it to you open?'

'No, he did not read it to me and he fastened it up.'

'How, then, did you know that it contained an application for money?'

'Well, I supposed so because he told me to wait and bring some money back.'

'Did you not smell something very disagreeable?'

'No, nothing at all,' said Fox. 'My smell is not very good and they must have opened the windows upstairs to let the smell out. Oh, they are two very wicked boys.'

Lawrence asked him to explain how Mrs Coombes's purse came to be found in his pocket.

'I put it there myself. Robert Coombes gave me that and a shilling at the same time, and that was the only money he gave me all the time I was there.' Fox was apparently contradicting himself on the issue of whether Robert had given him any money, but this seemed a sign of confusion rather than dishonesty.

Lawrence asked him if he would have stayed in the house if he had known what had been done to Emily Coombes.

'Oh, no,' said Fox. 'I would have run out of the house as fast as I could. I would not have stayed there if I had known it for a thousand pounds.'

The polling for the general election had concluded on 7 August with a Conservative victory. Lord Salisbury was appointed prime minister.

The new home secretary, Sir Matthew White Ridley, Bt, almost immediately addressed the matter of the penny dreadfuls. He told the House of Commons on 16 August that there was little prospect of restricting the publication of such works, as a Home Office inquiry of 1888 had been unable to demonstrate a connection between cheap books and juvenile crime. Under existing laws, only publications that were blasphemous, obscene or seditious could be banned.

Though the government declared itself powerless to act against the dreadfuls, the press continued to make a connection between the Coombes boys' books and their crime. The *Leeds Times* surmised that the brothers 'had lived in a world of hallucination', their brains addled by the cheap and fantastical stories that they kept in the back parlour. Confusing the real and the imaginary, they 'had begun to look on daggers as lead pencils, quite as harmless and innocent in making their mark'.

In an editorial on the case, the medical journal *The Lancet* explained the process by which the dreadfuls could foster violence. People of a lower evolutionary type, the journal said, had an ape-like tendency to imitation. If exposed to stories of suicide or murder, degenerate individuals might be impelled to act them out.

'Penny Dreadfuls Again', ran the headline in several papers when a fifteen-year-old errand boy stole a metal clock in London in mid-August. The mother of the boy said that his behaviour had been exemplary until he became keen on such stories – all he wanted now was to go to sea and read books about pirates. The magistrate looked over the samples of literature with which the mother presented the court, and shook his head ominously.

The journalist Hugh Chisholm suggested that the outcry over the penny dreadfuls was especially marked because the Coombes crime had come so soon after the exposure of the 'abominable' crimes of Oscar Wilde, a purveyor of 'non-moral literature' for the upper circles of the literary world. Wilde was in prison in Wandsworth, south London, having been convicted in May on twenty-five counts of gross indecency. The dreadfuls, said Chisholm, were the lower-class equivalent of Wilde's decadent productions.

Yet it remained impossible to prove a pattern of cause and effect: penny dreadfuls were continually being discovered in the bedrooms and pockets of young criminals and suicides, but perhaps only because they were in the bedrooms and pockets of most boys in Britain. In August a group of about twenty boys at a north-west London board school signed a petition to the newly assembled House of Commons that begged the politicians not to issue a ban. 'We read that some people who are too old to care about adventures put all the murders down to reading these tales,' they wrote. 'We do not think there is any truth in all this, and we hope you won't suppress any of the following papers.' The boys appended a list of their favourite journals.

The Home Office turned its attention to the welfare of the Coombes brothers. There were already rumours that Nattie had threatened suicide, and now Robert had become deranged enough to be locked in a padded cell. The *Lancet*, in its editorial on the Coombes case, referred to an 'epidemic of suicide' in Britain that was especially marked among the young. The Sunday paper *The People* reported that the number of suicides in London in the past month had far exceeded the figure for July 1894, and included at least five victims who were younger than eighteen: 'The peculiar state of the atmosphere in consequence of the excessive heat has been considered to have been the cause in many cases.' The home secretary told the governor of Holloway that the

Coombes boys should be kept under strict observation by the medical officer and the chaplain. They should be housed in the prison infirmary, he advised, given plenty of exercise, and kept away from other inmates.

Earlier in the century childhood had been prized as a time of purity and innocence, but by the 1890s darker interpretations prevailed. To those influenced by the theories of Lombroso, children were quintessentially base, not so much unblemished as primeval. 'The child is, naturally, by his organisation, nearer to the animal, to the savage, to the criminal, than the adult,' wrote Havelock Ellis in *The Criminal* (1890). 'Children are naturally egoists; they will commit all enormities, sometimes, to enlarge their egoistic satisfaction.' The celebrated psychiatrist James Crichton-Browne in 1883 urged parents to 'remember that children are not little nineteenth-century men and women, but diamond editions of very remote ancestors, full of savage whims and impulses, and savage rudiments of virtue'. Henry Maudsley, the other pre-eminent psychiatrist of the age, wrote in 1895: 'Whoever observes sincerely what a child's actual mind is, without being biased by preconceived notions of its primal purity, innocence, and natural inclination to good, must see and own that its proclivities are not to good but to evil, and that the impulses which move it are the selfish impulses of passion. Give an infant in arms power in its limbs equal to its passions, and it would be more dangerous than any wild beast.'

But the psychologist James Sully, an early researcher into child development, took a different view. Sully held that children were complex and vulnerable creatures, whose treatment by adults was decisive in forming their characters and fate. A child was 'not yet a moral being', said Sully in 1895, 'and there is a certain impertinence in trying to force it under our categories of good and bad, pure and corrupt'. He observed that the young confused fact and fiction because, to them, 'words are not dead thought-symbols, but truly alive'. Children often could not articulate their fears, even to themselves, and this only made those fears the more intense: 'how carefully are they wont to hide from our sight their nameless terrors, physical and moral. Much of the deeper childish experience can only reach us, if at all, years after it is over, through the faulty medium of adult memory.'

Robert and Nattie's father visited the boys in Holloway gaol frequently – fourteen times in four weeks, he said – and he remained in London when the SS *France* sailed for New York on 19 August (the chief steward of the *Spain* took his place on the ship). In early September, Coombes gave an interview to the *Evening News* in which he outlined the plans for his sons' defence: Robert would be defended on the grounds of insanity, Nattie on the grounds that he was wholly under Robert's influence. This was the narrative that Coombes had established when interviewed by the newspapermen in New York, before even speaking to his sons or the police: Robert was the leader and Nattie the follower; Robert was warped and Nattie was impressionable. Yet the boys' schoolteachers and neighbours made no such distinction: they characterised both brothers as quick-witted, competent lads. If either was naughty, it was Nattie, who, according to Mary Jane Burrage, 'cheeked' his mother and stole her food. By his own account, Nattie had gone along with the killing and its cover-up, and afterwards it was he who seemed the most alive to the danger they faced: he hovered in the background when they encountered adults; he fled when their Aunt Emily entered the house. Many commentators at first accepted that Nattie had encouraged Robert's

murder plan, but their father firmly steered the story so that
the boys – and their fates – were divided. Within days of the
New York interviews the Treasury had asked Baggallay to discharge Nattie so that he could be called as a witness. Coombes
was shrewd to focus on saving the son who might plausibly be
saved, but his strategy entailed turning one brother against
the other, and leaving Robert to bear the consequences of the
killing alone.

Coombes did not repeat his allegation that he had banned
Fox from the house, nor Captain Hadley's story about Fox
lurking in a gangway with a knife. Now that he was back
in England, he saw that it was hopeless to try to pin the
blame for the killing on Fox. There was no evidence that
the man had any prior knowledge of the murder, and the
worst that the police or the newspapers had been able to
dredge up about him was that he once had been charged as a
'suspected person' after being found in an East End railway
station late at night. He might be convicted of helping to
conceal the crime, but this would do nothing to exculpate
Robert or Nattie.

Coombes told the *Evening News* that his eldest son had
always been a most humane child, but was strongly drawn to
morbid subjects. On his most recent visit to see his boys, he
said, Robert appeared to have returned to his better self: he
was 'much affected' by the fact of the murder, 'and expressed
wonder that he could have killed his mother'. Robert seemed
bewildered, unable to fathom what he had done. Both his father
and Dr Walker saw signs in him of anxiety and distress.

On Monday 9 September, the September sessions opened at
the Old Bailey. The Common Serjeant, Sir Forrest Fulton,
addressed the Grand Jury that had been assembled to grant

the cases on the roster a 'true bill' and so enable them to pro-
ceed to trial.

Fulton remarked on the great number of cases before the
jury – 183 to be heard in the four courts over ten days – and
the unusual gravity of many of them. There was always a
build-up of charges over the six-week summer break, said
Fulton, but he could not remember a heavier calendar than
this. Nor could he remember a case of 'greater cruelty and
heartlessness' than the first that they were to consider, the
murder of Emily Harrison Coombes. He told the jury that
Nathaniel George Coombes would not be tried, despite having been charged under the coroner's inquisition, but would
instead be called as a witness for the Crown. John Fox would
be indicted as an accessory after the fact – that is, he would
be charged with having known of the crime and assisted in
concealing it. Robert Allen Coombes would be charged with
murder.

In Holloway on Tuesday, Fox, Nattie and Robert learnt that
the Grand Jury had returned true bills and that the trial might
be held as early as Wednesday, when a judge of the Queen's
Bench would come to the Old Bailey to hear the sessions' most
serious cases. Nattie was informed that he would appear as a
witness rather than a defendant, but would go in to the dock
with the others. Robert knew for certain now that he would
face the murder charge alone, and that his brother's testimony
might help to convict him.

Dr Walker talked to Robert that day about the forthcoming
trial. The boy at first seemed gleeful at the prospect of going
to the Old Bailey, telling the doctor that it would be a 'splendid sight' and he was looking forward to it. He would wear
his best clothes, he said, and have his boots well polished. He
started to talk about his cats, and then suddenly fell silent. A

moment later he burst into tears. Dr Walker asked him why he was crying. 'Because I want my cats,' said Robert, 'and my mandolin.'

On Wednesday, Justice Kennedy of the Queen's Bench went from the Royal Courts of Justice to take his seat in the Old Court of the Old Bailey. He announced that he did not intend to hear the Coombes case that day but would appoint any other day that suited counsel in the case. One of the prosecutors suggested Friday and Kennedy agreed. He confirmed that the charge against Nattie was being withdrawn.

Kennedy proceeded to hear two other cases on Wednesday (a fatal assault and a child rape) and two on Thursday (a woman charged with neglecting a baby who had died in her care, and a man accused of the manslaughter of his wife). Friday and Saturday came and went without the Coombes trial being heard. Instead, Kennedy dealt with a fishmonger's assistant who had accidentally killed another man in a fight about a woman; an American lawyer who had tried to blackmail a Dorset rector; a soldier who had shot at a woman who turned down his advances, and a thirteen-year-old servant girl accused of starting fires in her mistress's house. The jury was unable to reach a verdict on this last case. They were dismissed and a fresh jury appointed. Fox and Robert learnt that their trial would be held on Monday.

Remand prisoners were entitled to send a letter a day, posted at the government's expense, and on Saturday 14 September, Robert wrote to the Reverend Francis Shaw, a curate at a mission church off the Barking Road. The Coombes family went regularly to church — they were among only a fifth of Londoners to do so – and Robert and Nattie also attended Sunday school. It was said that the boys had been to church with John Fox even on the Sunday after the murder. According to the interview their father gave to the *Evening News*, Robert was a great favourite of the Reverend Shaw, and the curate had recently prepared the boy for confirmation. Coombes said that Shaw had offered to give evidence on Robert's behalf at the Old Bailey.

Francis Longsdon Shaw was the youngest son of a Derbyshire corn merchant. His mother had died in 1872, when he was a baby, and he was sent to board at a vicarage in Staffordshire. At the age of ten he had an epiphany during a mission service on a beach in the Welsh resort of Llandudno. Seven years later he was admitted to Trinity College, Cambridge, to read theology, and in May 1894 he was licensed to the curacy at St Andrew's, at the Plaistow end of the Barking Road. St Andrew's was a highly ceremonial church, known for its promotion of English plainsong. The parish had grown so dramatically since the church was built in 1870 that two of its curates – Shaw, who was twenty-three, and Allen Hay, another Cambridge graduate – were deputed to establish a mission a little further up the Barking Road. They raised funds by staging benefits in the parish hall (one featured a mandolinist called Miss Halfpenny and a ventriloquist and 'necromancist' known as Signor Ralpho) and were able to open St Martin's Mission in the summer of 1894. The Reverends Shaw and Hay had eschewed comfortable livings in the hope of bringing spiritual and practical relief to this deprived neighbourhood. They organised magic-lantern shows for local children, and they lived among their flock, lodging in ordinary terraced houses near the mission. Shaw was the most highly educated man that Robert knew.

Robert addressed his letter to the Reverend Mr Shaw at 583 Barking Road. 'Dear Mr Shaw,' he wrote.

I received your letter on last Tuesday. I think I will get hung, but I don't cares as long as I get a good breakfast before they hang me. If they don't hang me I think I will commit suicide. That will do just as well. I will strangle myself. I hope you are all well. I go up on Monday to the Old Bailey to be tried. I hope you will be there. I think they will sentence me to death, and if they do I will call all the witnesses liars.

I remain, your affectionate friend, RA Coombes

Robert had drawn two pictures on the letter. The first, captioned 'Scene I – Going to the Scaffold', was a sketch of three figures making their way towards a gallows, with the word 'Executioner' written above the first figure. The second figure, presumably, was Robert; and the third may have represented Fox, though he did not face a capital charge, or Nattie, though he faced no charges at all.

Beneath this drawing, Robert wrote: 'Will – To Dr Walker, £3,000; to Mr Hay, £2,000; to Mr Shaw, £5,000; to my father, £60,000; to each of the warders, £300.'

The second picture was entitled, 'Scene II – Hanging.' It showed a body suspended by the neck from a gallows, with a hand pulling the rope and a message issuing from the mouth of the dangling figure: 'Good-bye; here goes nothing. PS – Excuse the crooked scaffold. I was too heavy, so I bent it. I leave you £5,000.'

The letter was skittish, excited, switching between bleakness and gaiety, lightness and weight. Robert seemed full of bravado (he didn't care about death, only breakfast) and defiance (he would kill himself if he was not killed; he would denounce the witnesses as liars if he was convicted). In the captions to the pictures, he was both an airy 'nothing' on the gallows, and a being so heavy that he bent the wooden beam. The reference to his weight bending the scaffold was a joke – a piece of gallows humour – about the wobbly line of his drawing. The tone of the letter was unsteadily detached, as if Robert was half allowing and half refusing the sadness that had started to leak in when he wept in Walker's office about his mandolin and his cats.

On the day that he killed his mother, the explanation that Robert had given for her disappearance was that a relative had died and left them money. This was a veiled version of the truth: his mother was the relative who had died, and the boys and their playmate Fox were the inheritors of her wealth. 'All I know is that we are rich,' he had told his aunt. When Robert predicted his own death, in the letter to Shaw, he became the munificent benefactor. As if his love was money, he bestowed his bounty on the men who had shown him kindness: the prison warders, the Plaistow curates, the prison doctor and, most of all, his father. In this fantasy, death was not an absence but a release of riches.

PART III

THESE TENDER TIMES

9

COVER HER FACE

In the morning of Monday 16 September, Robert, Nattie and John Fox were taken from their cells to the yard of Holloway gaol, where they were ushered into the back of a horse-drawn van and fastened into narrow boxed compartments. A few warders accompanied them on the drive south to Newgate gaol, a four-mile trip that took half an hour.

The Black Maria discharged its passengers at Newgate, next to the Old Bailey law courts in the City of London. Until 1868 a gallows had stood just outside the prison entrance; as executions were no longer conducted in public, the gallows were now inside the yard, in a purpose-built shed fitted with a horizontal glass window. If Robert were to be sentenced to death, this was where he would be hanged. The most recent execution here had been that of Paul Koczula, a twenty-four-year-old waiter who had been found guilty of robbing and murdering his boss's wife at a German restaurant in Soho. Dr Walker of Holloway gaol had been present at the waiter's death. On 14 August 1894, he and the other witnesses had watched from benches in the yard as the hangman placed a noose around Koczula's neck and then pulled a lever to let him drop out of sight through a trapdoor in the ground.

The Coombes brothers and John Fox were led from the gaol to the Old Bailey courthouse through an underground passage known as Birdcage Walk. The roof of the tunnel was a heavy iron grating; the flagstone floor covered the graves of executed convicts.

Shortly after eleven o'clock, the warders guided Robert, Nattie and Fox up a small staircase that climbed straight from the Old Bailey basement into the prisoners' dock in the Old Court. Robert's shirt collar was turned up beneath his tennis blazer and Nattie wore a bow tie. Fox had spruced himself up a little, too. His wispy beard had grown fuller and blacker, and he sported a red handkerchief in his breast pocket.

Robert seemed to be suppressing laughter as he stepped in to the raised and bulwarked dock. Nattie 'gazed around like a visitor inspecting a new building,' said the *Star*, 'with a truly horrible unconcern'. Fox's expression was grave, and he trembled visibly as he looked about him.

Neither the boys' father nor their Aunt Emily was present, since both were waiting in a chamber reserved for the witnesses, but the forty-foot-square courtroom was crammed. The benches to the right of the dock were filled with reporters and newspaper artists, a gallery above the dock with members of the public. In front of the dock, in a well between the defendants and the judge, were the barristers-at-law who would defend and prosecute the case and the solicitors and government officials who had instructed them. The twelve men of the jury sat on benches in a box to the left, beneath three square windows that looked on to the dark granite walls of Newgate. Next to the windows were reflectors to brighten the room, and huge lamps for use when London became dense with fog – the city's 'pea-soupers' of soot and sulphur were at a peak in the 1890s.

Justice William Rann Kennedy, the judge who would conduct the trial, sat with two Old Bailey sheriffs opposite the dock. Behind them hung a crimson curtain and a gilded sword, above them a canopy and a carving of the Royal Arms. Robert peered over the dock railing at the judge, smiling broadly.

Kennedy, who was forty-nine, had smooth, clean-shaven skin, full cheeks, large brown eyes and a slightly downturned mouth, which gave him a doleful expression. He was well turned out in court, being one of the few lawyers in Westminster to adhere to the old custom of having his wig powdered and done up every morning. Before becoming a judge he had run a practice in Birkenhead, near Liverpool, specialising in maritime and commercial law, and had twice stood unsuccessfully as Liberal candidate in his constituency. Kennedy had been known at Eton and Cambridge as a brilliant classical scholar and linguist, but once appointed to the Queen's Bench in 1892 he proved ponderous, with none of the intellectual sparkle that had marked his academic career.

The case against Robert and Fox was to be presented by Charles Gill and Horace Avory, both of whom regularly appeared for the Crown at the Old Bailey. Earlier in the year, the two had prosecuted Oscar Wilde. Famously, Gill had asked Wilde to gloss a line from a poem by his friend Lord Alfred Douglas: 'What is the love that dare not speak its name?' It was the love between an older and a younger man, Wilde replied, 'when the older man has intellect, and the younger man has all the joy, hope and glamour of life before him'. Gill had also helped to convict James Canham Read, the murderer of Florence Dennis, in Chelmsford the previous winter.

Gill began by asking for Nattie to be discharged. The Crown had decided not to prosecute him, despite the West Ham coroner's belief that he should stand trial, because his evidence might help secure convictions against Robert and Fox. He was clearly less culpable than his brother, and he was the only person who could corroborate or refute the key details of Robert's confession and Fox's account of the aftermath of the crime.

After Nattie had been removed from the dock, the charges were read out by the Clerk of Arraigns. Kennedy asked Robert how he pleaded to the murder charge.

'Guilty,' said Robert.

His counsel, William Grantham, quickly intervened to inform the judge that Robert's plea was 'not guilty'.

'Tell him to say "not guilty",' said Kennedy.

'Not guilty,' said Robert, with another wide smile.

Fox was charged with 'receiving, comforting and abetting' Robert, in the knowledge that he had committed the murder.

'Not guilty,' said Fox.

Just as Gill was about to open the prosecution case, the proceedings were interrupted by an official who wanted to consult Justice Kennedy on a point of law. Kennedy left the room. While the court waited for his return, Fox and Robert were provided with chairs.

When Kennedy came back to the bench at noon, Gill rose to his feet again and ran through the facts of the case. A handsome man of forty-three, Gill was one of the finest advocates of his generation: his preparation for trials was thorough and intelligent, his manner in court unshowy, persuasive and scrupulously fair. His only mannerism was to remove his spectacles for emphasis, whether to signal surprise, doubt, indignation or encouragement. He was suspected of a lurking sympathy for many of the defendants he prosecuted.

The court fell silent when Gill began to reprise the story of the murder. Robert smiled and looked over attentively as the barrister described him buying a dagger with which to kill his mother and concealing it until his father had gone to sea. Gill told how Robert slipped the dagger under his pillow as he got into his mother's bed on the night of 7 July and how he rose before dawn to retrieve the knife, raise it above his mother's body and stab her in the bosom.

As Gill's account went on Robert became sullen and distracted, glancing around the room and then staring at the ground, though he smiled again when the advertisement that he had composed for the *Evening News* was read out to the court.

Gill told the jury that the Crown had made the fullest possible inquiries into Robert's state of mind and had passed to his counsel all the information that they had gathered from the Holloway medical officer.

He added that if the charge against Robert were to fail, that against Fox would automatically fail.

The judge queried this claim. 'Do I understand you, Mr Gill, to say that a person cannot aid and assist an insane person in the concealment of a murder?'

'No,' said Gill. 'I do not say that. I quite admit that I went a little too far in saying that Fox could not be convicted if the lad was insane.'

Kennedy accepted Gill's retraction and gave him leave to call his witnesses.

Robert and Nattie's aunt, Emily Coombes, was the first to be summoned. She entered the witness box to the left of the dock, between the judges' bench and the jury enclosure, and told the court that she had last seen her sister-in-law in the evening of Saturday 6 July. The boys had been playing in the garden, she said, 'quite happy'. She gave evidence about her subsequent visits to Cave Road, and then Robert's counsel rose to cross-examine her.

William Grantham, the twenty-nine-year-old son of a High Court judge, was educated at Harrow and Cambridge, and had been called to the Bar in 1890. He had been appearing at the Old Bailey since 1893, usually as prosecuting counsel in theft and burglary trials. His strategy in this case was to present Robert as deranged and – in some respects, at least – guileless.

In reply to his questions, Emily said that Robert's confession to her was 'quite open and frank'; the boy 'did not seem to feel his position at all'.

Grantham asked her about Robert's mother.

Aunt Emily said she had seen her sister-in-law nearly every day since Christmas. 'I had known his mother many years,' she said. 'She was a very excitable woman.' To be 'excitable' was to be impulsive, agitated, extravagantly emotional; it was a trait sometimes associated with drunkenness, sometimes with hysteria. According to the trajectory of degeneration set out by the French psychiatrist Bénédict Morel in 1857, it would be natural for such tendencies in Emily Coombes to become more acute in her son: a retrogressive family exhibited mild nervous disorders in one generation, neurosis or hysteria in the next, and psychosis in the third; the subsequent, and probably last, generation would be marked by idiocy.

The barrister asked whether Robert had seemed excitable.

'I have noticed him excitable many times,' she said. 'His mother gave him medicine for it when he complained of his head.'

Frederick Sherwood, on behalf of Fox, was next to cross-examine her. A solicitor's son aged thirty, Sherwood was educated at Oxford and had been appearing as counsel at Old Bailey trials since 1890. Sherwood hoped to persuade the jury that Fox was a trusting dullard, a warm-hearted old fool gulled by a brilliant child.

Sherwood asked Emily for her impression of Fox.

'Fox struck me as rather a stupid man,' she said.

Kennedy announced an adjournment for lunch.

When the court reconvened in the afternoon, Nattie was called to the witness box. He looked much younger than twelve, said the *Sun* reporter, who was struck by the 'grotesque' spectacle of 'this little lad testifying against his brother, scarce older than himself, for a horrible murder'. Nattie stammered slightly as he replied to Gill's questions.

Nattie told how Robert showed him the dagger, saying: 'This is the knife I am going to do her with,' and stuffed it up the back bedroom chimney. He related how Robert came to him on 8 July, having killed their mother, and held out the silver and gold watches. 'You can have one,' said Robert, handing Nattie the silver watch, 'and I will have the other.'

'My mother has beaten me several times,' said Nattie. 'She hit me on the Sunday before she died.' Asked why he was punished that day, he replied: 'I was naughty.' He reported that Robert was present during the beating, and afterwards said: 'If you cough twice that will show that I will do it.' There was some confusion about the day on which Emily Coombes had beaten Nattie. Robert had told the police that the beating took place on the Saturday. Nattie had told the coroner the same, but afterwards insisted that he was thrashed on the Sunday.

Gill asked whether he had coughed as agreed.

'I did not cough.'

Asked whether his brother had given any reason for the murder, Nattie said: 'Yes. He wanted to go away to some place – to some island – and live.'

Gill asked why Robert had gone into his mother's room in the week after the murder.

'He went to see if she was all right,' said Nattie.

Robert's counsel, Grantham, asked about the times that Robert ran away.

'My brother ran away from home suddenly on two occasions, I think. He took me with him – he asked me to go with him.'

Grantham asked how their father had reacted.

'Our father said nothing about it.'

Nattie confirmed that his brother had been 'funny in the head', having suffered from headaches and excitability.

What was Robert's manner after the murder? asked Grantham.

'He was quite calm,' said Nattie, 'and knew what he was saying then.'

Sherwood examined Nattie on behalf of John Fox.

'Mother was kind to Fox, too,' Nattie said. 'He used to come to the house pretty often. Sometimes he was not there for a week, but sometimes he stopped for a good time.'

Fox leant forward in the dock, listening anxiously to Nattie's answers.

'He used to saw up the wood and brush up the garden,' continued Nattie. 'When he worked in the house I and my brother talked to him from time to time. We knew him pretty well. I used to go out with Fox sometimes before Mother died. Sometimes I just went to the top of the street with him to see him off.'

Nattie said that he and Robert had spoken to Fox about twice since the arrest. 'He doesn't talk much. When he was staying in the house with us he did not talk very much. He is not very sharp. Sometimes we teased him.'

Horace Avory re-examined Nattie on behalf of the Crown. Avory was forty-four, the son of an Old Bailey clerk, and a sterner, more austere figure than his colleague Gill: he was wiry in build, with a small head on a long neck, pinched features and thin lips. He inquired further about the conversations between Fox and the boys, asking 'the most insidious' questions, said the *Sun*, in an attempt to prove that Fox knew about the murder, but Nattie gave him no satisfaction.

'We talked to him when we were generally playing cards,' said Nattie. 'We used to talk about who would win the game and that, nothing else. He used to tell us a tale sometimes.'

Avory asked if Nattie and his brother had discussed the murder in that period.

'After that Monday when Mother was killed my brother never talked about her. We never said a word to each other about it.'

'What was Robert going to do with your mother's body?' asked Avory. 'Did he ever say?'

Robert wanted to 'keep her', Nattie said. 'He said he was going to leave her up on the bed there, and put some quicklime over her. He said that soon after he did it, on the Tuesday, I think. After the Tuesday nothing further was ever said about it.'

The revelation that Robert had planned to preserve his mother's body with quicklime caused a stir in the courtroom. Avory sat down and Nattie left the witness box.

The rest of the afternoon's evidence turned principally on what John Fox knew of the crime. The K division police surgeon,

Alfred Kennedy, described the condition of Emily Coombes's body when it was found, and the multitude of maggots in the bedroom: 'on the bed alone there was quite a bushel of them, I should say'. A bushel was the equivalent, in dry goods, of eight gallons, or sixty-four pints. Dr Kennedy said that when he reached Cave Road on Wednesday 17 July, he could smell the decomposing body from the street. 'I am not asserting that the smell was equally diffused some days before,' he said, under cross-examination from Sherwood. Both the room door and the front door had been open when he reached the house, the doctor agreed, and the odour would have been much less intense before then.

The court heard evidence from several of the other witnesses who had testified in the West Ham court. Sherwood, in an effort to convince the jury that it was plausible that Fox had not been aware of the decomposing corpse, asked the Robertsons of 37 Cave Road if they had smelt anything odd.

James Robertson said: 'When I was in my garden I did not notice any smell coming from the house. I should not, because there are market gardens there at the back coming up to the Coombes' garden, and manure is often put there, and there are often large quantities of manure and smells there.' His wife, Rosina, testified that she had not noticed a bad smell either. The Coombes' and Robertsons' front doors were adjacent, she said, though their kitchen doors faced in opposite directions – the garden door of number 35 looked on to that of number 33. She had seen Fox playing cricket with the boys in the yard most evenings. 'They seemed pretty cheerful,' she said.

In his examination of Charles Pearson, the National Line officer, and John Hewson, the National Line cashier, Sherwood attempted to establish that Fox was both trustworthy and simple-minded. Pearson said that he had known Fox for three years: 'I have always found him honest, but he is not very bright as to intellect; I should think he is half-witted. He would not be put to do anything difficult, or any message that required much thought. I knew the Coombes knew him, and that he was in the habit of going to them and doing odd jobs there.'

Hewson said that Fox had lived in the docks for more than twenty years. 'Everybody knows him. He carried sailors' and officers' bags, and fetched things for persons from their houses, and posted letters. We are under the impression that Fox is half-witted, but otherwise well-behaved.' He told the court about Fox being caught in the fire on the *Egypt*. 'I think he was scared then.'

From the pawnbrokers, Sherwood elicited that there had been nothing shifty about Fox's behaviour when he had pledged the watches and mandolin. He 'appeared to be like a sailor', said Henry Goldsworthy of the Commercial Road. 'He did not seem very bright,' noted Richard Bourne of Plaistow. Many pawnbrokers were practised at giving testimony in court, since they frequently found themselves in possession of stolen goods. Goldsworthy had appeared at the Old Bailey as recently as the previous Monday, to testify to having been pledged an overcoat that formed part of a cargo stolen from a Jewish furrier at the Victoria Dock in 1893.

Justice Kennedy announced that the trial would be adjourned until the following morning.

At the close of the first day of the trial, the warders led Robert and John Fox back through the door in the dock and down the stairs to the Old Bailey basement, then along Birdcage Walk to the prison. Newgate had until 1882 been London's main gaol, but was now used only to house prisoners waiting to be tried at the Old Bailey, or to be executed in the courtyard. Even when sessions were in progress, the gaol lay half-empty. If a prisoner were to meet anyone while being walked through its corridors, the Newgate rules stipulated that he should turn to face the wall, put his hands behind his back, and wait until the other person had passed.

Robert and Fox were admitted through a thick iron door to a long stone corridor beneath tiers of cells. 'It was as if you were walking at the bottom of the hold of some great petrified ship,' observed the journalist W. T. Stead in 1886, 'looking up at the deserted decks.' Wire netting had been stretched across the well between the cells, to prevent prisoners from jumping to their deaths. The warders took Robert and Fox up the iron staircases to the balustraded walkways and into the cells in which they would spend the night.

The *Saturday Review*, commenting on the evidence presented in the Old Bailey, objected to Dr Kennedy's allusion to the 'bushel' of maggots in Emily Coombes's room: 'Why not two bushels, good doctor, or a dozen?' it asked. 'Give your evidence as to the cause of death directly, and leave the natural details to the charnel-house alone; there is enough for the jury to gape at.' The doctor's specificity had some relevance, though. The quantity and distribution of grubs helped to date the murder. A blowfly's egg took a day to hatch into a maggot, which fed for four days before moving away to find a dark nook in which its soft body could stiffen into a cocoon. Ten days later it would break out as a fly. Since the maggots in Cave Road had strayed far beyond their breeding and feeding grounds in the body's cavities, spilling on to the bed and the floor, it was evident that they had been alive for a week or more. Kennedy's evidence about the extent of the decomposition was pertinent to John Fox's claim that he had no notion that anything was wrong in the house; and it seemed proof of the callousness of the boys. Robert and Nattie had left their mother to rot, allowing the blowflies' offspring to consume her as if the insects were their proxies. It was an additional desecration.

Yet the court had also heard that after Thursday 11 July, when the corpse began to smell and the blowflies' eggs began to hatch, Robert only once stepped inside the room. He chose to pawn his beloved mandolin, to write begging letters and to doctor documents rather than venture into the chamber and renew his pillage of the family valuables. He had already covered his mother's face with a sheet and a pillow. Perhaps he failed to fetch more jewels or apply the lime because he could not bear to go near her changing body.

In the ten days that Robert and Nattie shared the house with their mother's corpse, reality was provisional for them; time was suspended. For as long as no adult knew about the murder, it had not quite happened. The boys continued to play: in the yard, at the park, in the parlour, in the street. They inhabited a make-believe world, in which Emily Coombes might be 'all right'; she might be 'kept'; she might even come back, as John Fox warned, to chastise her sons for making too much noise in the yard. The brothers tacitly agreed not to speak of the killing, and they chose the trusting, kindly Fox to sanction their pact. In this dreamlike moment, their lives had not yet been transformed, and their mother's had not been ended. As Nattie had said to his brother on 8 July – in awe, in horror, in simple disbelief – 'You ain't done it.'

The lawyers in the Old Bailey were presenting the court with opposed narratives: the prosecution told of a boy who was all head and no heart, a callous killer, while the defence depicted a boy whose reason had been utterly overthrown by his crazed emotions. There was no room for a story in which Robert was both scheming and desperate, ruthless and lost, in which he both knew and did not know what he had done and why he had done it.

Outside the Old Bailey in the evening of 16 September, newsboys were touting papers that carried the first reports of the Coombes trial. The *Spectator* noted, with disapproval, that they were being snapped up as quickly as if they had carried updates on a political crisis, a military battle or an important sporting event. In Islington, north London, a wax worker was offering models of the Coombes boys' and John Fox's heads for sale to showmen. Across the Thames, on the south bank, a penny theatre was staging a melodrama about the murder. Already the narrative of Robert Coombes's crime had been published throughout the country, illustrated by artists, and adapted for the stage. The appetite for news of the case, said the *Spectator*, 'reveals a strange and bad condition of feeling'. The *Saturday Review*'s distaste for the lurid detail supplied by Dr Kennedy was also a revulsion at the journalists and dramatists and wax modellers, the readers and audiences of London descending like vermin on the story of Emily Coombes's death.

THE BOYS SPRINGING UP AMONGST US

A light fog settled on London on Tuesday morning, but once it had cleared the day proved bright and very warm. In the Old Bailey, Charles Gill QC continued to make the case against Robert Coombes and John Fox. He called PC Twort to the witness box.

The constable described the events of Wednesday 17 July and read out Robert's confession to murder. In reply to questions from Robert's counsel, he confirmed that the boy was 'very frank and open' when he interviewed him: 'he told me all he knew without my asking him questions'. Nor had Robert tried to hide the murder weapon, said Twort, or to dispose of all the valuables in the house.

When Sherwood questioned him on behalf of Fox, Twort testified that Fox had sat in silence in the back parlour on the Wednesday afternoon. 'There was a good deal of talk amongst the women,' said Twort. 'Fox took no part in it. He took no notice. He did not seem to take any interest or appreciate the situation.'

Harriet Hayward of number 39 gave her evidence about the events of Wednesday 17 July. On cross-examination by Grantham, she declined to describe Robert as 'excitable'. 'I always looked on Robert as a bright, intelligent boy,' she said. 'I did not see any excitability about him.' She agreed that he had behaved honourably towards Fox when the crime was discovered: 'He took the blame off Fox and incriminated himself.'

When Sherwood asked her about his client, she said that she had seen Fox often at 35 Cave Road, chopping wood. She insisted on Fox's integrity and kindness, as she had in the magistrates' and coroner's courts. 'I always looked upon him as being very simple and good-natured,' she said. 'I don't believe he would hurt anyone. Mrs Coombes always spoke of him as being very trustworthy. When she went out she could always trust him in the place. I could see that the Coombes liked him. They all liked him. He was fond of playing with the boys.'

Inspector Gilbert described his search of the house and listed the items that the police had collected. A bloodstained piece of rag – the cloth left on Emily Coombes's bed – lay on the desk in front of him as he gave his evidence. In reply to a question from Grantham, Gilbert confirmed that he had found items on which Robert could have raised money. He handed Robert's nightshirt to the jury for inspection. The shirt had twenty or thirty spots of blood on the front and arms. Gilbert gave Robert's collection of penny dreadfuls to the judge.

'They are apparently sensational stories,' said Kennedy. He looked through the bundle and then laid it down on the bench by his side.

During Gilbert's evidence, Robert quietly laughed to himself. He began to make comical, grotesque faces at both the inspector and the judge. He stuck out his tongue at Justice Kennedy, who looked back at him severely. The *Evening News* noted that the boy had devised a game whereby he would smile and look intelligent, then pass both hands down over his face before removing them to reveal his eyebrows twitching and his lips moving, as if he were repeating words to himself. He would replace this distorted face in a flash with a bright, calm expression. The *London Daily News* interpreted Robert's changing faces not as a parody or impersonation of madness but as spasms of emotion. 'His callousness in the dock was extraordinary,' it reported, 'though now and then he buried his face in his hands. At other times, he made hideous grimaces at the Judge and witnesses.' He often looked 'more like an ape than a human being', said the *Sun*, 'mouthing in a meaningless way like an idiot'. As a defendant in a murder trial, Robert was not entitled to give evidence. His equivocal plea – 'Guilty' and then 'Not guilty' – and his strange dumb show were the only representations he could make. His performance was hard to read: some observers saw a clever boy mocking the proceedings; others a child who had lost control.

Once he had dismissed Inspector Gilbert, Gill had finished establishing the facts of the case. He would now summon witnesses to testify to Robert's character: Gill intended to show that the boy was rational rather than insane. First he called the headmasters of the three board schools that Robert had attended in Plaistow.

Robert and Nattie had been going to school since they were five. From nine o'clock to twelve o'clock each morning and from two to four each afternoon, they took classes in one of the large school buildings that had been established after the passage of the Education Act of 1870. A West Ham board school educated more than a thousand pupils, grouped in classes of between seventy and eighty. The infants (those children younger than seven) were usually housed on the ground floor, the girls on the next floor and the boys on the top.

The regime in the board schools was strict. Children were expected to rise when an adult entered or left a room, to answer 'Yes, ma'am', 'No, sir', 'If you please, ma'am' when addressing teachers, to form neat lines to file in and out of the building. When not at their lessons, they were taught to hold their hands behind their backs or to place them on their heads. They learnt to stand to attention at their desks and to march on the spot in unison. The teachers in East London schools checked the children's faces for dirt in the mornings and endeavoured to train their young charges not to drop the 'h's at the beginning of words. For discipline, they used the cane. Order, cleanliness and obedience were the chief precepts of the system.

Critics complained that the board schools espoused a rigid, mechanical style of learning, driven by the fact that their grants were awarded according to the number of children who rose by an academic 'standard' each year. There was little incentive to foster the children's creativity and self-expression. None the less, the towering school buildings were beacons of aspiration – 'oases', as one commentator described them, 'in the desert of drab two-storied cottages'. 'Each school,' said another observer, 'stands up from its playground like a church in God's acre ringing its bell.'

The Coombes boys' first school was in Limehouse, where they and their parents lived until 1890. The family then moved temporarily to Toxteth Park, Liverpool, where the brothers spent a year at St Bride's school. On their return to London in 1891 both boys attended Grange Road school, known locally as the Sewer Bridge school because of its proximity to the bridge over the Northern Outfall Sewer, which carried north London's effluent to the Thames.

'I am headmaster of the Grange Road school,' said George Hollamby, a fifty-three-year-old widower who lived in Stratford and had worked at the school since it opened in 1881. 'Robert Coombes was there in 1891, 1892 and 1893. He left in 1893, though there was a long interval of absence between 1891 and 1892.' The Coombes family had again spent several months in Toxteth Park in this period. It was on their return to London that they moved to 35 Cave Road.

'When he left he was in the fourth standard,' said Hollamby. 'His capacity was very good.'

The fourth standard, which Robert attained when he was eleven, was the level required to graduate from elementary school at thirteen. To achieve this standard, a child needed to recite eighty lines of poetry, read with fluency and expression from a passage chosen by the school inspector, write from dictation, making no more than three spelling mistakes, solve maths problems relating to weight, length and area, and be tested in drawing, singing and two other subjects such as grammar, geography, science or history. To prepare for the tests, the pupils memorised material in their 'readers', textbooks containing a miscellany of literary extracts and factual lists of kings, battles, rivers, British colonies, and so on. Inspectors visited the schools to examine the children in the autumn.

Robert's counsel, Grantham, asked Hollamby why the boy had left his school.

'In November 1893 he ran away from school,' the headmaster said. 'There was a slight trouble in the school with the teacher.'

Grantham asked whether a doctor had been involved in Robert's transfer from Grange Road to the nearby Stock Street board school.

'I know nothing about his being removed owing to a doctor's interference,' replied Hollamby. 'The school committee made a special order for his removal to Stock Street – that school was full at the time.'

Grantham asked whether Robert had suffered from headaches.

'While with me he complained of headache on more than one occasion,' said Hollamby.

Gill, for the prosecution, asked how often he had made such complaints, and to whom.

'He complained that his head ached to me or to the teacher,' said Hollamby. 'Not often.'

'I am headmaster of Stock Street school,' said Gill's next witness, Jesse Weber Smith, a forty-four-year-old teacher who lived in Forest Gate, north of Plaistow, and had been in charge of Stock Street since it opened in 1888. 'Robert was in Standard V when admitted. He passed that and was in Standard VI. I should say he was a very clever boy for his age.' The requirements for the fifth standard included a hundred-line recitation and the addition and subtraction of fractions. Since relatively few children attained this level, the class to which Robert graduated at Stock Street was smaller than those lower down the school, and dominated by 'clean-collar' boys from more respectable homes.

In cross-examination, Grantham asked Smith about the circumstances of Robert's transfer. Smith said that the West Ham school committee had made a special order for Robert's admission to Stock Street. 'Our school was full at the time – it was an unusual thing to make such an order.'

Grantham asked him how Stock Street differed from Grange Road school.

'There is very little difference between the schools,' said Smith. 'They are both public elementary schools. I suppose the exchange was made in consequence of a report by the attendance officer.'

Grantham asked him about Robert's behaviour. 'I gave the boy a good character while with me,' said Smith. 'He was a very good boy, who gave no trouble whatsoever.'

'He was very precocious?' asked Grantham.

'No,' Smith replied. 'I should not say that.'

Grantham was trying to suggest that Robert was mentally abnormal. Many scientists, Lombroso among them, held that precocity was a form of disease. 'Singularly precocious' children 'of extreme nervous constitution', observed the psychiatrist Henry Maudsley, were the 'outcomes of a process of degeneracy in the stock'. The *Dictionary of Psychological Medicine* advised that such children were more prone to madness than others.

The latest instalment of Thomas Hardy's new novel – subsequently published as *Jude the Obscure* – featured just such a child, a prematurely adult nine-year-old called Little Father Time. Little Time is an old soul in a young body, a figure of the despair and foreboding of the *fin de siècle*. He is tormented by the idea that he and his younger siblings are a burden to his parents and, in the chapter published in *Harper's New Monthly Magazine* in September 1895, he decides to kill the other children and then himself. They are found in their bedroom dangling from clothes hooks.

'The doctor says there are such boys springing up amongst us,' says the child's father, Jude; 'boys of a sort unknown in the last generation – the outcome of new views of life. They seem to see all its terrors before they are old enough to have staying power to resist them.'

The next witness for the prosecution was Charles Truelove, forty, another resident of Forest Gate and the headmaster of Cave Road school. Both Coombes brothers had transferred to this school when it opened in July 1894. The entrance to the boys' playground was through a decorative brick archway directly opposite the front door of 35 Cave Road. Truelove testified that Robert had left school for good on 30 May, having reached the age as well as the standard required by law.

'He was a very intelligent lad,' said Truelove. 'He passed the sixth standard with me and was placed in the seventh. He was a very good boy.' To pass the sixth standard, a boy needed to be able to understand proportion, vulgar fractions and recurring decimals (the education department ruled that questions involving recurring decimals would not be put to girls) as well as to recite 150 lines by Shakespeare, Milton or another canonical author, and to explain the allusions in the passage that he had learnt.

Nattie was still on the school roll, said Truelove. He had passed the fifth standard exams in the autumn and was now studying for the sixth. Nattie had attended school until Friday 5 July, said the headmaster, but was absent on the following Monday. This was the day of his mother's murder. 'I sent to ask about him,' said Truelove, 'and a verbal answer came that he had gone into the country.'

The testimony of all three headmasters contradicted the rumours that had been published in the papers about Robert's persistent truancy and disobedience. Rather, he emerged as a compliant and very able pupil, well liked by his teachers. He had flourished at school, the mysterious incident at Grange

Road excepted. Gill had succeeded in establishing that the boy was astute and rational, but in the process had made him a more sympathetic figure: sensitive, gifted, eager to please his elders.

Gill's last witness was Robert's employer at the Thames Iron Works, the shipyard at which he had taken a job a fortnight after leaving Truelove's school.

Johnson described himself as foreman plater at the Thames Iron and Shipbuilding Company Limited. He said that Robert was employed by the company in June as a plater's boy. 'He worked under my supervision and I considered his capacity was very good.'

Robert was one of about 3,000 employees of the Thames Iron Works, a company that manufactured and built vessels on the dry docks. When he joined 'the Limited', as the works were known locally, the yard was building a Japanese battleship, the *Fuji Yama*, a project that had been severely delayed by the ice and frosts of the winter. In June, in the heat, the construction was proceeding at a furious pace – the workers were putting 150 tons of iron on to the ship's frame each week.

The managers of heavily unionised industries such as shipbuilding and boilermaking found it much cheaper to hire boys than men. A couple of decades earlier, boys had been employed as apprentices to platers, riveters and caulkers, but the increase in automation meant that they were now more often used to run errands and mind machines. A plater's boy might also assist his boss in the workshop, cutting and shaping sheets of iron on a lathe, placing them on moulds and bending them into shape. The armour plates, more than fifteen feet long, three feet wide and four inches thick, were sent to the ship's skeleton to be riveted and welded into place.

The work in the shops and the dry docks was dirty and exhausting, and it could be dangerous. Some employees fell to their deaths from scaffolds over the ships, were crushed by iron sheets, burnt by red-hot bolts or blown up by exploding boilers. Most were eventually deafened by the roar of the yard. The hammers rang and pounded, the machines thrashed and whirred, the lathes shrieked through metal, the guns fired rivets into the plates.

Robert wanted to leave the shipyard almost as soon as he had started but his mother insisted that he stick with it: she had withstood years of relative hardship in the expectation that the family's collective income would rise when the boys went out to work. Though Robert's pay was far less than an adult worker's wage it was still a significant contribution to the family purse – typically, an assistant to a plater would earn between five and eight shillings a week. Boy workers handed their earnings over to their mothers, who usually gave them about sixpence back as pocket money. Since women controlled the household budgets, even men tended to give the bulk of their wage packets to their wives.

George Johnson informed the court that Robert worked at the iron yard until Monday 24 June, and came back for his money the next day. He left without giving a reason. Johnson provided him with a good reference for future employers.

Robert resigned from the ironworks on the day after the *France* reached London. He may have calculated that his father's return would both ease the immediate pressure on the family finances and shield him from his mother's wrath. Coombes brought home £9 2/- from his latest trip. Having not even known that his son had taken a job, he could not be angry with him for quitting it. But the problem of Robert's employment was left unresolved. Although he had chosen to leave the yard, it was humiliating for him to be without work. Other boys of his age took pride in being able to put food on the family table and pleasure in being able to buy treats for themselves: cigarettes, novelettes, music-hall tickets, fish and chips. To become a breadwinner was a step towards manhood, and it brought a rise in a boy's status within the home – at mealtimes, for instance, the wage earners would be served first and most generously. Without employment, Robert had no rights over the family provisions: the power to give or withhold remained with his mother.

After the iron plater's testimony, Charles Gill declared that the Crown's case was closed.

IT IS ALL OVER NOW

In the Old Court of the Old Bailey, William Grantham rose to make the case for the defence. Whereas most of the prosecution witnesses had been giving evidence for a second or even a third time, none of the defence witnesses had yet testified. Grantham told the jury that he intended to show that Robert Coombes was not in his right mind. He began by calling the boy's father to the witness stand.

Robert Coombes senior took the stand. He had 'nothing of the seafarer about him', observed the *Star*; he was 'respectable-looking', agreed the *Sun*.

Coombes recalled that his eldest son had suffered from headaches and excitability since the age of three or four. When the family was living in Limehouse in the 1880s, he explained, he had taken Robert to see a Dr Christopher Coward, who had prescribed medication for his headaches. He had continued to consult Dr Coward about Robert after moving to Plaistow in 1891, and – by correspondence – while the family was based in Toxteth Park, Liverpool.

'He was very ill at Liverpool from headache,' said Coombes, 'the same complaint, and in consequence of what Dr Coward told me I was specially careful.'

According to Coombes, Dr Coward considered Robert's brain particularly vulnerable to the pressures of schoolwork, as well as to the more obvious risk of being struck in punishment. 'He always told me never to chastise him anywhere near the head, or to touch him on the head, or to give him any home lessons to do.' When the family returned to London, Coombes asked the doctor to write a note about Robert's frailty to George Hollamby, the headmaster of Grange Road school.

Several medical manuals warned parents not to let children study too much. The stress of tests and homework was believed to cause 'brain irritation', headaches and worse. Over-education, claimed Wynn Westcott in 1885, could lead children to suicide by encouraging a 'precocious development of the reflective faculties, of vanity, and of the desires'. These theories, like the theories about penny dreadfuls, reflected a worry about the effects of education on the poor.

'The boy complained very often of his head at that time,' said Coombes, 'at intervals of a week or a fortnight, sometimes a month. At such times he would sit down and look very sullen, as if he was having a headache, and would speak to nobody.'

'In disposition,' he added, 'he was a very good boy.'

Coombes showed the court a certificate that Dr Coward had made out in 1891, which stated that Robert was suffering from cerebral irritation. This was a diagnosis given to patients who experienced headaches, restlessness, impulsive fits, peevishness or melancholia without any discernible organic cause. It was believed that the disorder could develop into epilepsy, though it could also fade away by adulthood. The term implied a physiological basis for Robert's condition but was in truth merely descriptive. It gave no real clues as to the cause of his disturbance, which could be anything from unhappiness to physical injury.

Coombes believed that the trauma of birth might have damaged Robert's brain. He was away when his son was born, he said. 'I think I had just gone to sea, or came home just afterwards, I cannot recollect. I know that my wife had a very bad time.' Robert had marks on his temples, he said, caused by the forceps that had wrenched him from the womb. He implied also that Robert might have been affected by his mother's temperament. 'My wife was a very excitable woman from the first,' he told the court, 'who very frequently laughed and cried at the same time.'

In 1893, Robert's difficulties recurred and he was moved from Grange Road school. Coombes described the problem as 'a difference with the teachers' and added that 'the other boys used to laugh at him'. The incident at school seemed to have made Robert a figure of mockery to his peers. Coombes said that Robert had complained of headaches ever since. This suggested that the boy's problems were exacerbated, even if they were not caused, by emotional distress.

Dr Coward died that year, aged fifty-four, and the Coombes family registered with John Joseph Griffin, who ran a practice in the Barking Road. 'When anything special occurred in consequence of his complaints of violent headache I had to take him to Dr Griffin,' said Coombes. In December 1894, he discovered that Robert had run away from home while he had been at sea, and he took him to see the doctor. Griffin recommended that Robert accompany his father on his next voyage. A change of air, in the form of foreign travel, was often prescribed for nervous complaints.

In January 1895, Robert and his father sailed to New York on the SS *England*, a sister ship to the *France*. One of the two assistant stewards on this trip was Robert's uncle Frederick, who had in the 1870s been an apprentice to his older brother in his ill-fated butchery business in Notting Hill. When the *England* set sail, London was enduring its coldest winter on record – the Thames had frozen over at London Bridge for the first time in eighty years. The ship was pelted with rain as she sailed out of the Thames estuary, and she ran into a powerful gale halfway across the Atlantic, accompanied by squalls of hail and very heavy seas. She was caught up in a hurricane, then a storm of thunder and lightning before she reached New York on 7 February. Robert and his father and uncle stayed in the city for a week before the ship cast off again into intense cold and high seas. The pitching of a cattle ship in a storm sometimes sent the cows crashing forward in their narrow stalls to break their knees or necks. The *England* took seventeen days to reach London, two days longer than usual, and Robert returned to Cave Road school on 11 March. Coombes claimed that the trip had done the boy good.

Gill cross-examined Coombes, asking him if there was a history of insanity in the family, and whether Robert had any intellectual impairments.

'I have not heard of insanity on my side of the family or my wife's either,' said Coombes. 'The boy always got on very well at school – he had no difficulty in learning. He is a very learned boy. He read a great deal.'

Gill indicated the penny dreadfuls on the bench. 'Has he been reading these sensational books for any length of time?'

'I am not aware that he read books of that kind,' said Coombes. 'There were good books in the house, such as the *Strand Magazine* and the New York *Century*.' The *Strand*, which sold half a million copies a week to a predominantly middle-class readership, had become famous in the early 1890s for publishing Arthur Conan Doyle's Sherlock Holmes stories. It advertised itself as 'cheap, healthful literature', 'absolutely pure'. The *Century*, formerly *Scribners,* was a prestigious American journal that ran pieces by the likes of Henry James and Mark Twain.

Justice Kennedy leafed through the penny dreadfuls. 'Here is *Jack Wright and the Fortune Hunters of the Red Sea*,' he said. 'They are what you would call sensational, but —'

Gill interrupted: 'You will see one called *Revenged at Last, or the Crimson Coat.*'

Kennedy continued his inspection. 'Well, some are apparently from the outside cover what one would call sensational, but one can't say exactly.' He threw down the books and turned back to his notes. 'There were good books found among these. Go on.'

Gill pointed out that Robert's collection consisted of 'books mostly relating to crime and criminals of some kind'.

'The jury shall see them for themselves,' said Kennedy. He seemed unwilling to make much of the penny dreadfuls.

Gill asked Coombes about Robert's job at the ironworks.

'I did not know that he got employment after leaving school till I arrived home.'

'Did you ever know him to suffer from any delusion?' asked Gill.

No,' said Coombes, but added: 'I have heard him say that he had heard noises in the night.'

Grantham rose to ask about the noises.

'He complained of hearing noises about the house,' said Coombes. 'The last time he complained of that was four months ago.' Coombes had been at home on some of these occasions, he said, and had not heard any noises himself.

This ended his testimony. Coombes had made it clear that he cared for his son and worried about his wellbeing: he had taken him to doctors for his headaches, to New York to try to restore his health. But it had also become apparent that he had been off-stage for many of the dramas of Robert's life: he was away at sea when his eldest boy was born, when he refused to attend school, when he left school and when he took his first job. Coombes seems to have shown no curiosity or concern about why both his sons had twice run away from their mother.

The next witness for the defence was Amelia England, the thirty-eight-year-old wife of a dock clerk, who lived at 33 Cave Road. The Englands' two older sons, like Robert and Nattie, had attended Grange Road school before transferring to Cave Road school when it was built in 1894. Mrs England's eldest son was the same age as Robert, and had just left school having passed the fourth standard.

'I am a next-door neighbour of the Coombes,' said Amelia England. 'I have known them for the last three years. I was very intimate with them.'

Grantham asked her to describe Emily and Robert Coombes.

'The mother was rather excitable all the time I have known her,' she said. 'Robert was very excitable indeed. I have on occasions gone to Dr Griffin for medicines for him. I knew he had pains in the head; he has complained in my presence. He has had very excitable fits.'

Gill, cross-examining, asked her to elaborate.

'I can hardly explain the excitement,' she said. 'If he could not get what he liked, he would fly into a passion, and then he would have these fits afterwards. I have known him to go right off into a fainting fit with them more than once. It was not always when he was in a great passion, but very often.'

Gill inquired how well she knew Robert.

'I saw him every day nearly all the time they were living there. He was a very bright, intelligent boy when spoken to, and a well-spoken boy.' She related how she had chatted to him in the street in the week after the murder. 'I spoke to him every day right up to the Friday in that week.'

Gill asked whether Robert enjoyed reading.

'He was fond of reading,' said Mrs England; 'passionately fond both of music and reading.'

Mrs England was dismissed, and Grantham called Dr Walker to the witness box.

George Walker had been a prison doctor for more than twenty years by the time he was appointed medical officer of Holloway gaol in January 1894. He frequently gave evidence at the Old Bailey about the men and women in his charge, and had already testified in three trials during the current sessions. His testimony did not always support an insanity plea – at the trial of a twenty-three-year-old woman who had killed her child in 1894, he said that he had seen no evidence of madness while she was on remand – but often it did. In June 1895, for instance, he had diagnosed kleptomania in the case of a woman who had stolen goods from the John Lewis department store.

The insanity plea had become increasingly common in English courts: in the 1860s, about 15 per cent of murderers were found insane, either before, during or after trial; in the 1890s the proportion rose to nearly 27 per cent. Yet the *Journal of Mental Science* observed in 1895 that the law on criminal responsibility was still in 'hopeless confusion'. At a meeting of the British Medical Association that summer, Henry Maudsley argued that madness often went unrecognised by the courts. He disagreed with the legal profession's narrow definition of madness, which held that a defendant was criminally responsible if he or she knew right from wrong at the time of his or her crime, a test formulated after Robert McNaughten tried to assassinate the prime minister in 1843. The 'right from wrong' test, said Maudsley, assumed 'that reason, not feeling, is the motive force of human action'. He argued that some acts of violence sprang from a desire so strong that it bypassed thought and lit straight into action. 'A disordered feeling,' Maudsley wrote, 'is capable of actuating disordered conduct without consent of reason.'

In reply to Grantham's questions about Robert, Dr Walker noted that the violence applied to Robert's skull when he was born would have exerted pressure on his brain.

'There is a distinct scar on his right temple,' Walker said, 'and on a very careful examination I noticed also a faint scar in front of his left ear. Those scars might have been caused by instruments used at the time of birth. The brain is always compressed more or less when instruments are used, and it would occasionally affect the brain of a lad. I believe children have suffered from fits afterwards.'

'I have noticed that the pupils of his eyes are at times unequal,' the doctor continued. 'The variability of the pupils showed that the mischief is not in the eye itself but is probably due to cerebral irritation.'

Walker told the court what Robert had said about the voices in his head, and about his mother throwing knives at Nattie and threatening to kill him. He reported that Robert had said that he had 'an irresistible impulse' to kill his mother.

Grantham asked if those had been Robert's exact words.

'I took down these words,' said Walker.

Walker said that his conversation with Robert the previous Tuesday – when the boy had shown excitement about the trial, then distress about his cats and mandolin – was indicative of cerebral irritation.

'I believe your opinion is also based on some letters written by him?' said Grantham.

'Yes,' said Walker. 'I have had a very extraordinary letter handed to me from him. The letter is inconsistent with the action of a sane person. It was written on Saturday last.' The Clerk of Arraigns read out Robert's letter to the Reverend Francis Shaw, in which he expressed his desire to die and gave instructions for the disposal of his imaginary fortune.

The letter carried two signatures, not only Robert's but also that of Charlie Sharman. Apparently Robert's father had hired Sharman to conduct his sons' defence. The solicitor may have been instrumental in publicising Robert's letter to the curate, since the document – and especially its threat of suicide – shored up the defence claim that the boy was insane. Equally, Dr Walker may have come across the letter in the course of his duties, since all the prisoners' correspondence in Holloway was vetted. Either way, Sharman's signature authenticated the document.

'Does that letter strengthen your opinion as to the boy's mental condition?' Grantham asked Walker.

'Yes,' said the doctor. He explained that he believed that Robert had been suffering from 'homicidal mania'. 'There are two kinds of homicidal mania,' said Walker. 'Sometimes the crime is committed on the impulse of the moment; sometimes with great deliberation and cunning.'

Grantham remarked: 'The reading of pernicious literature would have a bad effect on such a mind.'

Justice Kennedy intervened: 'It would have a bad effect upon the mind of any boy I should think.'

'But it would be worse for a boy suffering from mental affections?' asked Grantham.

'Yes,' said Walker. 'Certainly.'

'Homicidal mania' was a condition identified by the French psychiatrist Jean-Etienne Esquirol earlier in the century. A homicidal monomaniac, said Esquirol, became obsessed by the desire to kill, and after a murder achieved a sort of peace. 'The act accomplished, it seems that the attack is over,' he wrote, 'and some homicidal monomaniacs seem to be relieved of a state of agitation and anguish, which was exceedingly painful to them. They are composed, and free from regret, remorse or fear. They contemplate their victim with indifference, and some even experience and manifest a kind of satisfaction. The greater part, far from flying, remain near the dead body.' A maniac of this kind felt so lightened that he did not need to flee, his pain having been cast out and destroyed in the act of killing.

Esquirol specified that children could be prey to homicidal mania. Evidence of delusion was usually required to support the diagnosis, though some doctors argued that the murder itself could be the sole marker of insanity. All such syndromes were defined only by their symptoms; medics tended to believe that their origin was physiological – that they were diseases of the brain rather than the mind – and that they were therefore innate and incurable.

Under cross-examination by Charles Gill, Dr Walker acknowledged that in some of his conversations with Robert the boy had appeared sane. 'I should say the conversations were held in a lucid interval. He appeared to talk to me quite rationally and showed no insanity when I first examined him – that was the day after he was received into prison. He answered my questions intelligently. He appears to be a boy of more than average intelligence. He is well educated, and able to take advantage of the opportunities given him at school.'

So where, asked Gill, was the proof of delusion?

'I only find trace of delusion from the boy's own statement,' said Walker. 'Apart from the murder, I saw no delusion.'

Gill questioned him about whether Robert had really used the words 'irresistible impulse' in their conversation. The idea of irresistible impulse was sometimes invoked by defence counsel as an alternative to the traditional 'knowing right from wrong' test of insanity. It was an improbably technical phrase for a boy to use. Gill was implying that Walker had put words into Robert's mouth; or that, if Robert had indeed used the term, it might have been at the suggestion of his lawyer.

'"Irresistible impulse" is what I have written,' said Walker. 'I would not swear those were the very words he used, but he said something to that effect, either "impulse" or "irresistible impulse".'

Charles Gill also expressed scepticism about Robert's 'excitability', inquiring of Walker whether fits of passion could really be taken as evidence of insanity.

'A boy may be very passionate and may be vicious without being insane,' agreed Walker. 'Some boys do give way to extraordinary violent fits of passion, especially if they are interfered with and not allowed to have their own way; but I do not speak of those fits of passion, but attacks of mental excitement, as the father described it to me. That is very different.' He had himself witnessed the boy in a state of mental excitement, he said, and Robert's father had told him that he experienced these attacks every two or three months. Walker was making a distinction between a temper tantrum and an episode of confused thinking.

Gill asked whether Robert was in the throes of such an attack when he purchased the knife from Mrs Brecht's shop.

'He might have been under the influence of delusion when he bought the knife,' said Walker. 'I do not know that he was. He might have bought it while suffering from an attack of mania.'

'Do you seriously mean,' asked Gill, 'that he would go to the shop, select the knife, bargain for it and buy it while under the influence of mania?'

'Yes,' said Walker. 'Under the influence of homicidal mania these crimes are done with great deliberation.'

Gill asked if Robert had described the murder to him.

'The first time he told me he had no recollection of stabbing her,' said Walker, 'but remembered hitting her on the head with a truncheon. On another occasion he told me that he had stabbed her.' This was the first time that the truncheon had been cited as a murder weapon. Perhaps this, rather than the knife or the pillow, had been the means by which Robert had finally dispatched his mother after Nattie heard her groan. The police doctor had not mentioned finding a head injury during the post mortem, but Mary Jane Burrage had referred to seeing a horrible wound on her friend's temple.

Grantham intervened to ask Walker if he could explain why Robert had claimed that he had hit her with a truncheon.

'His different accounts of the crime showed loss of memory,' said Walker.

Sketch of the Coombes family home at 35 Cave Road, Plaistow, published in *Lloyd's Weekly Newspaper* on 21 July 1895, four days after the arrest of Robert and Nathaniel Coombes.

The Thames Iron Works, the West Ham shipbuilding company at which Robert worked as a 'plater's boy' in June 1895, and (*below*) the Japanese battleship *Fuji Yama* under construction at the yard that month.

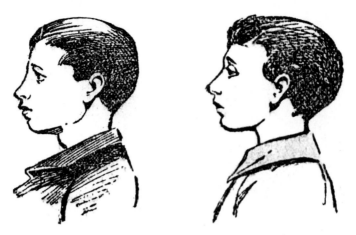

Newspaper sketches of Robert and Nattie Coombes,
aged 13 and 12 respectively, in July 1895.

Robert and Nattie's mother, Emily; their father,
Robert; and their friend John Fox.

Mary Jane Burrage, a friend of Robert and Nattie's mother; the
boys' aunt Emily; John Hewson, chief cashier of the shipping line
for which their father worked; and Detective Inspector Mellish.

A match at Lord's cricket ground in the summer of 1895 (*above left*), and a newspaper sketch of W. G. Grace at Lord's on 8 July, when Robert and Nattie watched him bat for the Gentlemen.

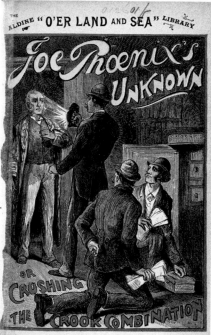

The young adventurer Jack Wright, the hero of one of the 'penny dreadfuls' found in the back parlour of 35 Cave Road, and (*right*) another of the sensational stories in Robert's collection.

Holloway gaol, north London, in which Robert and Nattie Coombes and John Fox were held in the summer of 1895, and (*below*) a cell and galleries at Newgate gaol, in the City of London, to which they were transferred for their trial in September.

Street view of Newgate gaol, with the dome of St Paul's in the background, and (*below*) Birdcage Walk, the passageway along which prisoners were led from the prison to the Old Bailey courthouse.

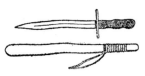

Robert Coombes and John Fox and Nattie Coombes in the Old Bailey on 16 September 1895, and the dagger and truncheon produced in evidence.

The Old Court in the Old Bailey in the 1890s, with the dock on the left, the judges' bench on the right, and the jury box by the windows at the back.

Speculative reconstructions of the crime and its aftermath, published in the *Illustrated Police Budget* on 27 July 1895 (*main image*) and the *Illustrated Police News* on 3 August 1895 (*inset*).

'Are you of opinion that he was not of sound mind?' asked Grantham.

The judge interrupted before Walker could reply. 'That is a matter on which the jury must form their own conclusion,' he said. Walker had frequently been permitted to give his opinion on a defendant's insanity in the Old Bailey courts, but Kennedy, implementing the most rigorous interpretation of the law, would not allow it.

Gill asked Walker a last question about Robert: was it compatible with insanity that the boy took himself off to Lord's on the day that he murdered his mother?

'I could not conceive anyone going to Lord's cricket ground and acting as the lad did after committing such a crime if he were sane,' returned Walker.

Walker's reply went to the heart of the puzzle of the murder. Robert's coolness before and after the killing could be read as evidence of culpability; and yet his very indifference might be the strongest sign that he was mad.

Charles Gill asked Dr Walker for his assessment of John Fox.

The doctor said that Fox had 'a badly shaped head and a highly arched palate'. 'He is slow in understanding what is said to him,' he added, 'and does not know common things you would expect an ordinary man to know. He is slow of apprehension. He has the peculiar hesitation in speech often noticed in weak minds.'

Grantham's next witness was John Joseph Griffin, medical attendant to the Coombes family since 1893. Dr Griffin was an Irish-born bachelor, aged forty, who lived and worked in a large terraced house in the Barking Road. He was the author of the sick note for Emily Coombes that Robert had altered in July.

Griffin testified that Emily Coombes was a 'hysterical' woman, 'very emotional, and subject at times to fits of crying and laughing. She used to laugh and cry with the least exciting cause. She was generally of a weak and nervous disposition.' He agreed that 'the nervous disposition and temperament of the mother sometimes affects the children', but stopped short of saying that Robert had inherited her weakness.

Griffin told the court how he had treated Robert for the 'disordered nervous system' and 'attacks of mental excitement due to cerebral irritation' that his predecessor, Dr Coward, had diagnosed. Robert's father usually brought him to a consultation, Griffin said, though the boy sometimes came with his mother.

'When the attacks were on him,' said Griffin, 'he had an irresistible impulse to run away without reason. I advised the father to take him to sea for a trip in consequence of those attacks.' By echoing Walker's use of the phrase 'irresistible impulse', Griffin supported the defence case that Robert had moments in which he could not control his actions. Yet the supposed symptom – the desire to run away 'without reason' – looked less like madness than misery. Griffin may even have perceived that Robert's problems were related to his mother: after all, he prescribed a journey that would enable him to escape her influence.

Justice Kennedy said that it seemed obvious that Robert was not suffering from mania.

'I never saw him in any condition of mania,' acknowledged Griffin. 'What I know is from what the father stated to me. He said his boy used to get up in the morning and complain of severe headache, and was restless, fidgety and excitable, and twitching in his limbs. His father used to put him to bed.

I gave him bromide of potassium to calm him.' Bromide of potassium was a sedative and depressant used to treat dis-orders of the brain. This was the medication that Amelia England had fetched for Robert when he became agitated. Though recommended in the *Dictionary of Psychological Medicine* as a safe drug, prolonged use could cause a con-dition known as 'bromism': the symptoms included stupor, paranoid delusions, pupillary dilation, insomnia, restlessness and psychosis.

Griffin said that he had seen Robert in Newgate the previ-ous day, and that his condition seemed to have developed into mania. 'He was in a condition of great mental excitement yes-terday,' said the doctor, 'and not responsible for what he was doing.'

The last witness for the defence was John Cossington, a West Ham attendance officer of thirty-six who lived in the Barking Road. Attendance officers were employed by the local authorities to ensure that children went to school. In the spring, the 'Punishment Men', as they were known, walked the streets of their district, compiling a register of all school-age children in houses rated at £28 or less. If a child did not turn up to at least seven of the ten school sessions a week, the officer would call at his or her house and issue a warning to the parents. If this was ignored, the parents were summoned to a magistrates' court and, unless able to justify the child's absence, could be fined five shillings.

'I had reason to make inquiries in October 1893 as to the boy's non-attendance at school,' Cossington told the court. 'I went to the mother.' Emily Coombes told him that Robert was 'sick through excitement'. 'When I did see the boy,' said Cossington, 'he was in a very sullen mood, and would not answer me.'

Emily succeeded in convincing Cossington of Robert's unhappiness and his need to be moved, even to an already oversubscribed neighbouring institution. At her urging, Cossington said, he had paid a visit to Dr Griffin, who lived across the road from him. 'In consequence of what I saw, read and heard from the doctor, and by request of the mother, that I would get him another school, I obtained a special order from the school committee for his removal from one school to another.'

Cossington did not allude to the nature of Robert's difficulties at Grange Road school. Nor did the defence press him on this, being keen to emphasise Robert's mental instability rather than the fact that he might have been mistreated by a teacher or bullied by other boys.

When cross-examined by Gill as to why Robert had left Grange Road, Cossington said only: 'The boy did not want to go back to the same school. He had stayed away from that school.'

Grantham did not call any further witnesses. As the defence was pleading insanity, any evidence of Robert's good character – such as the Reverend Shaw might have offered – would have done the boy no favours.

In his address to the jury Grantham said that this was one of the saddest cases ever to come before a court. He asked them to accept that Robert Coombes was insane, reminding them of the absence of motive in the case and the fact that the boy had not tried to escape. He began to expound the law on insanity but the judge stopped him, saying that the jury must take the law from him alone. Robert's counsel sat down.

Frederick Sherwood next urged the jury to acquit Fox. He insisted that the evidence showed that Fox knew nothing of the murder. The smell in the house, he said, 'only became acute on the opening of the door and disturbance of the corpse, and there is no reason for supposing that it was sufficiently present in the house as to induce Fox, a man of dull intellect, much given to smoking and used from his dock calling to unpleasant smells, to make inquiry as to its origin or investigate its cause'. Even if the jury believed that Fox knew of the murder, said Sherwood, 'he has not done a single act with the view of defeating the ends of justice or concealing the crime'.

Sherwood further submitted that if Robert Coombes were found insane, Fox must be acquitted: he contended that it was impossible in law to find Fox guilty of being accessory to an insane act. This was the same argument that Kennedy had dismissed when it was proposed by Gill at the outset of the trial. But now the judge said that he agreed. Bizarrely, he even complimented Sherwood upon his discovery of the point. The argument was in fact wrong, as several legal journals subsequently explained. Since 1882 the law had stipulated that the insane could be found guilty of committing crimes, even if they were deemed not to have been culpable, and others could therefore be found guilty of abetting such crimes.

Gill summed up for the Crown, submitting that Robert's insanity had not been proven. On the contrary, he said, the boy's actions showed him to be a lad of exceptional capacity. He conceded that Dr Walker's evidence was important, but, as the doctor had himself said, his diagnosis of insanity was based largely on the absence of motive for the murder.

The *Star* remarked that Gill adopted a 'studiously mild' tone in his final speech. He was respectful of the defence's medical evidence, and seemed to leave open the possibility that Robert was mad. 'Had Robert Coombes been a full-grown man,' said *Lloyd's Weekly*, 'the counsel for the prosecution would have resisted the theory of insanity, and possibly with success; but with so young a prisoner there seemed to be a desire all round to take the most lenient view.'

This leniency did not extend to Justice Kennedy. Though his role was supposed to be neutral, when he made his summing-up at 4.40 p.m. he set out the case against Robert far more strongly than Gill had done. The jury should not infer insanity, said Kennedy, because someone who had led an apparently blameless life suddenly committed a callous act. Nor should they jump to the conclusion that Robert was insane just because it was difficult to believe that a sane lad of thirteen could perpetrate such an atrocious crime. He had planned the death of his mother with skill and had displayed 'the most masterly sagacity' afterwards. The letter to Francis Shaw might be a sham, suggested the judge, written to simulate madness. Though Dr Walker had said that homicidal mania was often accompanied by cunning, Kennedy observed, 'even Dr Walker can not have known before such a case as this where the cunning and the madness were mixed up with so much pleasure and enjoyment of life'. He described Nattie, who was sitting in the courtroom surrounded by female relatives and neighbours, as 'a little slip of a boy wholly under the thumb of his elder brother'.

The one relevant question, Kennedy told the jury, was whether Robert knew that what he was doing was wrong. Repeating Sherwood's incorrect assertion, he added that if they did find Robert insane, they must also acquit Fox.

The sun set in the course of Kennedy's ninety-minute summing-up, and the gas was lit in the glass globes hanging from the courtroom ceiling.

At ten minutes past six o'clock, the jurors retired to consider their verdict. They returned at twelve minutes past seven.

Their foreman, a south London butcher of thirty-seven who had three infant sons, confirmed to the Clerk of Arraigns that they had reached a verdict: they found Robert Coombes guilty, said Harry Edis, but they made a strong recommendation to mercy on the ground of his youth, and because they did not believe that he realised the gravity of his crime.

Robert stood in the dock, his skin flushed, his eyes shining. He seemed at last alert to the seriousness of the proceedings. In the course of the day, he had, for the first time, heard people stand up in court to defend him. Several witnesses had spoken kindly, even warmly, of him – his schoolteachers, his father, Amelia England – and the doctors had done their best to absolve him of responsibility. Now the jury, too, was showing him compassion.

But Justice Kennedy refused to accept the recommendation of mercy. He insisted that the jurors again retire, and return with one of two conclusions: they must declare Robert guilty or guilty but insane.

They withdrew as directed but were back within two minutes. This time, in reply to the clerk's question, Harry Edis said that they found Robert Coombes guilty, but that he was insane at the time he committed the act.

Robert was composed as he heard the verdict, though tears ran down his cheeks.

The Clerk of Arraigns asked the jury: 'Do you find John Fox guilty or not?'

'Not guilty on the evidence,' said the foreman. Edis was keen to make clear that the jurors had acquitted Fox not on the technical issue of whether he could be an accessory to an insane act, but because they believed him to be innocent.

Fox was discharged. He left the dock and glided out through the courtroom, said the *Star*, like a somnambulist.

Robert turned quickly to a warder, smiling excitedly, and whispered something to him.

Nattie was 'looking on with an air of cold unconcern that was extraordinary', according to the *Star*; like Fox, he was probably more stupefied than indifferent.

The judge passed sentence on Robert. 'The only judgment I can give,' said Kennedy, with evident displeasure, 'is that the prisoner Robert Allen Coombes be detained in strict custody in the gaol in Holloway until the pleasure of Her Majesty be known.'

When Robert heard the sentence, his face convulsed, said the *Star*, as if he were about to break down in tears or to shout out in anger. He had been expecting the gallows, but a far weirder fate awaited him. Murderers detained at Her Majesty's Pleasure were usually given an indefinite detention in Broadmoor, a fortified criminal lunatic asylum that housed the most notorious killers in Britain.

Two Holloway warders quickly took hold of Robert and turned him to the door that led to the cells below the court. As they ushered him away he recovered his air of detached mockery. He laughed and remarked to one of his guards: 'It is all over now.'

12

BOX HIM UP

For the next week Robert waited in Holloway gaol for the Home Office to arrange his admission to Broadmoor asylum. *'Broadmoor!'* as R. J. Tucknor wrote in a short story for *Reynolds's Newspaper*: 'What visions of horror, ruined lives, and blasted aspirations, of madness and despair, does that single word conjure up!' The newspapers and journals of Britain, meanwhile, mulled over Robert's crime and his punishment.

The Lancet endorsed the verdict, approving of how, with 'sound common-sense', the jury had ignored the judge's insistence that only intellectual insanity could relieve Robert of responsibility: the boy's supposed motive for the murder was totally inadequate, the journal argued, and it was clear that he had a history of 'moral alienism' that had culminated in 'impulsive homicidal mania'. But few other commentators believed that Robert was mad. Rather, they concluded that the jurors had taken pity on him. 'In plain English,' said the *Star*, 'they didn't want to hang the boy.' *The Times* was glad

that in these 'tender times' they had found a way to spare him
the gallows.

The *Spectator* was appalled by such soft-heartedness: 'This
generation,' it announced, 'is going mad with pity.' For those
who wanted to see Robert punished, it was some consola-
tion, at least, that he was likely to remain in the most tightly
guarded asylum in Britain for the rest of his days rather than
be released – like most of those sentenced to life imprisonment – after twenty years. 'As he is thirteen years of age,' said
the *St James's Gazette*, 'it is, on the whole, more desirable to
pretend that he is mad, and so box him up in Broadmoor for
life, rather than to send him for penal servitude, with the high
probability that the carnivorous animal would be let loose
upon the world again at three-and-thirty.'

The language of racial atrophy pervaded the newspaper
coverage. If Robert was a bloodthirsty beast to the *Gazette*,
he was 'a half-formed monster' to the *London Daily News*,
and a 'monster of depravity' to the *News of the World*, while
the *Evening News* considered him among 'the waste products
of civilisation', 'one of the curiously morbid growths' of the
modern world. Before and during the Old Bailey trial, newspaper artists had depicted Robert as a classically handsome
boy with even and well-proportioned features. Nattie looked
feebler: some sketches emphasised the younger boy's hooded,
shadowed eyes and his weak chin. The illustrations published
by the *Star* immediately after the verdict were quite different:
Robert was jowly, dark and vacant, while Nattie was a pretty
child with fair curly hair. These were images drawn not from
life but from degeneration theory.

The *St James's Gazette* observed that Robert's schooling
had not made him more civilised but more savage, accentu-
ating rather than arresting the degenerative process: 'all that

elementary education did for Master Coombes was to pro-
vide him with weapons, as it were, to sharpen the claws of the
little tiger'. The *Daily Chronicle* noted that Robert showed
an eerie 'mixture of shrewdness and hysteria, ability and corruption', adding: 'This type is not rare. It might have been
foreseen as an outcome of the close-herded life of the English
town, as the price of some aspects of England's greatness.'
Robert Coombes was one of a new breed of urban lunatic,
said the *Chronicle*, a tribe of vicious, quick-witted degener-
ates who had replaced the 'grinning and harmless imbeciles
that sunned themselves in the towns and villages of an older
England'.

The *Saturday Review*, too, suggested that Robert's desolate environment had played a part in his regression. A lively-
minded boy in the affluent West End of London could play at
violence and adventure, the journal argued. He could scalp
Indians in his playroom, unearth treasure beneath the trees of
the square opposite his house: he had 'space and colour in the
actual events of his life'. But in West Ham, where the dingy
streets 'reeked with malaria from the marshes and smoke from
the docks', and the atmosphere was 'poisoned by exhalations
from earth sickened by its crowded life', Robert had been
driven not just to imagine but to enact his drama. 'Plaistow is
practical,' observed the *Review*, drily.

This journal expressed wonder that Robert had not been
scanned for the markers of degeneration: 'Did he show any
of the signs now recognised by the great Continental experts
as stigmata of physical and therefore mental degeneracy? It
was a test case for the application of the new knowledge.
If Robert Allen Coombes is a physical criminal or madman,
how about his brother, plainly an accomplice, and now turned
free on society to propagate a possibly degraded strain?'

A lifetime's detention in an insane asylum would ensure that Robert would not reproduce, but no restrictions had been placed on Nattie.

The *Pall Mall Gazette* argued that Robert and Nattie were so self-evidently depraved that both should simply have been put to death, regardless of whether they were mad. 'We must all be conscious of a pang of regret that these boys are not to be hung. It would be well if we could choke such moral abortions at birth, as we now choke physical ones. But since we cannot diagnose them at sight, it is surely wiser, cheaper, and kinder to dispose of them at once, when they do declare themselves, with no more excitement or doubt than a housemaid gives to the crushing of a beetle.'

Taking their cue from Justice Kennedy, most journalists concluded that the penny dreadfuls had not played much part in the murder. The *Pall Mall Gazette*, which in the past had inveighed against the dreadfuls, now declared that they were merely a scapegoat. 'When a boy of the lower class murders his mother or does similar things that he ought not to have done, what a blessing it is to get beyond elementary education, heredity, the social system – all the things we might dispute about – and find ourselves at one in blaming the penny dreadful for it all. Most of us have no idea what a penny dreadful is like. We only know that little boys buy them in dark shops in back streets, and that there is nobody to defend them. Therefore, down with the penny dreadful!'

'The truth is,' said the *Gazette*, 'that in respect to the effect of reading on boys of the poorer class the world has got into one of those queer illogical stupidities that so easily beset it. In every other age and class man is held responsible for his reading, and not reading responsible for man. The books a man or woman reads are less the making of character than the expression of it.'

The *Journal of Mental Science* agreed: 'It seems obvious that while stories full of bloodshed and horrors might help to confirm and encourage, and even to give direction to, a tendency already existing, they cannot be considered responsible for the origination of such a tendency.'

Others pointed out that there was no real difference between the trashy books in the back parlour of 35 Cave Road and classics such as Robert Louis Stevenson's *Treasure Island* (the hero of that novel, like Robert, was a boy 'full of sea-dreams', bewitched by 'anticipations of strange islands and adventures'). The Duchess of Rutland noted that there were 'guinea dreadfuls' as well as 'penny dreadfuls'.

Some journalists even expressed a rueful sympathy for Robert's fantasies. His murder plot was 'borrowed from the stock-in-trade not only of penny dreadfuls but of all the literature of boys' adventure', said the *Saturday Review*. 'The purchase of a knife from a marine-store dealer, the hiding of it, the secret talks with an admiring brother, the choice of pretexts for the deed (he would call it a deed), the signal from the other room, and the swift and sudden action – we know them all, and we can understand how they engrossed his mind to the exclusion of all else.' Robert yearned for 'the Island' of children's fiction, observed the *Review*, 'its rocks, no doubt, covering hidden treasure, its shores littered with attractive wrecks'. Even John Fox was a familiar figure of the genre: 'the faithful retainer, not fully in the confidence of his master but ready to serve him to the death, and possessed, no doubt, of a practical knowledge of islands'. The cosy retreat in the back parlour recalled the hideaway of a band of fugitives. Robert, Nattie and Fox 'played cards in their den, no doubt "with fierce oaths", and began their adventures by sleeping on unaccustomed couches'.

The *Star* reporter who attended the Old Bailey trial also recognised the boy's dreams. 'Alas! that island,' he lamented. 'We all wanted to get there in our day to live in a hut and shoot pirates and slavers, though happily the road there was less bloodthirsty than that which unhappy Robert Coombes chose.'

The origin of the crime was still a mystery. In their bid to secure an insanity verdict, Robert's lawyers had tried to wipe out motive rather than to find it: their medical witnesses had characterised the killing as a psychic spasm with no emotional content or meaning. The newspapers, too, placed the blame for the murder on Robert's physiology, though most argued that his degeneracy had rendered him immoral rather than insane.

Just one publication argued that Robert might be neither mad nor bad. The *Child's Guardian*, the journal of the National Society for the Prevention of Cruelty to Children, proposed that the cause of the crime lay not in the boy's disordered body but in the history of his home: specifically, in his relationship with his mother. 'Of the dead, we speak no ill in courts,' it observed in October in a piece entitled 'Boy Murderers'. 'Of the dead, in this particular case, we know no ill to speak, but we are of opinion that it is of great public concern to know what were the relations of the dead mother and her murderous child.'

The *Child's Guardian* suggested, as the lawyers had not, that Robert had assaulted Emily Coombes because she was physically brutal. This, after all, was what Robert had said. He had told the police that he had decided to kill his mother

because she had beaten Nattie and threatened them both; and
that he finally attacked her because she punched him as he lay
in bed. He had told Dr Walker that he had killed her because
she had thrown knives at Nattie and warned that she would
stick a hatchet in his head. The *Child's Guardian* pointed out
that Nattie had colluded in the murder plan. 'Was he, too,
insane?' it asked sceptically.

Legislation had been passed to protect children from violent parents – the Children's Acts of 1889 and 1894 stipulated
that physical correction should be 'reasonable' and 'within
the bounds of moderation' – but neither the police, the coroner, the solicitor nor the magistrate in the Coombes case
seemed to have inquired into the frequency, force or emotion
with which Emily beat her boys. They accepted Nattie's and
the neighbours' assurances that she was kind to her sons, and
ignored Robert's accounts of her threats and aggression. As
the *Child's Guardian* suggested, this was in part because it
was unseemly to speak ill of the dead, especially of a murdered woman: whatever she had done, she had not deserved
this. Most people in any case believed that parents were
entitled to punish their children by whatever means they felt
necessary; and the Coombes family appeared to be a respectable, churchgoing household, neither dissipated nor desperate. None the less the NSPCC, which had been prosecuting
parents for cruelty since its inception in 1884, had no difficulty
in believing the worst. 'That brute force begets brute force
and injustice injustice is beyond doubt,' it observed. 'That
there are thousands of parents – both fathers and mothers –
whose conduct to their children is worse than barbarous, the
records of this Society's work during but a few years places
beyond doubt.'

In a booklet published a few years later, the NSPCC reminded its inspectors of the need to interpret the language used by children. 'What the starved child calls stealing may not be stealing,' advised *The Inspector's Directory* (1901), 'yet as his parents call it stealing, the child calls it so, too. Never take a frightened, ill-treated child's *names* for its actions; find out, in particular, what those actions were.' This applied not only to Nattie's crime – the 'stealing' of food – but also to his punishment: the boys adopted their mother's description of the 'hiding' she administered, but the event may have been much more alarming than that term implied.

Violent parents not only inflicted physical suffering on their children, observed the *Child's Guardian*, but also caused psychological 'degradation'. As the older and favoured boy, Robert occupied a confusing position in his household: sometimes his mother punished him as a child, sometimes she enlisted him as a companion. The intensity of their relationship was particularly acute when his father was away, a closeness made literal on the nights that he slept alongside her. The NSPCC journal stopped short of addressing the oddity of a thirteen-year-old boy sharing his mother's bed, though such arrangements were usually witnessed only in slums and tenements that did not have enough space for adults and older children to sleep apart. A drawing in the *Illustrated Police News* picked up on the sexual symbolism of the murder scene: Robert is shown plunging a knife through the half-revealed breast of his mother while holding a truncheon at his groin. Pain is inscribed on the faces of both mother and son, one twisted in grief and the other in rage. Next to this image of savage and debauched frenzy, the newspaper published a sketch of Robert as a smooth-faced, clean-cut schoolboy standing in the dock.

The *Illustrated Police News* images dramatised the bewildering duality of Robert's behaviour: he was the good boy and the bad, child and man, beast and sophisticate. Robert 'appears to have two personalities', wrote the *Times* critic J. F. Nisbet, 'two memories which remain distinct'. His case played to the contemporary preoccupation with double selves. 'Every person consists of two personalities,' the French psychologist Pierre Janet had argued in 1886, 'one conscious and one unconscious.' Frederic Myers, a founder of the Society for Psychical Research, identified a 'subliminal self' that lay 'below the threshold of ordinary consciousness'. 'Two or more distinct trains of memory, feeling, will, may exist in the same personage,' wrote Myers in 1892. He proposed that the buried self communicated with the conscious mind by such means as auditory hallucination. Others speculated that unconscious selves might be revealed by hypnotism and mesmerism, or break forth spontaneously in somnambulism, epilepsy and homicidal insanity. 'Man is not truly one,' says Dr Jekyll in *Strange Case of Dr Jekyll and Mr Hyde*, 'but truly two.' By killing his mother, Robert had tried to resolve an intolerable tension, to simplify his divided self.

THE ILLUSTRATED
Police News

LAW COURTS AND WEEKLY RECORD

ESTABLISHED 1864.

No 1641. [REGISTERED FOR CIRCULATION IN THE UNITED KINGDOM AND ABROAD.]   SATURDAY, JULY 27, 1895.   Price One Penny.

BOYS MURDER THEIR MOTHER
REVOLTING CRIME AT PLAISTOW–SHOCKING DETAILS

HE SAID "WHEN I COUGH TWICE YOU DO IT" "THEN I DID IT"

WHERE THE MURDER OCCURRED

"YOUR MOTHER IS LYING DEAD UP STAIRS"

THE DISCOVERY OF THE BODY

IN THE DOCK

THE BOYS ON THEIR WAY TO THE CELLS

PART IV

THE MURDERERS' PARADISE

THOSE THAT KNOW NOT WHAT THEY DO

On Monday 23 September, six days after his conviction, Robert Coombes and two warders from Holloway gaol travelled by train to a village in Berkshire, forty miles south-west of London. Robert was wearing his cricketing trousers, his tennis jacket with gold piping and a pair of handcuffs by which he was attached to one of his guards. The day was blazing hot, but the boy was 'very cool and collected', reported the *Hampshire Telegraph*. 'He returned the glances of the passengers who travelled with him with careless smiles.'

A carriage met Robert and his guards at the railway station and they were driven up the hill and along the thickly wooded road to Broadmoor asylum, a group of tall, red turreted buildings encircled by a sixteen-foot wall.

The asylum gate was set in an archway flanked by towers and topped by a clock of black and gold. A turnkey unlocked the gate and the cab passed through the arch to a courtyard.

Robert was uncuffed, taken into the building and officially admitted to the asylum. His occupation was entered in the register as 'labourer in iron works', his crime 'murder of his mother by stabbing her with a knife'. He was sent to a bath-room, where an attendant watched over him while he bathed, and another took away his jacket and trousers and replaced them with a long calico nightshirt. His belongings were listed and stored. He was allotted a bed in one of the admissions wards in the asylum's central complex, where he would remain while his mental condition was assessed. Since he was consid-ered a suicide risk, he was observed closely.

During Robert's first week in Broadmoor the sun shone from dawn to dusk in a cloudless sky, and the temperature repeatedly reached 80 degrees Fahrenheit – it was the hottest September ever recorded. The admissions wards faced south, with a view through French windows to the open country at the front of the asylum: an undulating landscape of pastures, knolls and copses, run through by dark belts of pine and fir. Between the lawns and flowerbeds on the terrace outside the ward, a gravel drive was shaded from the bright sky by an avenue of limes. Below the drive the ground fell away gently in richly planted terraces to the foot of the ridge. The wall bounding the south-ern reach of the estate lay beneath the terraces.

It was as idyllic a prospect as a city boy like Robert had ever seen. In this pastoral setting the inmates of Broadmoor were returned to a kind of innocence: they were stripped of their freedoms and responsibilities, rendered as powerless and unencumbered as children. In Broadmoor they were unlikely to be reproached for their crimes. They entered a suspended existence, with little reference to the past or the future, a strange corollary to the dissociated, dreamlike state that often attended psychosis. The asylum was both gaol and sanctuary, fortress and enchanted castle. The spell by which the patients were bound within its walls could be lifted only at the behest of the queen.

Robert was interviewed by one of the asylum's four doctors within a few days of his admission. 'When questioned as to the murder of his mother,' the physician wrote in his notes, he 'at first pretended to have forgotten the occurrence: but subsequently admitted the deed.' Robert may genuinely, if briefly, have lost his memory of the killing, as he had done in Holloway. His grasp of the crime he had committed was fitful and unsteady. To survive the horror of the murder, Robert needed to forget. To recover from it, he would need to remember.

Broadmoor was built in the early 1860s to house the growing number of men and women found insane in the criminal courts. Its first patients were transferred from the Bethlem asylum in London in 1864 and the institution now held almost 500 men and more than 150 women. Just under half of the men had committed homicide, and about half of these had killed a member of his family. Robert became one of twelve male inmates who had murdered their mothers. Of the women in Broadmoor, who were housed in a separate part of the asylum, 80 per cent had killed one or more of their children.

In October, Robert was joined in the admissions ward by two more patients who had been convicted at the Old Bailey. Henry Jackson, an unemployed postman in his twenties, had suffocated his six-month-old baby. 'He seemed to hear a voice, not human, telling him to do the deed,' Dr Walker of Holloway gaol testified at his trial, 'and he felt he must kill the child; and after he had done it he felt a satisfaction.' Jackson was apparently suffering from the same species of mania – the compulsion to kill, the relief after killing – that Dr Walker had identified in Robert. Yet the insanity verdict in his case, too, masked the difficulty and unhappiness that lay behind his violent act. Henry Jackson's mother described the very tangible pressures on her son: he and his family were in a state of 'dreadful distress' after he lost his job, she said, having sold everything they owned in order to buy food.

The other arrival, Carmello Mussy, had shot at his land-lord before trying to take his own life. Mussy was an elderly Italian, wispy-haired, grey-whiskered, lame, his speech a garbled blur of French, English and his native tongue, often punctuated by sobs. The Old Bailey jury, moved by his vul-nerability, had found him guilty but insane. The judge com-plained afterwards that the jury's mercy was misguided: he had intended to give Mussy a light sentence, but the insanity verdict meant that the old man, like all the 'Pleasure Men' in Broadmoor, might never be free again. Robert's situation was similar. If he had been found simply guilty, his death sen-tence would almost certainly have been commuted – no one under the age of sixteen had been hanged in England since the execution in 1831 of the fourteen-year-old John Bell, who had killed another boy – but the combination of Justice Kennedy's intransigence and the jury's pity had ensured that his deten-tion would be indefinite. 'Those with long experience at the Old Bailey,' asserted the *Sheffield Independent* when Robert was convicted, 'remark that no case is on record of a person sentenced as a criminal lunatic ever being released.' This was a common misconception – several Broadmoor inmates were discharged each year – but most inmates did remain within its walls until they died.

After a few weeks, each new patient was assigned to one of Broadmoor's six 'blocks', which contained up to a hun-dred men apiece. The heavily staffed Blocks 1 and 6 – the 'back blocks', set against the woods behind the asylum – were inhabited by those patients who were considered dangerous to themselves or others. Blocks 3 and 4, which contained the infirmary and the admissions wards, were for the men who needed fairly constant supervision. Blocks 2 and 5 were the lightly staffed 'privilege blocks', for patients whose behaviour was more or less sane. Of the two, Block 2 was reserved for the more socially able and educated inmates. Robert, being young and therefore relatively impressionable, was sent to this building.

Block 2 sat to the side and slightly forward of the main complex and enjoyed fine views over the surrounding country. The building was 250 foot long and three storeys high. Most of its inhabitants were housed in single chambers, twelve foot long and eight foot wide, each furnished with a bed, a desk and a cupboard. Their windows were fitted with iron bars. Robert was issued with a toothbrush, hairbrush and comb and with a set of clothes: two day shirts, several sets of underwear and a flannel vest, a pair of strong grey trousers and a dark grey jacket.

Each morning, at 6 a.m. in summer and 7 a.m. in winter, Robert's door was unlocked and he rose to empty his chamberpot, wash himself with a flannel at a stand in his room, and dress for the day. He took a breakfast of tea, bread and butter in the Block 2 dining room. Afterwards, he and the other patients were released to the airing court for their first period of exercise. An attendant drew the bolts on the main door and then turned his key in the lock to let the men out, while another attendant stood by to count them as they passed: 'Three out, four out'. Security was tight in Broadmoor: there had been only six successful escapes from the asylum in thirty years, the most recent in 1888.

The Block 2 airing court encompassed several terraces below the main buildings. In spring its fruit trees blossomed against the weathered red brick of the asylum walls. In summer the beds brimmed with flowers, while sycamore and chestnut trees afforded shelter from the sun. A few attendants kept watch as the men played croquet, smoked and chatted, or walked alone. Some patients tended to their private gardens, small patches of land on which they could grow fruit and vegetables to eat or trade. The allotments were planted with strawberries, raspberries, cucumbers, tomatoes, plum trees, carnations. Thomas Henry Townsend, who had plotted to assassinate the prime minister in 1893, used to walk in the gardens gazing at the plants. 'I love beautiful things,' he explained. His failure to kill Gladstone, by his own account, stemmed from similarly tender instincts. 'He gave me such a sweet smile that he melted my heart,' Townsend would say, 'and I just couldn't pull the trigger.'

The patients were counted again as they returned to the block after each spell in the airing court: 'Five in, six in,' and so on. Once they were all back in the building, the door was closed, the bolts were rattled into their sockets, the key was turned in the lock and the ring buckled back on the attendant's belt.

Most of the patients' food came from the asylum farm, which grew crops and raised cows, pigs and sheep. The meals were prepared in a central kitchen and delivered to the block dining rooms. A typical dinner, served at about 12.30 p.m., was mutton, beef or pork, with potatoes or vegetables, followed by a steamed raisin or fruit pudding and accompanied by tea or weak beer. The Block 2 men were permitted to use knives at mealtimes, but the cutlery was counted out of the canteen as it was handed to the patients and counted back in once the meal was over. If the numbers did not tally, no patient could leave the block until the missing implement was found.

As well as the dining hall, the ground floor of Block 2 housed a pantry, a scullery, the attendants' offices, a billiards room and a day room. The day room had an open fireplace, upholstered benches along the walls, plants and flowers in pots and vases, and chairs and tables at which the patients could read and write or play card games. Through the barred windows, they could see the shallow valley and hills beyond the asylum. The tables were scattered with weekly periodicals, such as *Punch*, and daily newspapers, from which the attendants had snipped out any articles that they believed might hurt or excite a patient's feelings. Block 2 was the only block to have its own library; the books, which were chosen by the chaplain, included Hardy's *Jude the Obscure*.

The inmates' health, comfort and cleanliness were monitored closely. The common areas were heated by open fires and by warm air fanned up through grates in the floor; the temperature was regulated to 60 degrees in the day rooms, 55 in the dining room, 50 in the corridor. In 1896 the Block 2 urinals were supplemented with teak-seated flushing lavatories. The asylum's own plant burnt coal to supply gas for lighting and, from 1897, its engine house was able to run hot water to the blocks. On one evening a week, Robert took a warm bath. An attendant supervised, handing him a brush and carbolic soap with which to wash himself and carefully measuring the water temperature with a thermometer (the bath was heated to between 90 and 96 degrees Fahrenheit). As Robert grew older, an attendant shaved his face three times a week, while another stood by to ensure that the razor remained in his colleague's charge. The attendants were watchful about any means by which a patient might harm himself or others: no matches were allowed in the wards (the attendants lit the inmates' cigarettes, pipes and cigars), no mops, brooms or pokers were left lying about, all cupboards were kept locked, all fires extinguished at bedtime.

When dark fell, the common rooms and corridors were lit by mantled coal-gas lamps. Robert was given a supper of bread, butter and tea before being sent to bed at 7.45 p.m. and bolted into his room at eight. He slept under a sheet and blanket on a horsehair mattress stuffed and sewn in an asylum workshop. Throughout the night, the attendants made regular trips down the long corridors, checking on the patients by shining torches through narrow, glazed apertures in the bedroom doors.

The Broadmoor superintendent was Dr David Nicolson, who at the time of Robert's admission had run the asylum for almost a decade. Nicolson was tall, broad and jowly, with a bulbous nose and a drooping walrus moustache. A protégé of the pioneering Broadmoor superintendent William Orange, Nicolson took a liberal and humane line on crime and insanity. He was an outspoken opponent of criminal anthropology: the idea of hereditary criminality was a dangerous nonsense, he said in July 1895, 'because it does not include circumstance and motive in the computation, and because without these no standard of capacity, or of conduct, or of responsibility can be regarded as trustworthy or even possible'. Nicolson also held a broad view of what constituted an insane crime, and would have had no difficulty with the idea that Robert Coombes's murder of his mother, though premeditated, was an act of madness: 'an insane man has frequently a definite purpose of committing the act,' he said, 'and a clear knowledge of the results'.

Since he believed that madness was at least partly caused by a person's surroundings and experience, Nicolson tried in Broadmoor to foster an environment conducive to sanity. Unlike prison governors, he rarely employed attendants with military backgrounds. 'I prefer to train up an ordinary man,' he said; 'perhaps it might be a labouring man or an artisan – because there is not so much of the "toe the line" business on their part as a soldier naturally has, and which is necessary in prisons; there is more of the element and idea of nursing with us; that is to say, we have to get the inmates to rub along somehow from day to day.'

In keeping with the precepts of 'moral management' established earlier in the century, Nicolson impressed on his attendants the need to be gentle and sympathetic towards the patients. They were encouraged to accommodate erratic behaviour and to quietly ignore delusions. The *Handbook for the Instruction of Attendants on the Insane* (1885), known as the Red Book, advised asylum attendants to 'exercise such tact as will comfort the depressed, soothe the excited, and check the impulsive, irritable and destructive'. Some of the patients, observed *The Attendant's Companion* (1892), 'like elder children, may be trusted to do many things for themselves; others, like younger children, must have everything done for them'. In the asylum, Robert was treated as a child among children.

The Broadmoor staff used no mechanical restraints, such as straitjackets and fetters – there was not even a padded room on the premises. Instead, an attendant was taught to summon help if a patient became unruly, and then to try with one or more other staff to hold the patient until he or she was calm. If a struggle was unavoidable, the attendants were warned never to place their knees on an inmate, nor to twist his or her limbs in any way. The asylum rules stipulated that kindness and forbearance should be the touchstones of the patients' treatment. Drugs were used sparingly: morphine was occasionally dispensed as a sedative, brandy as a tonic.

The only therapies were the tranquil setting, the steadiness of the staff and the pattern of the days.

The attendants at Broadmoor were better paid than those at other asylums (most earned between £45 and £80 a year, while the Chief Attendant received £130), and some remained at the institution for life. In 1895 almost 80 per cent of the staff had served at Broadmoor for more than five years, and 60 per cent for more than ten. They did not always live up to the standards set out in the rule books but very few incidents of ill-treatment were recorded in the ledger of staff misdemeanours. Rather, the attendants were occasionally penalised for being late or drunk, for sitting down in a day room to read a newspaper or take a nap, for leaving the medicine cabinet open, miscounting the inmates, flirting with female patients, or failing to notice a missing spoon.

Within a few months of Robert's arrival, Nicolson was succeeded as medical superintendent by Richard Brayn, a dapper, clean-shaven man who had previously worked as a doctor in the prison service. He was employed on a salary of £900 (his deputy earned £500 and the two other doctors in the asylum £225 and £180 a year). Brayn gained a reputation as a strict superintendent, though this was based principally on the fact that in his first years he increased the use of solitary confinement in the back blocks. His views about the inmates were similar to those of his predecessors. He would remind visitors to the asylum that his charges were morally innocent: they were patients, not prisoners, and they had no need to expiate their crimes.

Brayn and Nicolson worked together on Home Office assignments before and after Brayn took charge of the asylum. In October 1895, when Robert had just been admitted to Broadmoor, the two doctors were asked by the home secretary to appraise the mental condition of Oscar Wilde, who was still being held at Wandsworth prison. After examining Wilde, Brayn and Nicolson concluded that he was not mentally ill, but suggested that his conditions be improved: he should be moved to a prison outside London, they recommended, and given more food, more space and more books. They advised that it was dangerous to his mental wellbeing to deprive him of a wide range of literature. Wilde was transferred in November to Reading gaol.

Under Brayn's stewardship, the life of Block 2 continued as before. The well-known war correspondent George Steevens, on a visit to Broadmoor in 1897, was taken by Brayn to the Block 2 day room. A dozen or so patients were sitting around, some reading and some playing cards. Like the other journalists who toured the asylum, Steevens was asked not to identify any of the inmates but was otherwise free to report on what he saw. The day room, wrote Steevens in an article published in the *Daily Mail*, 'looked like the smoking room of a comfortable but unpretentious hotel. . . Here was a quiet, trim, scholarly-looking man who had pushed his wife over a cliff; there a rougher, ragged-bearded elder who had throttled his senior partner; there, reading the *Daily Mail*, a mild-eyed visionary whose mission in life is to kill a royal person.' Steevens noticed two attendants in dark blue uniforms standing by like waiters, 'quiet, decorous, tactful, but vigilant'. The patients bade the superintendent 'Good afternoon' and paid no more attention to his guest than the residents of a gentlemen's club would have paid to another member's visitor.

Robert Coombes was the youngest inmate of Broadmoor by several years – there were no other patients below the age of twenty – and only the fourth boy ever to have been admitted to the asylum. Yet the mature and cultivated manners of some of his fellow residents concealed crimes quite as desperate as his own.

Among the patriarchs of the asylum was an engineer called Nathaniel Currah, from Lambeth in south London. In 1887 Currah's thirteen-year-old daughter Beatrice had pleaded with her parents to let her join George and Olga Goring's troupe of acrobat cyclists, and they had reluctantly agreed. Beatrice spent the next year on tour with the trick cyclists, in England, France and Germany, sometimes performing five times a night at different theatres and music halls. Over the months, she became sickly and weak. The Gorings disguised her skeletal legs by wrapping her shins in bandages and tights before she was seen on stage. One night she was so feeble that she dropped a young boy in the troupe, a slip that provoked hissing from the audience. In June 1888, the Gorings decided that she was too ill to perform and sent her home to Lambeth. Beatrice's condition worsened, and in December she died of consumption.

Upon his daughter's death, the once amiable Currah went mad with grief. He would wake screaming in the night, and by day he shuffled about muttering to himself, swearing, and tying knots in lengths of string. He tried to prosecute the Gorings for cruelty and neglect, but he met with no success in the courts. One night in June 1889 he made his way to the stage door of the Canterbury music hall in Lambeth and waited until George Goring and his entourage arrived in their private omnibus. As Goring alighted, Currah lunged forward and stabbed the acrobat in the stomach. 'I've got you this time, old boy,' he cried. He then drew a pistol and shot himself.

Goring died of his wounds. Currah survived to be charged with murder. The Old Bailey jury found him unfit to plead – being 'undeniably insane', in the words of the doctor who examined him, 'full of hallucinations and illusions' – and he was sent to Broadmoor without standing trial. Currah had tried to punish both of the men whom he blamed for Beatrice's death: Goring and himself. His act of violence was driven, like the crimes of many inmates of the asylum, by a deranging fusion of rage and shame.

In Broadmoor, Currah became again a peaceful, jovial fellow. When the celebrated author and journalist George Sims visited the asylum in the late 1890s, he found Currah in a day room smoking a briar-root pipe. The grey-haired, ruddy-faced old man engaged the visitor in conversation. He proved eager to discuss Sims's writings, particularly a series of poems about the plight of the poor. Sims was struck by Currah's warm, lilting voice and his soft blue eyes. As he left, he noticed that Currah returned to reading a copy of Charles Dickens's *Little Dorrit*, a novel in which the young heroine comforts and forgives her aged imprisoned father.

Several of Robert's fellow Block 2 inmates had more directly destroyed their children. Richard Oakes, a chemist, had been confined in the asylum since 1890, when he and his wife had been so financially desperate that they had decided to poison themselves and their eight-year-old son, Arthur. In a suicide note, Oakes explained: 'We have, God forgive us, taken our darling Arty with us out of pure love and affection, so that the darling should never be cuffed about, or reminded or taunted with his heartbroken parents' crime.' The strychnine quickly killed the boy but the dose was insufficient to kill the parents, and when their landlady found them both were lying in a blood-soaked bed, having tried to finish themselves off by cutting their throats with razors. They were charged with murder and attempted self-murder, found guilty but insane and sent to Broadmoor. In the asylum, Oakes was tranquil and well behaved and showed no signs of insanity. He rarely saw his wife: the Broadmoor men had no contact with the women except at chapel on Sundays, and even then the men were all seated on the ground floor, facing the front, by the time the women were allowed to file in to the first-floor gallery. An attendant found Oakes dead in his room in Block 2 in November 1895, aged sixty-four, apparently having suffered a heart attack. He was buried in the asylum cemetery.

A few months later George Pett, a retired grocer from Brighton, was admitted to the asylum. In February 1896 Pett had pushed his two daughters into the sea from a flint promenade on Brighton beach and then jumped in after them. He left his hat on the promenade, having tucked inside it a note addressed to his wife, explaining: 'Life is unendurable'. Pett and his younger daughter were fished out of the water alive but the twelve-year-old Lilian had drowned. At Broadmoor, Pett was initially placed under keen observation, since he had made an attempt at suicide, but when his mood improved in June he was transferred from the infirmary to Block 2. He put on weight after his transfer, the attendants reported; he became cheerful and talkative; and he seemed to enjoy playing billiards and reading the newspapers.

Some of the block's elders were distinctly eccentric, among them a doctor who wrote to the royal family to pledge outlandish sums of money for the building of hospitals. 'From time to time,' recalled a fellow inmate, 'his sense of identity became confused. Every Good Friday, for instance, he would plead indisposition and retire to bed, remaining invisible in his room till early on Easter Sunday morning he would make a dramatic reappearance.' Another doctor in the block, Archibald Campbell, had been the superintendent of a private asylum in Cumberland until he was convicted in 1898 of having carnal knowledge of a lunatic. Three maids had seen him having sex with a female patient in a laundry cupboard. Although it had become apparent at his trial that Campbell had been very drunk at the time of the crime, several of his fellow alienists testified that he had been suffering from a bout of insanity. The jury concurred and it was arranged that he be sent to Broadmoor. 'He has no symptoms of actual insanity,' reported Brayn after his fellow superintendent's admission, 'but he is very conceited, egotistical and boastful, and has an exaggerated sense of his own capabilities and importance.'

As well as doctors, the asylum housed several would-be writers. Isaac Jacob Mauerberger, a Polish journalist arrested in 1887 for sending death threats to Lord Rothschild, was composing a series of treatises on Jewish social and philosophical questions, later published under the title *A Voice from an Asylum*. Roderick Maclean, who had fired a pistol at Queen Victoria in 1882, wrote sonnets for other Broadmoor inmates at a shilling a time. His attack on the queen, which was the last of the eight attempts made on her life by different men, had been partly provoked by her failure to acknowledge receipt of a poem he had composed about Prince Albert. The most scholarly inhabitant of Broadmoor was both a medical and a literary man: William Chester Minor, an American army surgeon who had killed a ship's stoker in London in 1872, had during his two decades in the asylum become a prolific and treasured contributor to the inaugural edition of the *Oxford English Dictionary*. Minor was provided with an extra room in Block 2 to accommodate his library of rare books, which he was using in the late 1890s to furnish the new dictionary with thousands of quotations a year.

For the rich men in Block 2, there was little restriction on how they could spend their money. Some wore frock coats and fancy ties instead of the dark grey asylum uniform. Some ordered pheasants and other delicacies from London or from the local village, Crowthorne. Some employed poorer patients as personal servants. On one of his visits to the asylum, George Sims was invited into a bedroom (probably Dr Minor's) that was hung with fine engravings, furnished with a Chippendale bookcase that held dozens of first editions, and decorated with vases of cut flowers. The occupant offered Sims an expensive cigar and rang a bell to order coffee, which was brought to the room on a silver salver.

Robert was one of the few lower-class patients in Block 2, but a year after his admission another working lad was assigned to the building. Alfred Gamble, a former assistant to a greengrocer in Chapel Market, Islington, arrived in Broadmoor in 1896, at the age of sixteen. He had been arrested twice in 1895, the first time on suspicion of the murder of Sydney Dowling, a two-year-old boy who was found in a bin, his naked body wrapped in a sack and his mouth stuffed with a page from the *Daily Telegraph*. Gamble had been seen handing Siddy a piece of fruit outside his house that morning. 'I ain't done nothing at all,' Gamble said when questioned. 'I only gave him a pear. I wouldn't kill a child. Other people knows that.' He was discharged for lack of evidence. A few weeks later William Cattel, aged three, went missing while on a trip to a sweetshop. He was discovered in a stable in Islington, still alive but with severe wounds to his lower body. He too was wrapped in a sack and his mouth was stuffed with chaff and dirt. This time the evidence against Gamble was compelling:

the greengrocer for whom he worked had sent him to the
stable on an errand that day; he had been seen in the vicinity
with Willie Cattel; and the child had been found in a sack
marked with the name of Gamble's employer.

A tall, thin boy, Gamble appeared before the magistrates
in December in a dirty red scarf, an untidy frock coat and
corduroy trousers. He was charged with maliciously wounding a child and remanded at Holloway pending his trial at the
Old Bailey. Gamble was found unfit to plead (Dr Walker of
Holloway pronounced him an imbecile) and in January 1896
he was sent directly to Broadmoor. 'The case belongs to the
same group as the Plaistow murder,' observed the *Journal
of Mental Science*; 'that of crimes by "instinctive" juvenile
criminals.'

Like Robert, Gamble was placed in the gentlemen's block on
account of his age rather than his social standing. The boy's
vulgar manners irritated some of his fellow inmates. Archibald
Campbell, the disgraced asylum superintendent, took a 'great
dislike' to Gamble, according to an attendant, and complained
that his loud voice 'went through his head' to such an extent
that it made him want to 'blow his brains out' – it was unclear,
from the attendant's report, whether he wished to blow out
his own brains or those of the boy. Gamble was employed as a
servant by Sherlock Hare, a former barrister who was among
the more combative residents of Block 2. Hare sometimes gave
the lad paintings as gifts, and sometimes accused him of poi-
soning his supper.

Events from the wider world occasionally penetrated the
cloister of Broadmoor: in 1897 the asylum took part in the
celebrations of the queen's sixtieth jubilee (one patient ate
a jubilee medal, though it passed through him without ill

effects); in 1899 all the asylum's pigs contracted swine fever and were slaughtered; in the same year a few of the attendants and one of the doctors were called up to serve in the Boer War.

Even more occasionally, the affairs of Broadmoor were exposed to the world. In the summer of 1898 a new inmate caused a small furore in the press. Jonathan Lowe, a middle-aged night porter, was charged in April with murdering his former landlady. Both of the medical witnesses at the trial believed Lowe to be insane, but the judge refused to allow the defence to examine them; he guided the jury towards a guilty verdict and sentenced Lowe to death. Afterwards, the Home Office asked Brayn and Nicolson to interview Lowe – the Criminal Lunatics Act of 1884 gave the home secretary the power to order a medical inquiry if there was doubt about the sanity of a condemned prisoner. The doctors reported back that Lowe had been infatuated with his landlady to the point of monomania. He had come to believe that she had a mystical influence on him, and when she ignored his letters to her he became depressed and suicidal. They concluded that this was a 'very clear case of insanity'. Upon reading Brayn and Nicolson's report, the home secretary repealed the death sentence and sent Lowe to Broadmoor.

A few weeks after his admission, Lowe gave a glowing account of his new home. 'The superntend, the doctors and all the atendents are all very kind and respectfull to the patents,' he wrote to a friend in July. 'We have about five hours and half out in the gardens every day. There is books to read, periodicals, and the daly paper to read; biliards, bagatle, cards, demonios, chess, draphs, and everything that is nessery fer our amusement. Band plays out in the grounds, and there is plenty of musick amongst the patents themselves. We have our beer and tobaco and plenty of fruit; in fact, I am very comfortable. I am very well satesfied with my lot.'

Lowe's friend sent a copy of this letter to the *Globe*, which printed it in full. Newspapers all over the country followed suit, several of them appending outraged editorials about the luxurious conditions at the asylum. *Lloyd's Weekly* reported that many of the inmates were perfectly sane, and that the attendants were 'highly amused at the tricks which must have been used to fool doctors and juries so as to secure admission' to this 'murderers' paradise'. The lunatics and pseudolunatics, the paper's informants claimed, 'eat, drink, laugh, and grow fat'.

Brayn felt obliged to defend the asylum's practices to his employers. In a memorandum to the home secretary, he wrote: 'Recreation, in the form of entertainments and games of various kinds, has long been universally recognised as an important remedial agent in mental diseases, and as a valuable means of treatment now forms an essential part of the routine of every lunatic asylum. The days are long gone by when the irrational beliefs and violent acts of lunatics were dealt with by harsh measures of punishment, as if they were voluntary.' Jonathan Lowe, he said, 'is a man of low mental development who has spent a considerable portion of his life in the workhouse and amidst more or less sordid surroundings, and to him the comforts of an Asylum may appear attractive by comparison, but the greater number of the inmates, who are capable of appreciating it, consider that the privileges accorded to them in Broadmoor are a very poor compensation for the loss of their liberty'.

A former inmate of the asylum wrote a letter to the press that echoed Brayn's point: detention in Broadmoor was 'a living death', he said. 'To be separated from all you hold dear on earth is a terrible thing to one who has any love for home; it was to me. . . With all the kindness, there are many in Broadmoor who wish they had been hung.' He signed the letter 'An Ex-Madman'. The correspondent – John Brailsford, who had killed a fellow lunatic in a Birmingham asylum in 1859 – sent a copy of his published letter to Brayn, with a note attached. 'I am very thankful for all the kindness I received at Broadmoor,' he told the superintendent. He added that he often thought of his fellow inmates; he had learned to love and respect many of them and he wished that they could be free.

The pain and despair of Broadmoor patients was most evident in the back blocks, where the men sometimes lashed out in horror or rage and the attendants wore padded jackets with hidden buttons to protect themselves from injury. Robert and the other residents of Block 2 came across the inmates from other blocks rarely, in communal areas such as the infirmary, the chapel and the hall. Some of the more disturbed men were vacant and abstracted, some aggressive, some caught in dreams of divinity or fantasies of persecution. These were patients closer to the deranged squires in Robert's penny dreadfuls. One elderly inmate, said to have killed his mother in 1849, would inform passersby that he had great mysteries, comets, suns and fires fastened to his shoulders. Another announced: 'My name is T Perkins, and I have been murdered here, by those that know not what they do, because they have ether in their heads, for Christ's sake.'

In the back blocks, the most violent patients were locked in their rooms for hours at a time. Towards the end of the 1890s, the lunacy commissioners who made annual inspections of

Broadmoor censured Dr Brayn for his excessive use of this practice.

Among the more frequently secluded inmates of the back blocks was Thomas Cutbush, who had been admitted in 1891, aged twenty-six, after attacking and wounding two women in south London. He was a dark, slight, sharp-eyed and educated man, described in his medical notes as 'very insane'. He would deliver disjointed soliloquies as he sat in his room: 'You can buy a box of sardines for six pence,' he said. 'If I take my food there's mercury in it. My coat is not good enough. I will see Sir Edward Blackall of Scotland Yard. It is all a fraud. If I had any knife from the pawn brokers I would settle the whole damn crew of the cut throats.' Cutbush used to promise to 'rip up' the attendants with a knife and when his mother leant over to kiss him at the end of a visit he tried to bite her face. He sometimes attacked other patients – one Block 2 man (Arthur Gilbert Cooper, a curate who had cut his vicar's throat in 1887) was hit hard in the face by Cutbush when he encountered him in a corridor in 1891. Three years later, two reporters from the *Sun* newspaper visited Cutbush in Broadmoor. He greeted them with silence, and they wrote an article in which they identified him as Jack the Ripper, the perpetrator of the Whitechapel murders of the late 1880s.

Even in Block 2, the anguish and disturbance of an inmate occasionally interrupted the calm routines. One morning in May 1897, George Pett, the affable grocer who had drowned one of his daughters off Brighton beach, was found dead in a fellow patient's room, having hanged himself with cord from a hinge on the window.

Robert, too, seems to have suffered a breakdown. In November 1898, at the age of sixteen, he was sent from Block

2 to the more closely supervised Block 3 and kept there for fourteen months. He had arrived at the asylum smooth and blank, his rage and fear sealed over. It may have been the kindness as much as the strangeness of Broadmoor that eventually cracked him open: not just to sensations of anger and anxiety now, but also to grief.

TO HAVE YOU HOME AGAIN

Among the papers that the police found on the writing desk in 35 Cave Road on 17 July 1895 was a letter written by Emily Coombes to her husband. It was composed on Sunday 7 July, the older Robert Coombes's fifty-first birthday and the day before Emily's death.

Although Coombes had left home as recently as 4 July, the postal services were so swift that Emily had already sent him a parcel and received a note in return. She probably sent the parcel to Gravesend, in Kent, where his ship stopped on its passage out of the Thames. She had addressed her latest letter to the pier in New York at which the *France* would dock more than two weeks later. It was not read out in any of the court hearings because it had no direct bearing on the case, but it had probably been read by Robert, who wrote his own letters at the same desk in the ten days after his mother's death. When the Coombes boys were charged with murder the letter was copied for the West Ham magistrates' court and retained in its files. The transcriber could not make out all of Emily's last written words, and many of the allusions are in any case unclear: it was a hurried note, an instalment in a conversation. Yet the letter casts some light on the younger Robert Coombes's story – not so much on the mystery of why he killed his mother as on the mystery of how he might recover from having done so.

> My Darling Husband,
>
> I received your welcome letter from ? and pleased you received the things safe. Robert I do miss you. Emily was down and was not doing anything and no money for rent. I don't know what they will do. I gave her the coat I could not help doing so – young Robert did not like to see her crying not like some one told me – never mind Robert don't go away by thinking there is some one comes to your house far from it. I am quite surprised at you – after all these years and the nice little home you have got it takes keeping up also your boys are not the same – they can eat more than you can but my love you don't look at that. Well did you find your ? I wish you all the love and Good wishes and long life on your birthday and only wish you had been home for it – never mind. I trust you will soon xxxx. I have not seen anything of your mother or Annie. I am writeing to Mrs Cooper – going there this week if she at home. Robert I have sent you the paper mind and will send next Sunday also for you – not quite so bad never mind write untill you get the next one. I can just see you having a fine lark. Well dear the boys sends there love to you and hopes you are well & longing to have you home again also myself and accept true love from me.
>
> From your, ever True and Faithfull Wife
> EH Coombes

Emily and her husband had evidently quarrelled just before he left for New York. He had voiced a suspicion that she had 'some one' secretly come to the house in his absence – a lover, maybe, since Emily seems at pains in the letter to insist on her fidelity; or a debt collector or impoverished friend, given how she justifies her expenditure. Robert and Nattie, in that close-quartered house, had probably heard their father accuse their mother of promiscuity or profligacy. In the letter Emily is flustered, defensive, upset. She tells her husband how much she and the boys miss him, though he has been gone for just three nights, and reminds him what she has to put up with – the demands of his sister-in-law, the appetites of his sons, the responsibility for his 'nice little home'. As if to calm herself, she repeats the phrase 'never mind' after each burst of indignation or worry. She mentions that she has sent him a paper with news 'not quite so bad' as the last one. That Sunday's newspapers reported that American beef slaughtered at Deptford, the chief cargo of the National Line, was still selling poorly but was fetching slightly more than it had in the previous week – meat sales, particularly of American beef, had been badly hit by the drought.

The letter evokes something of the atmosphere of agitation and strain in 35 Cave Road on the weekend of the beating and the murder. Emily was a highly strung woman, and she seems to have been wound tighter still by her argument with her husband and his departure for America. That Sunday was hazy with heat – the temperature rose to 80 degrees in the shade – and she faced a long summer alone with her restless, hungry boys. She does not allude in the letter to her fury with Nattie for stealing food, nor to her thrashing of him. Perhaps all that unfolded later in the day.

For though her letter is threaded with anxiety, Emily emerges from it also as the tender wife and mother whom her friends described. She is warm, sympathetic, alert to the unhappiness of others. She tells her husband that she has impulsively given his sister-in-law a coat that weekend, presumably to sell or pawn, and that Robert was distressed to see his aunt upset. She insists on her eldest son's sensitivity – his capacity to care – as she had insisted to the attendance officer that he was suffering at school. Whatever cruelties and confusions Emily Coombes may have inflicted on Robert, she also loved him. She believed that he was a boy who could feel sorrow as others did.

IN THE PLASTIC STAGE

Robert was allowed back to Block 2 on 8 January 1900, two days after his eighteenth birthday. Upon his return he immersed himself in the life of the asylum.

About half of the Broadmoor inmates were deemed stable enough to work on the estate: they were assigned jobs in the workshops, on the farm, in the laundry, in the kitchens and bakehouse, and as carpenters, bricklayers and cleaners. 'Suitable occupation,' advised the Red Book for attendants, 'has a most salutary effect on both the body and the mind. It diverts the Patient from his morbid fancies, and leads his thoughts into a healthy channel.'

Robert worked in the tailors' shop, part of a three-pronged building behind the central hall. Amid the smells of the horse-hair and leather in the adjoining mattress-makers' and boot-makers' shops, he and the other tailors made and repaired the dark blue uniforms of the staff, and the underclothes, bedlinen and grey suits of the patients. They cut the winter jackets and trousers from heavy cloth such as Melton, corduroy and fustian, the summer wear from flannel and drill.

Each working patient was given an extra meal a day (an eleven o'clock lunch of bread, cheese and oatmeal) and paid about five shillings a month, an eighth of the going rate for labour. Robert could use his wages, which were entered as credit in a book kept by the Broadmoor steward, to order extra provisions such as tea and tobacco, or seeds to plant in his allotment.

Robert's supervisor was Charles Leach Pike, a master tailor who had joined the Broadmoor staff in 1895, aged twenty-three and newly married. One of eight occupational attendants in the asylum, Pike was paid a salary of £57 to train and oversee the men in his workshop. The attendants were enjoined in the Red Book not to 'hold themselves aloof from their charges or be content with supervising them', but rather to 'join heartily in their occupations and amusements, and work both with and for the Patients'. Pike heeded this advice. He was vice-captain of the Broadmoor Cycling Club, a keen pianist and a frequent performer in the asylum's theatrical entertainments. The costumes for the shows were put together in his workshop. As accompanist to the Broadmoor string band, Pike inspired several of the inmates in his charge to take up music. Robert learnt to play new instruments – the violin, the piano and the cornet – and he became an enthusiastic member of the asylum's brass band.

Brass bands were amateur, working-class ensembles, of which there were tens of thousands in Britain at the turn of the century, whereas string bands had more refined, upper-class antecedents. The editor of the *British Bandsman* complained about the class distinction, finding 'no reason why Tom who plays the cornet, should be in a lower social or musical grade than Dick, who plays a violin'. It was a mark of the oddity of Robert's position, as a working-class lad among the educated lunatics of Block 2, that he played both brass and string instruments, and probably was a member of both bands. The bands performed in concerts in the hall; at staff balls at Easter and Christmas; at ceremonies in the asylum grounds. In the summer of 1900, the brass players gave a concert on the Broadmoor cricket pitch to celebrate the relief of the siege of Mafeking, the South African town that Colonel Robert Baden-Powell had held against the Boer forces for seven months.

Charles Coleman, the Principal Attendant of Block 2 and the member of staff most directly responsible for Robert's welfare, was another passionate performer and musician. Born in Dorset in 1850, Coleman had been a drummer with the Dorset Militia before joining the staff of Broadmoor in 1873. He lived in Crowthorne with his wife and children, among them a daughter who was an attendant in the Broadmoor women's wing. Coleman played in the string band and performed with gusto in entertainments in the hall. He was a well loved figure in the asylum, especially prized for his comic turns in seasonal revues: his impersonation in November 1900 of a statue of Alexander the Great had the audience helpless with laughter.

From his office on the ground floor of Block 2, Coleman wrote detailed, sometimes dryly humorous reports to the asylum's Chief Attendant about the upsets and altercations on the block, taking care to follow the guidance in *The Attendant's Companion*: 'never say that a patient *thinks* this, or *imagines* that, or *feels* the other. You cannot be sure of what a patient thinks or imagines or feels. All that you can be sure of is what he *says* and *does*, and your reports should be strictly limited to his sayings and doings.'

Several of the reports relating to Block 2 inmates featured the irascible and increasingly paranoid barrister Sherlock Hare, who had been admitted to Broadmoor in 1892, aged forty-one, after attacking a newspaper editor in Burma. Over the years, Hare complained to the Block 2 attendants that the cook had prepared him poached eggs instead of omelette; that other inmates had made fun of his name; that his chops had been poorly cooked (he wanted to take this up with the home secretary); that attendants and patients had blown tobacco smoke in his face; that the doctors had inoculated him with syphilis; and that he had been accommodated in a single room – he said that he supposed only murderers were allowed two, a barbed reference to William Chester Minor's double suite. When Hare insisted that someone had been sitting on his bed while he was in the airing court, Coleman investigated, and established that the bedclothes were rumpled because Hare himself had sat on the bed to put on his boots before going outside.

Another of Coleman's reports described a spat between Hare and a patient called Ben Hewlett, a widowed policeman who in 1887 had attacked his nine-year-old son with a chopper. In a Block 2 corridor, wrote Coleman, he saw Hare push Hewlett and Hewlett push Hare back. When Coleman intervened, Hewlett said that Hare had started the scuffle. Hare denied it and called Hewlett a liar. 'And you,' replied Hewlett, 'are a lunatic.' Coleman gently advised Hewlett to return to work, and Hare to repair to his room.

The flags at Broadmoor were flown at half-mast upon the death of Queen Victoria in January 1901, and the asylum observed a day of mourning. The next year the patients assembled in the hall to watch a series of short films – probably the first moving pictures they had seen – of the coronation of Victoria's son as Edward VII. They were now detained not at Her Majesty's but at His Majesty's Pleasure.

A few local shocks were felt at the asylum in the opening years of the new century: a fireball hit the gatehouse during a thunderstorm in 1900, smashing off a chimney pot; in the same year an attendant's three-year-old son fell into a water butt on the estate and drowned; in 1902 an attendant was invalided out of Broadmoor after being stabbed fifteen times in the face by a patient in the back blocks. On 3 December 1902 Coleman hurried to the aid of William Chester Minor, who was crying out in pain. 'He had cut his penis off,' wrote Coleman in his report to the Chief Attendant. 'He said he had tied it with string, which had stopped the bleeding. I saw what he had done.' The sixty-eight-year-old lexicographer had long been tormented by sexual fantasies and delusions, and he had lopped off his penis, he said, 'in the interests of morality'. He was taken to the infirmary. Three months later he had recovered and was back in his Block 2 quarters.

Robert remained rational enough to stay in Block 2. The attendants kept an eye on him, as he was still considered fragile, but he seemed now to be able to tolerate the pressure of dark thoughts, to sit out a low mood rather than snap under its strain. 'RAC rather depressed this evening,' wrote an attendant in a note of 4 October 1901; 'he says he is alright.'

Robert took part in many of the asylum recreations. He excelled at billiards, which was played on a frayed old table in one of the two day rooms at the front of Block 2. Many inmates liked to watch the matches, and some acted as bookmakers, setting odds on the result of a tournament and taking bets in batches of tobacco, cigarettes and cigars. Each male patient was allotted an ounce of tobacco a week, drawn from the government stock of contraband seized by Customs & Excise officers.

Dr Brayn used to tell how he once consented to play billiards with a patient, who proceeded to win the game.

'There you are,' said the superintendent. 'I knew you would beat me.'

'Ah, sir,' remarked another criminal lunatic, consolingly, 'to be expert in billiards is the sign of a misspent life.'

Robert was also one of a small group of patients who played chess, continuing a tradition established by inmates such as Edward Oxford, the first of the eight men to try to assassinate Queen Victoria, and Richard Dadd, a patricide who while at Broadmoor had decorated the asylum hall with a series of fantastical murals. Robert proved a talented chess player, as did his fellow Block 2 inmate Reginald Saunderson.

Saunderson had been admitted to Broadmoor in the same year as Robert, at the age of twenty-one. He was a pale, tall young Irishman of aristocratic descent, with deep-set grey eyes. In November 1894 Saunderson had absconded from an institution for 'mentally deficient boys' near London and cut the throat of a woman in Kensington. He fled to Ireland, where he surrendered himself to the police. It emerged that, like Robert, he had taken an obsessive interest in the capture and trial of James Canham Read; the day on which Saunderson turned himself in, 4 December 1894, was the day of Read's execution.

Unlike Robert's family, Saunderson's parents were rich enough to hire doctors to help to save him from the gallows. The famous alienist Lyttelton Forbes-Winslow interviewed Saunderson and reported that the young man told him: 'Everything around me appears to me as if in a dream, and I have no recollection of having committed the murder of which you speak; had I done so, I cannot understand the wickedness of the act, or what I should suffer in consequence. I hear, and have heard for some time, and do at the present moment hear people speaking to me, who apparently are hidden behind the walls; I have been persecuted by these voices for a long period of time, urging me to do the various acts, and I believe in their reality.' On the basis of this suspiciously comprehensive and precise fulfilment of the definition of insanity, Saunderson was found unfit to plead and sent straight to Broadmoor.

Both Saunderson and Robert took up correspondence chess, a form of the game that had become popular in the last decades of the nineteenth century. Each match was conducted by post, one move at a time, and could last for several months. Saunderson was at one point playing seventy-one correspondence games simultaneously. He secured many of his opponents through the offices of Frideswide Rowland, a former Irish women's chess champion who ran competitions in the *Weekly Irish Times* and the chess journal *The Four-Leaved Shamrock*. By way of thanks, Saunderson used to post boxes of asylum-grown strawberries to Mrs Rowland every summer. He was a 'bright, pleasant' correspondent, she recalled, and a strong player.

In 1902, to mark the coronation of Edward VII, Mrs Rowland advertised in the pages of *The Four-Leaved Shamrock* for volunteers to take part in an Ireland v England match. Saunderson and Robert both signed up. Saunderson was allotted to the Irish team, since he had been born in Dublin, and Robert to the English. The standard was high: the forty or so competitors included the future English correspondence chess champion and the future Irish over-the-board champion. In all, 111 games were played, with a point being awarded for a win and a half for a draw. Saunderson lost his match but Robert beat his Irish opponent, and when the competition concluded in 1904 England won by 68½ points to Ireland's 42½.

Saunderson ceased his correspondence with Mrs Rowland soon after this match. She later heard that the Broadmoor authorities had limited the patients' participation in chess, as the game was proving 'too exciting' to some on the cold damp days that they were confined in the block.

In the summer months, both Robert and Saunderson played cricket for the Block 2 team, as did Alfred Gamble, the costermonger's boy who had attacked young children, Arthur Gilbert Cooper, the curate who had cut his vicar's throat, and Roderick Maclean, the would-be royal assassin and aspiring poet. Dr Brayn often captained the Block 2 side, while John Baker, his deputy, led a team drawn from the patients in Blocks 3, 4 and 5 (Blocks 1 and 6, the back blocks, did not field any players). On other occasions, the Block 2 attendants and patients played together, or a team of gardener patients played a combined team of tailors, upholsterers and boot-makers. As well as adhering to the usual rules of the game, the patients had to observe the asylum's strictures on cricket: they were to walk to the field in a 'compact manner', flanked by attendants, and during a match had to keep a distance of twenty yards from those attendants assigned to form outposts; if they wished to relieve themselves, they had to do so at a designated spot supervised by a member of staff.

The fixtures were organised by the Broadmoor chaplain, the Reverend Hugh Wood, a first-class cricketer who in the late 1870s had played for Cambridge University and then for the Yorkshire county team. Wood arranged up to seventy matches at the asylum each season in the early 1900s, and oversaw the laying of a new pitch within the walls in 1903. The Broadmoor

First XI increasingly competed against teams fielded by local institutions such as Sandhurst Royal Military College and the Windsor police. Robert played in a side that beat the Reading Gas Company in 1907. In the same year he was listed in the local paper, the *Reading Mercury*, as one of the batsmen who helped the Broadmoor side to victory over Crowthorne.

By the asylum's standards, Robert was a decent batsman – he was usually placed halfway down the batting order – and an able bowler. He shared the bowling duties with Dr Brayn, George Melton (a railway-van boy who hit his mother on the head with a hammer in 1896), Henry Spurrier (a lance-corporal who knifed a fellow soldier in 1899), Kenneth Murchison (a renowned Boer War gunner who had shot a reporter through the head in Mafeking in 1899) and Thomas Shultz (an office boy who attacked his boss with an axe in 1904).

Of the players in the Block 2 cricket team, the one whose crime most closely recalled Robert's was a lad called Frank Rodgers, admitted to Broadmoor in 1904 at the age of fifteen. Robert was by then twenty-two; Frank took his place as the baby of the asylum.

Frank had a more moneyed and educated background than Robert. At the beginning of 1904 he had been living in a large house called The Gables in the pretty village of Meldreth, near Cambridge. The Rodgers family had recently moved from London in the hope that the peace and seclusion of the countryside would help to cure Frank's mother, Georgina, of her weakness for alcohol. Frank's father, a City solicitor, commuted daily to London, leaving Frank and his mother at home with Frank's sisters Winifred and Queenie and his older brother William. Georgina continued to drink heavily.

One evening in April, Frank and Winifred returned from a visit to a friend's house to find their mother drunk. While the children ate their supper, Georgina lay dozing in an armchair in the dining room. Afterwards Frank went upstairs and Winifred went to the drawing room to play the piano. A few minutes later Frank entered the drawing room with a revolver in his hand. 'I have shot Mother,' he told Winifred. 'It is for the best.'

Winifred rushed out to find her mother lying in the hallway with a bullet in her neck. She quickly summoned a doctor, while Frank took his youngest sister, the six-year-old Queenie, across the road to a public house. He asked the landlady if Queenie could stay there for the night, as he had shot his mother. He then sat down to read a newspaper.

Winifred and William followed Frank to the pub. 'Frank,' said William, 'why did you do it?' 'I did it for Queenie's sake,' Frank replied. He repeated this to Winifred: 'It is for Queenie's sake. She cannot live the life we have had for the past two years.'

When the doctor arrived at The Gables he found Georgina Rodgers dead. Frank confessed readily to him – 'I have done it' – and handed him the revolver, saying that he had taken it from his brother's drawer. A policeman came to arrest the boy.

At Frank's trial for murder, Winifred confirmed that their domestic life had been very unhappy for the past couple of years because their mother had so often been drunk. Frank was their mother's favourite child, she said, known by the others as 'Mother's boy'. William then testified: Frank had been restless for many weeks, he said, often rising from his bed in the middle of the night to lock the bedroom door. The family doctor confirmed that Georgina Rodgers was nearly always inebriated when he saw her. He said that Frank had told him that for the past two or three months he had frequently sensed his mother standing right behind him, looking over his shoulder, but when he turned she seemed to disappear. Frank had also told him that as he advanced on his mother with the revolver he heard a voice say, 'Do it quickly'. Finally, two alienists appointed by the Crown gave evidence. The first said that Frank was unable to tell right from wrong because his determination to put an end to his family's trouble had narrowed his mind. The second said that Frank had become convinced that 'there was no other way out of it'. The press described Frank's manner in court as gentlemanly, intelligent, polite.

The boy's plight aroused the compassion of many. 'The sympathy of the whole neighbourhood appears to be with young Frank Rodgers,' noted the *Hertfordshire and Cambridgeshire Reporter*, observing that the boy had 'brooded over the unhappy conditions of things at The Gables and in this state of mind committed the terrible deed, perhaps feeling prepared to suffer himself for the sake of his little sister Queenie and the rest of the family'. The jury, without leaving the box, arrived at a verdict of guilty but insane.

The home secretary was uneasy about sending Frank Rodgers to Broadmoor. He asked Dr Brayn how the boy would be accommodated. 'I should propose to place him at first in one of the infirmary wards,' replied the superintendent, 'where he would be under the constant supervision of an attendant day and night.' This was the same arrangement that had been made when Robert was admitted and, again, when he became unstable at the age of sixteen. Brayn explained that if Frank was sufficiently rational he would be sent on to Block 2, to reside with 'patients of the better class'.

Frank was admitted to Broadmoor in June and transferred to Block 2 in July. He engaged in many of the same pursuits as Robert. He followed the cricket in the newspapers and was a keen participant in the asylum games. He and Robert played their first game together in July; Robert was the leading scorer of the match, making sixty-three runs before he was caught out by Alfred Gamble. Frank also took up the violin, practising on four evenings a week in the winter months, and became a member of the string band. He learnt to play chess. He taught himself French and shorthand and was given lessons in mathematics by the chaplain. He grew apples and strawberries on his allotment.

Frank's father sent him hampers containing oysters, French bread, cuts of rabbit and pork, bottles of Lea & Perrins Worcestershire sauce and copies of the *Boy's Own Paper*. This magazine was a middle-class version of the story papers found in Robert's house, having been founded as an antidote to the dreadfuls – it was full of tales of adventure and derring-do, but firmly pinned to the virtues of valour, self-sacrifice, the defence of Empire. Frank was a voracious reader. While on remand in prison, he had read both Jules Verne's *Twenty Thousand Leagues Under the Sea*, the submarine fantasy of 1870 that inspired the Jack Wright stories, and Thomas Anstey Guthrie's *Vice Versa: a Lesson to Fathers*, a novel of 1882 about a schoolboy and his father, a City merchant, who exchange bodies and inhabit each others' lives. The boy's father is taught how trapped a lively-minded boy can feel when he has 'no money and few rights', 'virtually no way to assert himself in the world around him'.

Dr Brayn wrote to the Home Office with his observations about Frank Rodgers's crime. 'Defect of will power and the influence of puberty were no doubt largely responsible,' said

the superintendent; 'he is still in the plastic stage of adolescence and very susceptible to extraneous influences.' In
another memo he summed up the cause of the murder as
'Domestic worry. Adolescence.'

Adolescence had been identified only recently as a distinct developmental phase, notably with the publication in
1904 of the American psychologist Granville Stanley Hall's
*Adolescence: its Psychology and its Relations to Physiology,
Anthropology, Sociology, Sex, Crime, Religion and Education.*
Hall described the adolescent years as the occasion of 'a
marvellous new birth' but also a time of 'storm and stress',
characterised by conflicts with parents, moodiness and risk-
taking. This period, he suggested, was 'pre-eminently the
criminal age'.

'At no time of life,' Hall said, 'is the love of excitement so
strong as during the season of the accelerated development of
adolescence, which craves strong feelings and new sensations,
when monotony, routine, and detail are intolerable.' A love of
cheap fiction was one of the symptoms, Hall wrote: at about
the age of twelve many boys were seized by a 'reading craze',
and in their eagerness to 'have the feelings stirred' they sought
out 'flash literature'. They became subtly imprinted by such
fiction, he suggested, acquiring a half-conscious, shadowy
fantasy world, impossible to articulate except, sometimes, in
action: 'There is now evolved a penumbral region in the soul
more or less beyond the reach of all school methods, a world
of glimpses and hints. . . Perhaps nothing read now fails to
leave its mark. It can not be orally reproduced at call, but on
emergency it is on hand for use.'

There were many correspondences between the histories of
Frank Rodgers and Robert Coombes. Both were bright boys
and passionate readers. In the months that preceded their

matricides both suffered from headaches, nightmares, irritability. They had been their mother's favourites before becoming their destroyers. After the killing each calmly confessed (though Robert took longer to do so), and seemed relieved rather than tormented by his act; in explaining his crime, each boy cited a need to protect a younger sibling. One of the alienists who examined Frank Rodgers for the Crown reported that the lad's 'immature judgement. . . had for some time led him to believe there was moral justification' for the matricide: 'He thought it was the right thing to do.' Dr Brayn agreed that Frank had become 'convinced that his mother's death was imperative'. Robert too had imagined that there was justice and necessity in the killing of his mother.

Both boys seemed to have unacknowledged motives for murder. They chose to present themselves as the defenders of weaker children but were also driven by fear. Frank had imagined his mother creeping up on him; he had locked his door against her at night. His claim that he did it for Queenie served to mask his anxieties. By invoking Nattie's thrashing as the motive for the murder, Robert similarly played down or displaced his own dread of an unsteady and overwhelming mother.

Frank and Robert drew their murder plots from the fiction-fed shadowland that G. S. Hall had described. For much of their childhood, storybooks had offered these boys an escape from anxiety, and when they found themselves in crisis they framed their solutions in the language of those books. Frank's was a *Boy's Own* narrative of chivalric heroism, Robert's a more muddled and lurid penny adventure of rescue and revenge, self-sacrifice and self-interest. The purity of Frank's narrative aroused compassion in his audience; Robert's tawdrier story invoked disgust as well as pity. Unlike Frank,

Robert lied and dissembled after the murder, and he stole his mother's money. The heroes whom he emulated included not just the noble knight but also the independent lad setting out to sea in search of a new life, and the clever criminal outwitting the establishment. Robert aspired to be a hero, to protect and rescue Nattie. He aspired to be a villain, cool and notorious, free of all feeling.

In 1905 Frank's father applied to the Home Office for Frank to be conditionally discharged, and Dr Brayn advised that since the boy seemed sane there was no need for him to remain in the asylum. The home secretary refused the application, on the grounds that to discharge him so soon 'would encourage popular belief that sane murderers are sent to Broadmoor and released after a short time' but the next year agreed that Frank could be entrusted to his father's care. The seventeen-year-old left Broadmoor on Christmas Eve 1906. He was one of 175 patients to be discharged between 1896 and 1910 (of these, forty-nine relapsed and were re-admitted to the asylum). Frank took a job as a clerk in his father's office in the City; at home in the evenings he practised the violin with his sister Winnie.

Frank Rodgers was married in 1910, four years after leaving Broadmoor, and by 1911 he and his wife had a baby daughter.

In 1910 another young criminal was admitted to Block 2. Patrick Knowles was born in 1894 in Teesside, north-east England, to a shipyard ironworker and his common-law wife. As a child, he sold matches for a living. In 1903, when he was nine, Patrick killed a one-year-old boy by burying him on a piece of wasteland and then attempted to abduct and kill two other infants. He was apprehended and charged with murder.

The Home Office asked Drs Brayn and Nicolson to examine Patrick. They pronounced him insane – or rather, 'of unsound and unformed mind in consequence of childhood and immaturity of development', a phrasing that suggested that most children were legally mad. On the basis of this assessment, the Home Office announced that rather than face trial the child would be confined in Broadmoor at His Majesty's Pleasure. Unknown to the press and public, Patrick was instead conditionally discharged and sent incognito to an industrial school for poor and delinquent children. Only in 1910, when he was sixteen, was he transferred to Broadmoor, and even then the Home Office had doubts about whether it was a suitable place for someone so young. 'I fear this is the only course open,' read a note on Patrick's file. 'It is not a satisfactory thing to send a boy of 16 to Broadmoor, but it has not worked badly in the case of one or two other boys of that age.'

Dr Brayn was still running the asylum when Patrick was admitted, but he retired a few months later. In his fifteen years in charge, he had reduced the use of solitary confinement to even fewer hours than when he had taken over, and increased the life expectancy of the inmates. He was succeeded by his deputy, John Baker, an unmarried Aberdonian born in 1861, who had written papers on epilepsy, criminal anthropometry and infanticide. In the most recent of these, published in 1902, Baker observed that many of the female patients in Broadmoor had killed their babies in a fit of 'transient frenzy', a single, fleeting episode of psychosis.

Patrick Knowles, like the other young patients, was placed in Block 2. As he had already learnt the rudiments of tailoring at the industrial school, he was given a job in the tailor's shop with Robert. The tailor, Charles Pike, described Patrick as a painstaking and intelligent worker, quiet, respectful, obliging and of a happy disposition. Dr Baker echoed Pike's appraisal: far from displaying 'inherent vicious or criminal tendencies', said Baker, Patrick's conduct and demeanour were exemplary and he was a favourite with both staff and inmates.

In December 1911, after thirteen months in the asylum, Patrick was discharged to the care of the industrial school at which he had already spent seven years, and where he was now to remain until he was able to support himself. The head of the school wrote to the Home Office to ask for funds to help the lad to emigrate. He explained that he feared that Patrick would otherwise be tempted to go back home to Teesside. The headmaster saw the boy's home as the source of his troubles; Dr Brayn, too, had believed that Patrick's crime was rooted in his 'squalid' family life. The press usually interpreted juvenile atrocities as evidence of the innate, hereditary nature of criminality and madness. The staff at Broadmoor, on the contrary, saw young murderers as the most malleable of their charges; they suspected that the causes of their violence often lay in their unhappy circumstances, and that they might flourish under different influences. The doctors who dealt with avowedly insane children often detected emotional as well as physiological causes for their outbreaks of unreason. To get better, such patients needed to recognise the pain that they had endured as well as the pain that they had inflicted.

Charles Coleman, the Principal Attendant of Block 2, was promoted to Chief Attendant of the asylum in 1906, but at the beginning of 1912 was obliged to retire. Coleman had served at Broadmoor for almost forty years. The band played at his leaving ceremony, and Samuel Smith, who succeeded him as acting Chief Attendant, made a eulogistic speech of farewell.

For many years Dr Brayn had taken the view that Robert, though 'rational and tranquil', was not fully stable: despite his apparent sanity, the superintendent worried that he might become dangerous again, whether to himself or others, if he were set at liberty. As Brayn told a visiting journalist, many patients whose behaviour was perfectly normal within the asylum walls could revert once they were in the wider world. To illustrate the point, Brayn introduced his visitor to a quiet, well-spoken inmate who was tending a flowerbed, and explained that the man had once been discharged from the asylum as cured and within three days had smashed his wife's head to a pulp with a hammer. But Brayn's successor, Dr Baker, was more optimistic about Robert's chances. When Robert petitioned the Home Office for his discharge in February 1912, Baker wrote to the home secretary in support of his application. 'I have the honour to submit, herewith, a petition from Robert Coombes. . . He is a good tailor, a member of the Asylum band and cricket team. . . In my opinion his prayer might receive favourable consideration without undue risk.'

The Broadmoor authorities could not release a patient unless to the care of a person or agency prepared to oversee his or her return to normal life and to report back to the asylum if anything went awry. Since no member of Robert's family was able to look after him, Dr Baker recommended him to a Salvation Army colony at Hadleigh, Essex, which occasionally took in the asylum's discharged men. Robert was offered a place at the Hadleigh colony in March, and the Home Office agreed that he could be conditionally discharged.

When Robert had been admitted to Broadmoor in September 1895, some newspapers had predicted that his spell in the asylum would be short and unhappy. 'He is not likely to trouble the Broadmoor authorities very long,' said *The Sunday Referee*; 'within a few years he will probably die raving mad.' As it turned out, Robert spent seventeen years in the asylum, and was the longest-serving of the eight men set free in 1912.

On Friday 15 March, at the age of thirty, Robert packed his belongings and said goodbye to the staff and his friends. In the office of Samuel Smith, the acting Chief Attendant, he changed into a going-away suit that had been cut and stitched for him in the tailor's shop and he handed back his uniform. Robert left the asylum in the custody of Charles Pike, the tailor attendant, who had been assigned to accompany him on his journey out of Broadmoor and back to Essex.

PART V

WITH TRUMPETS AND SOUND OF CORNET

SMOOTH IN THE MORNING LIGHT

The king was George V, who had succeeded to the throne on the death of Edward VII in 1910. The prime minister was H. H. Asquith, a Liberal, whose party had regained power in 1905 after a decade of Conservative rule. Asquith's government was contending with a surge of discontent. Hundreds of thousands of workers had gone on strike in 1911, protesting about their conditions and wages: cotton weavers in Lancashire, sewing-machine makers on the Clyde, dockers and carters in London, railwaymen and seamen throughout the country. Even schoolchildren went on strike in September, demanding shorter hours and free pencils. In November, scores of women stormed Parliament to insist on their right to vote.

The unrest continued into the new year. A million coal miners were on strike when Robert left Broadmoor in mid-March, and a band of suffragettes had been smashing shop windows in London. An Essex woman – the wife of W. W. Jacobs, author of the horror story 'The Monkey's Paw' – was charged with breaking four windows in Earl's Court Road.

'I have done this because I think it is my duty as the mother of five children,' Eleanor Jacobs explained to the magistrate.

'What!' said the magistrate. 'Your duty as a mother of five children to smash property up!'

'Yes,' she said. 'That is the only way we can protest against the action, or rather the inaction, of the Government in refusing justice.'

The magistrate was so baffled by Mrs Jacobs's statements that he thought that she might be demented, so he had her remanded for seven days while a doctor investigated the state of her mind. She was found sane and sentenced to a month's hard labour.

Because of the coal shortages caused by the miners' strike, only half of the trains were running, but Robert and Charles Pike managed to make their way by rail through London to Essex. The Salvation Army Farm Colony at Hadleigh overlooked the Thames Estuary a few miles from Southend. It sat on a hilltop by the ruin of a thirteenth-century castle, above a scrubby foreshore piled with cockleshells. The sharp winds from the river and sea carried a salty reek of fish and algae. The Essex clay was springy and sticky underfoot. At the colony headquarters, Pike gave Robert into the care of the Salvation Army officers and then headed back to Broadmoor.

The Salvation Army had been founded in East London in 1865 by the self-styled 'General' William Booth and his wife, Catherine. It was an evangelical, working-class Christian movement that focused on social reform. During Robert's childhood 'Sally Army' bands had paraded the streets of West Ham with their drums and trumpets, blasting out the joy of salvation, while the Army missions offered practical help to the poor. Booth had established the colony on the Essex badlands in 1891, in the hope that it would help to solve two apparent problems of the day: the fragility of the overstretched Empire and the physical decline of the urban working class. In 1910 the novelist Henry Rider Haggard explained in his book *Regeneration* that as Booth had become acquainted with the histories of the destitute men on the streets of London, he realised 'how closely a great proportion of human sin is connected with wretched surroundings'. To attempt 'not only the regeneration of the individual, but also of his circumstances', Booth proposed to take wrecked men out of the urban slums, restore them to health and productivity, and then ship them out to people the wilds of Canada and New Zealand. In this way, the teeming city would be relieved of its tramps and wastrels, and the empty imperial outposts filled up with fresh colonists. Booth's project gained extra urgency in the wake of the Boer War: in 1899 it had emerged that 8,000 of the 11,000 Mancunians who volunteered for service in South Africa were so physically feeble as to be unfit for service. 'Back again to the garden!' urged the general.

About 200 men were living in the Hadleigh colony in 1912, many of them derelict alcoholics picked up from the streets of London. All were unemployed. 'We came down in a farm wagon,' recalled one colonist, 'half a dozen lads from the train, and there it was, smooth in the morning light, and the castle standing on the highest part like it was watching still over the fields. I was going to stay here! No foggy smoke, no screeching noise, and no more shivering and standing idle in the bitter wind and rain and sleet at a dockyard gate.' Most of the residents were eventually discharged to paid work or to a colony overseas. Within a fortnight of Robert's arrival, forty-two men – almost a quarter of the Hadleigh population – were despatched to Canada.

At Hadleigh, Robert slowly accustomed himself to a degree of freedom. There were no locks or bolts on the bedroom doors, no walls around the estate. He worked again in a tailor's shop, on the main parade of buildings along the dirt track known as Castle Avenue. Other colonists made bricks, grew fruit or tended the colony's poultry. Several million bricks, marked with the initials SALIC (Salvation Army Land and Industrial Colony), were carried by barge to London each year: the Bricks I site produced a red, wire-cut brick suitable for bridge- and sewer-building; Bricks II turned out the yellow brick that was used in ordinary terraces such as Cave Road; and the kilns of Bricks III fired a superior red brick, suitable for the construction of villas. The extensive market gardens grew mint for sale in London and rhubarb for Southend. The tomato houses and orchards produced tons of fruit for local markets. The poultry were the pride of the colony: Hadleigh's fancy fowl often won prizes in national competitions. As at Broadmoor, most of the men also farmed their own allotments, which was considered good training for those who would emigrate and live off the land. General Booth's emphasis on the garden had a moral charge: to tend to a plot implied a taming of one's own nature, a process of self-civilisation exemplified in Frances Hodgson Burnett's novel *The Secret Garden* (1911), in which the renewal of a wild and ruined garden transforms a sour girl and a hysterical boy into loving, fit and happy children.

Religious services were held in a corrugated-iron hall on Castle Avenue, known as the Citadel. These could be intense and noisy events, especially when a colonist experienced a revelation and knelt at the Citadel's wooden seat to repent his sins and pledge himself to God. The atmosphere owed more to the exuberant, heady spirit of the music-hall than to the restrained rituals of the Anglican Church. General Booth liked to cite Psalm 98: 'With trumpets and sound of cornet make a joyful noise before the Lord, the King.' More than fifty musicians played with the Hadleigh colony's renowned brass band.

To begin with, Robert was provided only with basic board and lodging but he was soon rewarded for his work with tokens to spend within the colony, and later with a few shillings' pay a week. In the summer of 1912 he wrote to the chief steward at Broadmoor to request that he forward him some of the credit that he still held at the asylum: five shillings was sent to Robert in June, another fifteen in July.

Robert's bedding and dining arrangements improved over time. The seaweed mattress and rough covers with which he was first issued were replaced with a firmer mattress and softer blankets. He was promoted from the first section of the refreshment rooms, where he sat on a bench at a bare table and fetched his food from a bar, to the second section, where he was served by a waiter, and then to a third, in which he sat on a chair at a table dressed with a white cloth and was brought thinly sliced meat on white crockery.

The longer-standing residents of Hadleigh were moved from dormitories to individual rooms in one of the colony's farmhouses. By June 1912, Robert had been given a room in Castle House, an eighteenth-century building overlooking the castle ruins. He could see the tall chimney of Southend electric power station to the east, where the Thames opened into the sea, and the long stretch of Southend pier.

After Emily Coombes's murder, Robert's father had moved out of the house at Cave Road and taken lodgings in the Barking Road. He was back at work on the SS *France* within weeks of the Old Bailey trial but on his return from New York in November found time to visit his son in Broadmoor. The next year the National Line sold both the *France* and the *England*, as Coombes had feared, and he had to find work as a steward with other companies. In 1903 he married a twenty-three-year-old barmaid called Ada White, a dock foreman's daughter who worked in the Ordnance Arms pub in the Barking Road. In the summer of 1912, she fell ill with pneumonia while he was at sea. She died in their house in East Ham in July, with one of her husband's sisters at her side.

John Fox returned to anonymity after his acquittal, and seems to have died or emigrated by the end of the century. His friend and protector John Lawrence died in 1898 in a vast new lunatic asylum in Woodford, Essex. Fox and Robert's solicitor Charlie Sharman was declared bankrupt in 1896 and he was suspended from practice when it emerged that he had been stealing from his clients. The next year he was charged with sexually assaulting another of his clerks – the case was heard by his friend Ernest Baggallay, who immediately dismissed it. By 1912 Sharman was again working as a lawyer. He subsequently developed a sideline in organised crime, selling stolen bonds on behalf of an international gang of mailbag thieves.

Both of Robert's grandmothers had died by 1912: Mary Coombes in Bow in 1900, leaving about £1,000 to be shared between her five children, and Tryphena Allen in Liverpool in 1904. Robert's aunt Emily had been widowed, while his uncle Frederick, who had accompanied him on the voyage to New York, had married, had a child, and set up as a grocer in Clerkenwell. Robert's aunt Mary Macy, who had taken charge of Nattie, was still living in Liverpool. Her husband had died in a home for retired seamen in Staten Island, New York, and two of her five children had emigrated to Australia.

There is no record of whether Nattie visited Robert in Broadmoor, and Nattie's job, like his father's, had made it impossible for him to offer to look after Robert upon his discharge, but the brothers met after Robert left the asylum. Nattie remained the smaller of the two: he stood at five feet two inches, while Robert had grown to just over five feet seven inches tall. Nattie's hair had darkened to black and his eyes to grey, whereas Robert's hair was still brown and his eyes blue.

Nattie had become a ship's stoker, first with the Merchant Navy, sailing between England and Australia, and from 1904 with the Royal Navy, sailing with the Home Fleet from Chatham in Kent. Stokers performed the most gruelling of shipboard duties, tending to the fires and furnaces that powered a steamer's engine. The stoker was 'the lowest class of sailorman', reported Robert Machray in *The Night Side of London*: 'his work brutalises him; the heat in the interior of the steamboats drives him mad'. The stoke hole that contained the furnaces was hot, shiny, slick with oil; its cranks whirled and its pumps pulsed to propel the shafts that turned the ship's screws. The stokers – stripped to the waist, black with coal, a film of pale ash sticking to their sweat-beaded skin – averted their heads from the spit and flare of fire and steam as they opened the furnace doors. Their hands blistered in the heat; their eyes tingled and smarted. By 1912 Nattie had been scarred above his left eyebrow and on the back of his right forearm. The stokers 'come and go in the blazing light and half gloom', observed the authors of *Ocean Steamships*, 'like nightmares from fantastic tales of demonology'.

In June 1913, Robert and Nattie's twice-widowed father fell ill on board the *Rossano*, the cargo ship on which he was serving as chief steward. He was put ashore on 2 July at Puerto de la Luz, a coaling port on the island of Las Palmas, off the Atlantic coast of Africa, and was admitted to the town's Queen Victoria hospital. On 6 July, the day before his sixty-ninth birthday, he died of cancer.

Nattie was halfway across the Atlantic in July 1913. He had been lent by the Royal Navy to the recently established Royal Australian Navy in January, and in June had been appointed to serve as a leading stoker on its flagship, the HMAS *Australia*. The *Australia* was a giant battlecruiser that consumed coal at a tremendous rate: to run her at full speed, fifty stokers had to keep feeding the furnaces hard. When she stopped to refuel at the Caribbean island of St Vincent on her maiden voyage that August, it took twenty hours for the whole crew to load 2,000 tons of coal through manholes in the deck. 'I have been down many coal mines,' remarked the ship's padre after visiting the stoke hole, 'and preached considerable about hell, but I never saw anything equal to this yet.' The ship reached Sydney in September, and in October 1913 led the fledgling Australian fleet in a ceremonial procession into the harbour. The largest warship in the southern hemisphere, the *Australia* toured the country for the next few months, being greeted with excitement wherever she docked. The coming of the Australian fleet was hailed by the defence minister as the most memorable event in the continent's history since the arrival of Captain Cook.

A week after Nattie reached Sydney, Robert travelled from Hadleigh to the Probate Office in London to execute his father's will. Because their stepmother had died, he and Nattie were the heirs to the £186 in the estate. Though not rich, they were now men of moderate means.

Back at Hadleigh, Robert got permission to leave the colony and follow Nattie to the Antipodes. He sailed on 2 January 1914 from Gravesend in Kent on the Royal Mail steamer *Otranto*, as one of about 400 third-class passengers. When asked for his next of kin, he provided the name and address of Charles Pike, the master tailor and supervisor at Broadmoor. He gave his own occupation as 'tailor'.

This was the first sea voyage that Robert had made since his trip to New York with his father when he was thirteen. The ship steamed down the widening reaches of the river, the Essex marshes falling away to the left, the Kentish hills to the right. She sailed out to the Atlantic and then into the Mediterranean, stopping to collect and deposit mail and passengers at Gibraltar, off the Spanish coast, at Toulon in France, at Taranto in Italy and at Port Said in Egypt before passing through the Suez Canal to the Red Sea and the Indian Ocean. At Colombo in Ceylon a touring Australian cricket team boarded the vessel for the last leg of the voyage. Passengers of all classes played sports and games on deck and attended a fancy-dress ball.

After six weeks at sea Robert disembarked in Sydney. The city was the capital of New South Wales, one of the six Australian territories that in 1901 had joined together as a commonwealth of federated states. Since federation, some 400,000 Britons had emigrated to Australia, swelling its population to almost five million.

Nattie had lodgings in Newcastle, a hundred miles north of Sydney. Robert took the train 550 miles south-west to Melbourne in Victoria. He found work there as a clerk.

SUCH A HELL OF A NOISE

When war broke out in August 1914, the Australian prime minister promised Britain an army of 20,000: 'While the Empire is at war,' he said, 'so is Australia.' Robert Coombes travelled back up to Sydney from Melbourne to volunteer for service. By the time he joined up in September, the number of soldiers in the new Australian Imperial Force had already exceeded the total that the prime minister had pledged. About a quarter of the men in the AIF were British-born.

The army offered Robert a form of stability – after nine months of civilian life, he regained the structures and certainties of an institution – and the pay was good. Australian privates earned six shillings a day, more than any other Allied troops; they were sometimes referred to by the British, who earned a single shilling a day, as the 'Six-Bob Tourists'. The coming of war also gave Robert a chance to embark on the voyages of adventure of which he had dreamt as a boy.

Over the last three months of 1914 Robert trained in a series of camps in south-eastern Australia, taking part in parades, drills, route marches, physical jerks for up to sixteen hours a day. He was taught to turn in formation, to stand to attention, to form fours. In the absence of uniform, he and his fellow soldiers drilled in shirtsleeves or singlets, dungarees and white hats. They slept twenty-three to a ten-man tent. The diet, everywhere, was meat stew, bread and jam.

Robert was assigned to the 13th Battalion, which was composed mostly of men from New South Wales and was one of four battalions in the 4th Infantry Brigade. Though the men of the 13th were a various lot – among them accountants and labourers, bushmen and clergymen – they gained a reputation as sturdy, independent types; strapping country lads with a breezy disdain for authority. In the 'Battalion of Big Men', Robert cut a slight figure: he weighed a little over eleven stone and his chest measured thirty-four inches, the minimum required in the early days of the war. He needed spectacles to correct the vision in his left eye. At thirty-two, he was older than most of his comrades; but, having spent so long in Broadmoor, he was also far less worldly. He had acquired a reserved, educated manner among the gentleman lunatics of Block 2. He knew little of drink or money, and in two decades had barely spoken to a woman.

When the uniform for the extra troops arrived, Robert was issued with boots, puttees, cord breeches, a grey collarless shirt made of Merino wool, a loose khaki jacket and a felt 'slouch' hat, its brim turned up on one side. Each tip of the jacket collar was adorned with a badge of a rising sun, the emblem of the AIF.

In October, the 13th Battalion formed a military band. Since there were no official bands in the AIF, the unit had to obtain its own instruments and sheet music and to draw musicians from the ranks. The 13th was lucky: a Miss Margaret

Harris of Sydney donated the instruments and the commanders were able to find good performers among the troops. Robert was one of about twenty-eight men selected from the 900-odd in the battalion. He was provided with a cornet, the instrument that usually carried the main melody in a military band piece; it could produce a rich, mellow sound, warmer, rounder and more lyrical than the piercing bright notes of the trumpet.

On 22 December the band marched through Melbourne at the head of the 13th and played the battalion on to the HMAT *Ulysses*, the flagship of a fleet carrying some 12,000 Australian and New Zealand soldiers to war. During the six-week voyage to the training camps in Egypt, the band rehearsed daily. On the troop deck or in the officers' mess each evening, it played ragtime tunes, British army staples such as 'It's a Long, Long Way to Tipperary' and waltzes such as 'Dancing by the Moon' and 'Pink Lady'. A favourite number was 'Australia Will Be There', a new song that both promised the nation's allegiance to Britain and asserted its independent identity. The bandmaster had arranged for the music to be printed just before the *Ulysses* sailed, and the battalion band popularised the anthem throughout the AIF.

'Our band is improving wonderfully,' Private Byron Hobson of the 13th Battalion confided to his diary. 'The band played on our troop deck last night,' he wrote on New Year's Eve, 'and we had a fine time ragging and dancing. . . I have never heard such a hell of a noise before.'

The regime on the *Ulysses* was relaxed and the atmosphere irreverent. The soldiers wore dungarees, padded about barefoot, sunbathed, read books, played cards and chess. To while away the days at sea, the 13th and the 14th, a sister battalion raised in Queensland, held a bun-eating competition, a cricket match (won by Robert's battalion team) and a blind boxing match (a bloody affair, also won by the 13th). Yet the passage was slow and the diet of stew monotonous, and though Robert was used to a circumscribed life some of his companions rebelled against the constraints. When the ship docked near Colombo in mid-January a group of men (mostly of the 14th Battalion) escaped into town on small craft, got deliriously drunk and ran naked through the streets, mauling women. Back on board the ship, the language became so blue as the weeks passed that the minister warned the troops that they would be ostracised from polite society if they persisted in using the 'Australian adjective' (bloody). In another sermon, he reflected aloud on how Man lived from moment to moment, not knowing what the next day would bring – 'Stew!' hollered the congregation.

Even the music had started to grate on some. 'I only realised tonight what getting too much of a good thing meant,' reported the nineteen-year-old Private Eric Susman on 25 January, after a very hot afternoon on the Red Sea. 'We have all been interested in our brass band, and have listened to it day by day, and have appreciated its continuing proficiency. But now, the continual blare is becoming boring and nerve-racking. We get too much of it, too many marches and "patriotic selections". Anything for a comic opera selection, or a tango dance played by a string band!'

When the *Ulysses* sailed through the Suez Canal at the end of the month, the troops lining the banks greeted the new arrivals with cheers. The Australians yelled back: 'D'you want some stew?' They disembarked in Alexandria on 1 February 1915 and took the train to Cairo. From there, the men marched the last three miles to the camp at Heliopolis. The band's clarinets, trumpets, euphoniums, bassoons, tubas, bugles, cornets, cymbals and drums were transported by truck.

The presence of the Australians was designed to discourage any local dissent in Egypt, which the British had declared a protectorate in December. The 13th trained hard in the hot dust and sand, engaging in sham fights, drills, night manoeuvres, trench-digging, twenty-mile marches through the desert. Egypt was 'Bum – very bum', concluded Private Susman: 'Hell with the lid on.' The men complained among themselves about the incompetence of their officers, particularly their commander, Colonel Granville John Burnage, whom they dubbed 'Granny', and his stiff, rule-bound side-kick Major Walter Ellis.

The soldiers bought drugged cigarettes and embroidered sateen souvenirs in the Cairo bazaars, and paid for sex in the brothels. Outside the city, they climbed pyramids and rode donkeys and camels, pursued by street vendors who cried out 'eggs-a-cook!' as they pulled boiled eggs from the folds in their gowns. The soldiers were strange and comical to the Egyptians, too, with their weird pets (one battalion brought a kangaroo as a mascot) and futuristic vehicles. The AIF had an armour-plated desert truck that the troops called 'The Terror', the name that the dime-novel hero Jack Wright gives to an electric carriage that he has invented to ride across the American West. The Australian soldiers had been raised on the same penny fiction as their British counterparts.

Robert's band performed at church parades and funeral services and on marches. At the start of a night march through the desert, they stood in two feet of sand as they played their boys out with 'Here We Are, Here We Are Again'. After a forty-eight-hour sandstorm they played them into camp with 'The End of a Perfect Day'. On 1 April they performed for the troops by moonlight in a palm grove by the Nile. Even Private Susman was by now smitten with pride: 'Our band,' he told his diary, 'is at present the crack band of the military forces in Egypt.'

Robert and his fellow bandsmen doubled as their battalion's stretcher-bearers, the soldiers who would administer first aid on the battlefield and carry wounded troops to safety. The size of a band roughly corresponded to the number of stretcher-bearers required by a battalion, and it was convenient to train them as a group. Captain Cyril Shellshear, the battalion medical officer, taught the musicians to dress and bind wounds, to fashion slings and splints for broken limbs and to load a man on to a stretcher. The collapsible wood and canvas stretchers were fitted with leather halters that the bearers could strap over their necks to spread the load. They were also taught to carry the wounded without the aid of a stretcher: hoisted over a bearer's back in a fireman's lift or sitting on two bearers' clasped hands.

In April the Australian troops learnt that they were to sail for Turkey as part of an Allied plan to seize the Gallipoli peninsula, gain control of the Dardanelles strait, capture Constantinople and knock Turkey out of the war. On 11 April, recalled Sergeant Charles Laseron of the 13th, 'we left Heliopolis and marched to the station with the band playing and everybody swinging jauntily, much bucked-up by the prospect of immediate active service'. In Alexandria, they boarded a filthy tramp steamer and set out to sea, the band performing 'The Marseillaise' as they sailed past the French troop ships in the bay.

The 13th Battalion soldiers were known for the excellence of their trench-digging and their marching, for the speed with which they could load their guns, and for a cool, stubborn spirit known as 'hide'. The flippancy of some could shade into a harsh contempt. As they lay in the dark ship crossing the Mediterranean, horse urine dripping on to them from the deck above, they sang to the tune of 'Onward, Christian Soldiers':

Onwards ragtime soldiers
Fed on bread and jam
For our bloody colonel
We don't care a damn.
See our gallant major
Strutting on ahead,
And our only prayer is –
May God strike him dead.

On 17 April the steamer anchored off the Greek island of Lemnos, sixty miles west of the Dardanelles, and on the night of 24 April the battalion band gave a final concert. The men roared for encores. 'Good old band!' they cried at the close. In the morning Robert put his cornet into storage and buckled on the armband that marked him out as a stretcher-bearer, the initials 'SB' embroidered in red wool on cream cloth. At 10.40 a.m. the battalion sailed for Gallipoli.

As the ship anchored near Suvla Bay in the afternoon of 25 April, the men of the 13th looked out at the thin beach, the sheer, scrubby rock face behind it, the shells bursting from the mountains, the rifles flashing and snapping in the dust and smoke. The first waves of Australian and New Zealand – or

Anzac – troops had landed on the peninsula in the early hours of the morning and were fighting in the hills while Allied battleships bombed the Turkish positions from the bay.

At 9.30 that night the soldiers began to clamber down the rope ladders on to a destroyer, from which they were transferred to rowing boats that carried them closer to shore. A few of the men were hit by Turkish bullets before they reached land. The rest climbed out of the boats with their heavy packs and waded to the beach, where the bullets continued to whip down among them.

Hundreds of soldiers were wandering about on the beach, having retreated from the front line dazed or wounded. The Turks, though initially outnumbered, had used their superior artillery to inflict great losses on the Australians and New Zealanders, driving the invaders back so that they now held only a broken line of ridges close to the bay. The new arrivals were told to head up the slope to plug a gap in the line.

The soldiers of the 13th were under constant fire as they climbed the hill past scores of dead and wounded soldiers. When they reached the narrow, jutting ridges at the head of the valley they began to dig in. As they dug they fought, shooting at the Turks across the flat fields between the trenches. The Australians were exposed if they moved even a few feet back, and the Turks were, in places, barely forty yards in front of them. Above the steady clink of the shovels, the shells screeched. 'The noise is hell,' wrote Hobson in his diary.

The bearers were kept busy from the start. When Robert heard the cry 'Stretcher-bearer!', he and a comrade hurried forward with a stretcher and a pannier of supplies: scissors, bandages, dressings, water, morphine tablets. They would staunch and bind an injured soldier's wounds, lay him on the stretcher and carry him away for treatment. Regimental bearers usually took the wounded only as far as a dressing station or ambulance just behind the front line, but in the chaos of the Gallipoli landings they had to haul them all the way down the ravine to the shore. Robert and the other bearer would edge through the gravelly gully with their load, dodging bullets and shells from the hills, using their bodies as brakes as they slipped on loose stones. At the casualty clearing station on the beach, which was often itself raked with artillery fire, they handed over the wounded. Then they climbed back up, grabbing at tufts of scrub along the tracks, their hands and clothes snagging on bristles as they picked their way through rocky fissures to fetch the next casualty.

In these first days and nights, the bearers worked with courage and tenacity. All around them men cursed and screamed, crazed by thirst or pain or terror. Some of the bearers collapsed from exhaustion as they struggled down the gullies, and then rose to carry on. 'The stretcher-bearers are great,' attested one soldier. 'They go up and down all the time in the open, carrying the wounded through a withering shellfire. It's magnificent to see them. They are the real heroes of the affair, because they are unarmed and exposed to everything.' Private Ray Lingard, a twenty-one-year-old 13th Battalion bearer, explained in a letter to his uncle: 'The Turks are waiting for you to just bob up so as to have a smack at you. We stretcher-bearers are not protected by the Red Cross, so you see they are at liberty to blaze away as much as they like.' The bearers came to symbolise the 'mateship' that was forged at Gallipoli: a spirit of unflagging, selfless devotion that was the kernel of the Australian soldier's identity. At night they dug graves for the dead.

The bearers slept in the hillside below the ridges, where they were frequently assailed with shells. 'One landed within seven or eight yards of my dug-out, but luckily did not explode,' wrote Private Lingard. 'It buried itself about seven feet in the ground . . . We were trying to cook some tea, but shells kept landing and throwing up heaps of earth in the air all around us.' The troops treated the danger like play, the proximity of death as a wild joke. 'I never laughed so much in my life as I did when those big shells were landing,' said Lingard.

The bearers needed unusual resilience to endure the passivity of their role: they were required to witness savage violence, to step forward to comfort the wounded, while never lifting a hand against the enemy. The *Official History of the Australian Army Medical Services* observed that 'the courage required of the stretcher-bearer was of a peculiar and (so to speak) unnatural quality; not the instinctive response of the courageous animal to attack, but an acquired and "conditioned" inhibition of the instinct to flight; a deliberate disciplining of the mind and will through the impulse of "self-respect".' The bearers were 'servants at once of humanity and of hatred, of the Geneva Convention and of the Military Command'. Unlike other soldiers, they had to suppress their impulses to defend themselves or others.

This passivity made the bearers especially prone to nervous collapse. The 13th Battalion bearer James Dow, who was later diagnosed with neurasthenia, described the agony of watching a friend slowly die in the dugout beside him. 'What makes us mad,' he wrote in a letter to his parents, 'is that they snipe you and you cannot revenge your mates.'

On the night of 2 May, the 13th was instructed to attack the Turks from one of the ridges at the top of the valley. As the soldiers advanced under cover of fire from the British gunships, they sang 'Tipperary' and 'Australia Will Be There', the swell of their voices flooding down the valley behind them to the beach. They fought furiously through the night, digging fresh trenches on the plateau beyond their ridges, but when dawn broke they found that the battalions that should have protected their flanks had failed to arrive. Exposed on all sides to Turkish shells and machine-gun fire, the men of the 13th were mown down. 'It was just hell pure and simple,' wrote a private, 'with the gates wide open.'

Robert and the other bearers ferried dozens of men down to the beach, many with their limbs blown off or their bellies split open. At the 4th Brigade Field Ambulance station, Lieutenant-Colonel Joseph Beeston operated on the casualties. 'Some of these are very ghastly,' he wrote in his diary. 'A shell will carry the whole of the intestines away, others half of the abdomen. Nothing can be done for these unfortunate fellows but fill them up with Morphia, and await the end.' In total, the 13th had now lost more than half of its 934 men, and fourteen of its twenty-five officers. The commander of Robert's company, Captain Brache, fell down a ravine on the night of 2 May and broke his back. Major Ellis, the battalion's second-in-command, was hit by a sniper and died the next day.

The once-derided Colonel 'Granny' Burnage had been continually in the front line in these first days on Gallipoli. He led his troops into action and steadied them when they wavered. 'He is as brave as a lion,' said Private Hobson, 'and we have grown to love him.'

General John Monash, the commander of the 4th Brigade, reflected in mid-May: 'We have been fighting now continuously for twenty-two days, all day and all night, and most of us think that absolutely the longest period during which there was absolutely no sound of gun or rifle fire, throughout the whole of that time, was ten seconds. One man says he was able on one occasion to count fourteen, but nobody believes him!' The general had come to know the sound of each projectile: 'the bullet which passes close by has a gentle purring hum, like a low caressing whistle, long drawn out. The bullet which passes well overhead has a sharp sudden crack like a whip. . . Our machine guns are exactly like the rattle of a kettledrum. The enemy's shrapnel sounds like a gust of wind in a wintry gale, swishing through the air and ending in a loud bang and a cloud of smoke, when the shell bursts. Our own artillery is the noisiest of all. . . ear-splitting, with a reverberating echo that lasts 20 or 30 seconds.'

The men of the 13th continued to attack the Turks and to defend themselves, with bullets, bayonets, handmade bombs, neither advancing nor retreating from their positions on the ridge. Of all the troops, the stretcher-bearers made the most forays into the lines of enemy fire. Corporal Harold Sorrell, a Methodist divinity student and one of the 13th Battalion bearers, reported to his parents that month: 'There is not a front line trench in the whole of the field into which we have not been. I have been hit four times, and have had countless narrow shaves. One morning I had just dressed a man's broken leg, and was lifting him on to a stretcher when the sniper's bullet whizzed under my arm, and drew blood on the three knuckles, and entered the patient's neck, fortunately not killing him.'

Many of the dead lay in a wheat field between the two front lines, swelling in the heat. During an armistice on 24 May, hundreds of Turkish and Allied troops walked in to the no-man's land between the trenches to collect the bloated, maggot-infested corpses for burial. The men tied handkerchiefs around their faces to stave off the smell. When the truce came to an end at 4.30 p.m., the Australians exchanged cigarettes and souvenirs with their Turkish counterparts and wished them well. Then the fighting resumed.

The Turks blew in a section of the trenches occupied by the 13th on the night of 29 May: there was a muffled roar as the earth rocked, the underside of a cloud glowed red with the reflected explosion, and men were buried where they stood or lay. The Turks then threw their bombs. 'Grenades like showers of peas,' wrote a lieutenant, 'and the noise and the flashes and confusion in the darkness, together with thick curtains of acrid smoke, made this portion of the line a terrible Hades.'

'The stretcher-bearers worked like heroes,' recalled Private Hobson. When Colonel Burnage was wounded, the bearers went quickly to his aid, but he told them to leave him until all the other injured men had been evacuated.

After this attack the 13th Battalion, bearded and scrawny, finally went into rest in the valley.

General Monash and Colonel Burnage congratulated the troops on their courage and endurance, giving special praise to the stretcher-bearers. In the official 13th Battalion history, the bearers were described as 'magnificent, without exception', and Robert was one of eleven men in the force of almost a thousand to be singled out for the service they had given in the days after the landing. He and the divinity student Harold Sorrell were also lauded for their 'exceptionally splendid and gallant work' in carrying the wounded down from the ridges in the attack of early May, and in risking their lives to gather and bury all the bodies that they could find.

The official historian of the AIF rated the 4th Brigade's defence of the ridges above the valley as one of the four finest Australian achievements of the war. For Robert, the achievement was very particular. In Broadmoor, every aspect of his life had been regulated, from the temperature of his bath to the location of his tailoring shears; on the ridges of Gallipoli he was subject to unfettered sensation and danger. Some of the sights and smells and sounds were weirdly reminiscent of the scene in his mother's bedroom at Cave Road: the groaning bodies, the sweet, ammoniac stink of rotting flesh, the descent of the flies. This time, though, it fell to Robert to save the wounded and to honour the dead.

The Australians were effectively in a state of siege: 20,000 men were occupying an area less than three-quarters of a mile square, bounded on one side by the ridges, on another by the narrow beach. From their camp in the valley, the men of the 13th looked up at the crest above them, scorched bare by gunfire; and down at the Aegean Sea, pink and yellow as the sun rose and sapphire at noon.

Some of the troops in the valley dug trenches and tunnels, while others were sent to the beach to unload the barges and distribute supplies. They shifted crates of bully beef and cheese, bags of sugar, boxes of biscuits and ammunition; they loaded water on to mules to carry up the hills by night, and wounded men on to boats that would take them to the hospital ships in the bay. Those working on the beach could hear the shrill whistles of the small craft, the rattle of anchor chains, the hiss of steam and the hoots of trawlers as well as the constant din of battle in the hills and of shells hitting the shore. Many of the men stripped off to bathe in the sea, cooling themselves in the water until gunfire lashed up the foam.

In June the heat in the valley rose to 84 degrees. The men were ankle-deep in dust, and constantly pestered by flies: house flies were breeding at the manure heaps, blowflies in the bodies of the dead. The flies settled on the latrines and the mess tins, floated in mugs of tea. The troops had only to open their mouths for the flies to dart in. Captain Shellshear had trained his stretcher-bearers in sanitation but the rate of infection was such that by the end of July, 80 per cent of the men had contracted dysentery, or 'Gallipoli gallop'. The stench of excrement and decay drifted out to the boats in the bay. Hundreds of reinforcements were shipped in to take the places of the wounded, the sick and the dead.

In August the 13th took part in two further failed attacks on the Turks, in the mountains to the north of Monash Valley, and again suffered terrible losses. The stretcher-bearers were overwhelmed by the task of carrying the wounded to safety; many were themselves injured or killed.

Robert had escaped serious injury in his first six months at Gallipoli, despite being hit at least twice by shells and once by a bullet, but in November he contracted hepatitis and trench foot. Rain, snow and blizzards assailed the peninsula, and Robert's toes swelled, blackened and burned in the icy water that flooded the trenches. That month the Allies at last decided to give up on the Gallipoli campaign. In preparation for an exit, they instructed the soldiers intermittently to fall silent, to accustom the Turks to an absence of noise in the Allied trenches. On 10 December, Robert's fellow bearer James Dow reported to his parents that only six of the original 13th Battalion bearers remained on the peninsula. The others, said Dow, had been 'shot off'.

On 12 December, Robert became one of 900 men to sail for Egypt on the hospital ships. The rest of the Australian troops were stealthily taken off the peninsula over the next week. The attempt to eliminate Turkey from the war had failed, but the evacuation, at least, was a success.

About 10,000 AIF soldiers spent the Christmas of 1915 in hospital in Egypt. Among the white marble columns of the former Palace Hotel in Heliopolis, Robert was supplied with toothpaste and soap and clean pyjamas, and tended by Australian nurses in starched uniforms. He asked that Nattie be informed of his whereabouts.

Nattie was also serving with the Australian forces. The *Australia*, on which he was a stoker, had taken part in a mission to occupy the capital of German New Guinea in August 1914 and had since covered more than 40,000 miles chasing two German destroyers across the Atlantic. In the heat of the tropics, the stoke hole grew so hot that the stokers took off all their clothes. 'The perspiration dripped down their naked bodies into their boots, out of which they poured it in streams,' reported the engineer-commander, 'but we kept after the Germans without losing a knot.' The journey was interrupted only by the dirty and exhausting business of loading fuel from colliers stationed off tropical islands. Towards the end of 1915 the *Australia* was sent to patrol the North Sea, where the crew were issued with rabbit-skin coats to protect them from the bitter cold. Nattie was promoted stoker petty officer, the equivalent to the army rank of sergeant. He received the news of Robert's ill health on Christmas Day.

Robert was discharged to a camp on the other side of the Nile in January 1916 but instead of being returned to the 13th Battalion was transferred to one of the sanitary sections that were being set up to oversee hygiene in the field. He was

The gatehouse to Broadmoor Criminal Lunatic Asylum, photographed in 1910, and (*below*) the upper terrace of the asylum, with Block 2 on the right.

David Nicolson (*above left*), superintendent of Broadmoor from 1886 to 1896, with Richard Brayn, his successor; an asylum terrace in the early 1900s (*above right*); and (*below*) a plan of the male quarters in 1902 – Block 2 is in the bottom right-hand corner.

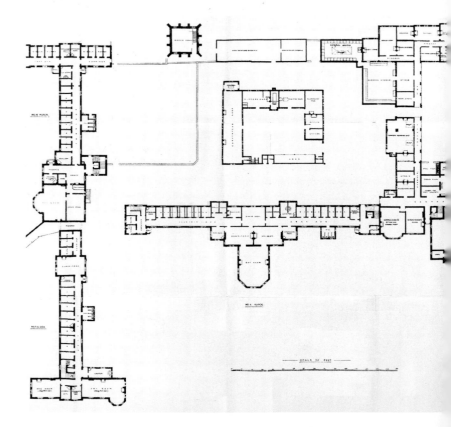

The Broadmoor cricket team in 1905 – none of the players is identified, but Robert Coombes may be the man sitting on the grass second from left.

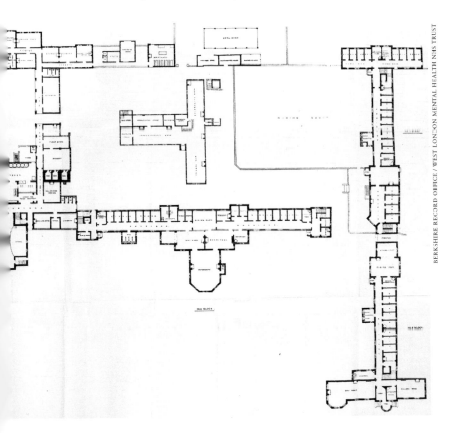

Dormitories of the Salvation Army colony overlooking the Thames at Hadleigh, Essex, in the early 1900s, and (*below*) a plan of the colony in about 1912.

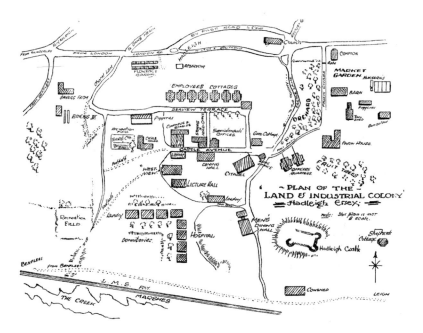

AUSTRALIAN WAR MEMORIAL

An Australian training camp in northern Egypt at the beginning of the Great War, and (*below*) the 13th Battalion band soon after its formation in Australia in November 1914. Robert Coombes is probably the soldier in spectacles in the back row, third from left.

AUSTRALIAN WAR MEMORIAL

Gallipoli, 1915: Anzac
troops attacking the
Turks (*top*); an Australian
recruitment poster (*above*);
and stretcher bearers on
the beach (*right*).

Australian troops on the Western Front in October 1917, and (*below*) the 45th Battalion band in northern France in March 1918 – Robert is in the front row, holding a cornet, behind the biggest drum.

Robert Coombes in the late
1930s or early 1940s and
(*below*) a photograph taken
in 1928 of the Orara river,
near which he lived.

promoted corporal, which entitled him to an increase in pay
to ten shillings a day and gave him authority for the first time
over other soldiers.

Robert's unit formed part of the 4th Division, which
included the 13th Battalion and also a new 45th Battalion,
to which half of the men of the 13th had been transferred.
From March onwards, the division guarded the Suez Canal
and trained in the desert nearby. The men were again plagued
by insects in the intense heat; Robert and the other sanitary
officers helped to limit infection by burning manure and
building box-latrines. On 25 April, the first anniversary of
the Gallipoli landings, the Prince of Wales visited the camp
to watch the division compete at water sports in the canal.
General Monash pinned blue ribbons to all the men who had
served in the Dardanelles and red ribbons to those, like Robert,
who had taken part in the landing. These early recruits would
become known as 'the Adventurers', 'the Originals' and 'the
Pioneers'.

Robert sailed from Alexandria for Marseilles with the
4th Division's medical section on 1 June 1916, then took a
three-day rail journey north to French Flanders. The British
commanders urgently needed the Australians to reinforce the
Allied line along the Western Front. After the sand and dust
of Egypt, the Australian troops were dazzled by the colour
of France in June: the green fields, the blue cornflowers, the
scarlet poppies, the tiny white blossoms in the hedgerows.
Grateful villagers pressed strawberries and cigarettes on the
soldiers when the train stopped at the stations along the track;
at longer halts, Australians dashed in to the villages to buy
chocolate and wine.

Behind the lines in Flanders, Robert and the men in his
charge built latrines and urinals. They erected incinerators to

burn rubbish, manure and faeces. They cleaned the streets and billets, supervised the baths in which the troops came to wash and the laundries that disinfected their lice-ridden uniforms. They tested the drinking water. The sanitary officers urged the troops to bury their waste in shallow trenches or shell holes, or, better still, to defecate in pits, pans or biscuit tins covered with fly-proof lids. They told the cooks to wash their hands with soap, to disinfect their implements, to burn food waste, and to use grease traps when disposing of dirty water. Robert was promoted acting sergeant.

That month Robert was recommended for a Military Medal for his service at Gallipoli, especially at the landing and in May. He was 'one of the few survivors of the 13th battalion stretcher-bearers', noted the citation, 'who were thanked by Col Burnage & Major Ellis for services during the first 2 days'.

In July the 4th Division was ordered south to the Somme, and at the beginning of August they reached the town of Albert, a few miles behind the front line. The golden statue of the Virgin Mary on top of Albert's cathedral had been jolted out of place by a bomb, and the Madonna now pitched forward over the town square, clutching her infant son. From the streets of Albert at night, the men could hear the bombardment at the front line, see the sky flush red with shellfire. Two men in Robert's sanitary section were wounded in an attack.

The division was sent in to battle on 5 August, with the objective of holding on to the village of Pozières, which had just been won back from the Germans. The Germans were waging a vigorous counter-attack, in which they shelled the Australians with explosives and shrapnel day and night. The stretcher-bearers and ambulance units struggled to convey the wounded back to safety. Some of the sanitary men doubled as medics, treating prisoners of war and their own troops. At night, sanitary squads went out to bury the dead.

On 16 August, after eleven days in the trenches, the 4th Division was sent back north. It had succeeded in retaining Pozières, but at a cost of a thousand men. The Australian Imperial Force as a whole had lost 28,000 soldiers in six weeks on the Somme, more than in the whole eight-month campaign at Gallipoli. Its troops had been exposed to the full force of industrialised war.

Both at Gallipoli and on the Western Front, Robert had seen comrades unstrung by the intensity of the fighting, and the incidence of shellshock in the 4th Division was particularly high. But he was still stable. His fellow Broadmoor inmate Frank Rodgers, who had killed his mother in 1904, was also now serving in France. Sergeant Rodgers proved a very capable soldier, according to his British Army papers: 'Honest, sober, hardworking, & intelligent.'

In Belgian Flanders that autumn, Lieutenant-Colonel Sydney Herring, the commanding officer of the 45th Battalion, decided to form a military band. Herring had served with the 13th in Egypt and at Gallipoli, and he had seen how a band could lift the spirits of the troops. On a visit to London in the spring he had bought a set of instruments, paid for by the men of the 45th, and when the battalion was sent north in October he launched a search for musicians. A few of the surviving bandsmen-bearers of the 13th had been moved to the 45th – including Ray Lingard and Harold Sorrell, both of whom had sailed out of Melbourne on the *Ulysses* – but Herring requested that Robert be transferred to the battalion to lead the new ensemble.

Robert was known as a good soldier as well as a fine musician, and his service record was clean: he had served for two years without missing any days in the field to venereal disease and without being cautioned for any misdemeanour such as insubordination, drunkenness or absence without leave. Herring confirmed his promotion to sergeant once he had been transferred to the 45th. Robert was given a cornet, a badge with three chevrons and a lyre, and an increase in pay to ten shillings and sixpence a day. Later in October, the *London Gazette* announced that Robert Allen Coombes had been awarded the Military Medal for the courage that he had shown at Gallipoli. Robert asked that a copy of the announcement be forwarded to Nattie.

Nattie – now chief petty officer stoker, a senior noncommissioned rank – had chosen to remain with the Australian fleet rather than return to the British navy when his term of service expired. His ship had still not seen any combat. On a foggy day in April 1916 the *Australia* collided with another Allied vessel while on patrol near Scotland, sustaining a forty-foot gash in her side, and she was being repaired when the Allies joined battle with the German navy off Jutland in May. 'It was too bad!' complained Nattie's fellow stoker Reginald Stephens. 'The men were absolutely sick about it! We had, during the war, done more running than any other battlecruiser in the navy – and then, owing to an accident, we missed the biggest naval battle by a few hours.' For the rest of the year the *Australia* continued her uneventful patrol of the North Sea.

Robert proved an effective bandmaster, alert to matters of discipline and deportment as well as musical direction. He sometimes rehearsed the musicians alongside his old band in the 13th Battalion. At the 45th Battalion headquarters, where he was stationed with about ten other sergeants, he made friends with William Alabaster, a twenty-three-year-old carpenter from East Ham who had emigrated to Australia in 1912. Bill Alabaster led a unit of pioneers in engineering and construction tasks. He was a tall, fair-haired, jovial chap, who had sailed for Egypt on the same ship as Robert and had served with him at Gallipoli.

The AIF no longer used its musicians as stretcher-bearers: after the devastating losses on the Somme in the summer, the commanders had decided that the depletion of battalion bands was too damaging to morale. Instead, Robert and the band marched their battalion into the front line, then worked behind the lines before marching out to meet the troops as they returned from the action. The 45th was constantly on the move – it struck camp once every five days, on average, during its two and a half years on the Western Front – and the band sometimes led the way on the marches between billets. When the battalion was resting, the musicians staged concerts for the men. In place of the crazed racket of the front – the roar, scream and bark of artillery – the band made sweet, stirring music, summoning the numbed troops back to themselves with plangent, sentimental tunes, rousing martial marches, playful rags. The bandsmen struck notes of innocence, defiance, fellowship, pity, romance with a sincerity that briefly pierced the Australian soldiers' armour of laconic mockery, their fabled coolness and 'hide'.

In late October the battalion was sent back to the Somme, where it remained through the terrible winter of 1916/17, being rotated in and out of the front line as the snow gave way to fog and freezing rain. The mechanisms in the men's rifles froze; the bolts jammed with mud. On the coldest nights, hoarfrost formed on the men's greatcoats even as they sat in their huts with the braziers lit, and their breath froze into icicles where it touched the wool of their balaclava caps. There were spells of rest and pleasure. Robert and two other sergeants spent Christmas Day 1916 with a French family they had befriended, eating jelly and cream, drinking wine, singing and playing games before rolling back to camp in the early hours of Boxing Day.

In the thaw of 1917, the mud sucked at the soldiers' boots as they moved between camps. The troops trudged through flooded shell craters in fields strewn with dead men and dead horses, wrecked wagons, scorched and blasted trees. The Germans often targeted the support lines, and the Australians became accustomed to the strangled shriek of a descending shell, the roar and flare as it hit the ground, the sight of a 'cobber' blown to bits where he stood. 'We live in a world of Somme mud,' wrote Private Edward Lynch of the 45th Battalion. 'We sleep in it, work in it, fight in it, wade in it and many of us die in it. We see it, feel it, eat it and curse it, but we can't escape it, not even by dying.' In the dismal village of Dernancourt, the battalion hid from the German planes during the day in the cellars of ruined buildings, coming out at night to repair roads and bridges and to dig graves. 'We hate this hole,' wrote Lynch. 'We're as mud-stained, wet and weary as the place itself.'

The British commanders were increasingly assigning the Australians to the more difficult actions on the Western Front – a tribute to the effectiveness of the soldiers, and the reason that the AIF suffered a higher percentage of casualties than any other Allied force. The 45th was awarded thirty-seven decorations for bravery at Gueudecourt in February 1917. In June it took part in an elaborately planned action at Messines Ridge, in Belgian Flanders, which opened with the Allies detonating a million pounds of explosives next to the German trenches, instantly killing 10,000 enemy soldiers. The blast was heard in London and felt across southern England. In the fighting that ensued, Bill Alabaster led the parties carrying grenades, ammunition and water from the 45th Battalion headquarters to the troops at the front line, across open ground raked by artillery and machine-gun fire. Herring recommended him for the Military Medal. The 45th lost seven officers and 344 other ranks over four days of combat.

'We're a pretty casual sort of army all right,' observed Private Lynch, 'yet notwithstanding this, the battalion has never lost a position to the enemy and much of their worth lies in this casual-going attitude. They'll stand amidst a tornado of screaming, crashing death and pump bullets into an enemy attack, or attack the strongest-held enemy position with the same casual air that they'll chuck, or fail to chuck, an off-handed salute to the British staff officers on the Strand.'

Robert and his friend Bill Alabaster went on ten days' leave in September 1917. They crossed the Channel to Folkestone and then caught a train to Victoria station in London. Most Australian soldiers on leave in the capital called at the AIF headquarters in Horseferry Road, near Victoria, to store their packs and collect their back pay before setting off to see the sights, make merry in the pubs and music halls, and call on British family and friends. Robert joined Alabaster on a visit to his parents' home in Forest Gate, just north of Plaistow.

When the two returned to France at the beginning of October, their battalion was taking part in an attack on the Germans at Passchendaele. The landscape was desolate: gaunt, stubby trees rose from sodden fields; the bodies of soldiers lay mired in the mud. Under fierce bombardment in the atrocious terrain, the Allied assault ground to a halt in early November. Again the 45th Battalion suffered heavy losses: seventy-four men were dead and 210 wounded, altogether about a third of its force.

After Passchendaele, the 45th was granted a long period of rest in the north. By now Robert and the other veterans of Gallipoli had spent more than three years at war. A photographer took a series of pictures in their camp in March 1918. In one of these, Robert sits at the centre of his military band of twenty men, clutching a cornet. In a photograph of the non-commissioned officers, he and Bill Alabaster are seated side by side, smiling a little.

In late March the Germans launched a massive offensive in the Somme, and the 4th Division, which had already taken part in more fighting than any other Australian unit, was summoned to shore up the line. The 45th Battalion moved swiftly to the front. On the roads near the Somme the men passed hundreds of French villagers fleeing the Germans, and then came upon the ruins of Albert, grey with smoke, the leaning Virgin still catching the sunlight.

Near Dernancourt, the village in which it had been so miserably housed during its first winter in France, the 45th helped to halt the German attack, losing almost 250 men in the process. Bill Alabaster was one of them. On 5 April he was hit by a shell while going into the line. Robert saw his friend lying in a trench, wounded in both thighs. 'I've got badly smashed,' said Alabaster. Two stretcher-bearers carried him to a clearing station, and from there he was taken to a military hospital, where he died.

On 8 August, the 45th Battalion took part in a triumphant Allied advance near Amiens, capturing 400 enemy soldiers and an immense quantity of artillery. A few days later Robert and his band were sent to perform in the Grand Theatre in the port of Le Havre, where they shared a programme with the celebrated Anzac Coves pierrot troupe. Band and battalion were reunited towards the end of August.

The Allied armies continued to advance on the Germans, and that autumn Robert was granted special leave to return to Australia, a privilege given to those who had served continuously since 1914. He sailed south on 23 October. Nattie had transferred in August to the Australian destroyer HMAS *Swan*, which was engaged in anti-submarine patrols in the Mediterranean and Adriatic. Both brothers were at sea when the Armistice was declared on 11 November.

Robert reached Sydney on Christmas Day 1918. He and the other soldiers were greeted by the governor-general of New South Wales, plied with flowers and cigarettes, taken on a 'joy ride' through the flag-lined streets to a welcome-home buffet and tea. At Gallipoli, declared the commander of the AIF, Australia had 'leapt into manhood – or rather I should say into nationhood by the valour of her sons'. Robert was returning to a land that believed itself to have finally come of age in the Great War, a country that he had helped to define.

Of the 32,000 men to volunteer for the AIF in 1914, Robert was among the 7,000 still serving in 1918. He came back to Australia with the knowledge that he could not only stay steady in a harrowing and chaotic world but could act with honour. He had saved lives.

EPILOGUE

Another Boy

I began researching Robert Coombes's life in the summer of 2012, after coming across an account of his arrest in an old newspaper. I was intrigued by the story, so I looked up the transcript of the trial at the Old Bailey, then more articles about the case. Some of the reports dubbed the matricide 'The Plaistow Horror'; others called it 'The Plaistow Tragedy'. The story of Emily Coombes's murder and its aftermath did seem at once tragedy and horror show, a tale to make you recoil in disgust and to pull you close in pity. I was fascinated by Robert: in his court appearances he seemed hollow, light, scoured clean of feeling; and yet the killing suggested a catastrophic disturbance, an unbearable intensity of emotion. There was something disjointed and fractured about his story. At the time of the murder, many believed that Robert simply had no feelings for others – that he was, in modern terminology, a psychopath. Others held that he was weird because he was insane – that he suffered from a psychotic illness. I wondered whether his strangeness might have sprung more from events in his life. I wanted to know if his history had a bearing on his crime, and I decided to find out what I could about his boyhood.

I read the file on the case at the National Archives in Kew, which contained transcripts of the witness statements and of the letters written by Robert and his mother. I studied apprenticeship and cemetery records at the London Metropolitan Archives in Islington, and crew agreements at the National Maritime Museum in Greenwich. I researched the Coombes and Fox families on genealogy websites and in newspaper archives. I traced and read as many as I could of the penny dreadfuls that had been found in 35 Cave Road, along with books, journals and newspapers that discussed the board school system, the London docks, pawnbroking, cheap literature for boys, degeneration, the Thames iron yard, cattle ships, the politics of East London, household budgets, boy labour, the law on insanity and on child protection. At the local archives in Stratford, I looked at the electoral rolls, the registers of the district's schools, and maps and photographs of late-nineteenth-century West Ham. I visited Southend-on-Sea and the places in Plaistow in which the Coombes family and their friends had lived. The stretch of houses that included 35 Cave Road had been demolished, but most of the terrace was still standing, as were the playground walls of the school opposite Robert and Nattie's house. I walked down the Barking Road to the now defunct docks and the site of the iron works and tried to imagine being there in 1895, when the district thundered with machines, reeked of coal tar and carcasses, explosives and glue. In West Ham, wrote the novelist Arthur Morrison, 'the air was electrical'; there was, according to the Liberal MP Charles Masterman, 'everywhere a stirring and an agitation'. Here more than anywhere in England, it seemed that the world was transforming as the century turned, mutating at unnatural speed, throwing up freaks, portents, atavistic selves, precocities and perversions. It was a time of tumult and foreboding.

In Robert's home, too, the atmosphere had become charged with an unease that verged on menace. Emily Coombes was volatile, and Robert believed that she was dangerous. She threw knives, he said, and threatened death. His anxiety had already spiralled into fits and faints, spells of silence and withdrawal, a tendency to hear noises and feel pains in his head. His previous attempts to extricate himself and Nattie by running away from home had ended in failure, and the bromides that he was given for his headaches and attacks of excitement may have intensified his dissociation and disquiet. By July 1895 he was more alienated than ever, unsettled by the wrench of leaving school, the brutal monotony of the iron yard, the heavy heat of the summer. His father's visit usually brought some respite, but this time Coombes and his wife had argued – about sex or money or both – and Emily had been left jittery and aggrieved. Robert's own shame and frustration were resolving into a fury against her.

The boys spent the stifling days of 6 and 7 July at home with their mother. In the evenings Robert joined her in the marital bed, as he often did in his father's absence. At some point that weekend, Emily thrashed her younger son for taking food and threatened the older boy. Robert had already bought the knife. Now he made his promise to Nattie. His mother had become a monster to him, like the serpent with which Jack Wright grapples in the cave beneath the sea.

Only a couple of matricides a year were reported in the British press in the 1880s and 1890s, and it has remained a very rare crime. Between 1968 and 1978 an average of six males killed their mothers in Britain each year, of whom about two were admitted annually to Broadmoor. In the United States, about 2 per cent of all homicides recorded between 1976 and 1998 were murders of a parent. Adolescent boys who kill their mothers are rarer still, but a few studies have been made of such crimes. Compared to other young murderers, young matricides rarely have a history of violence. Compared to older mother-murderers, they rarely have a history of psychosis. Their mothers tend to be dominating and intrusive; their fathers, typically, are passive or absent figures. The boys are more likely than their adult counterparts to have been mistreated, whether sexually, physically or emotionally. In many cases, they have tried to run away from home before the killing, and afterwards they often show relief, as if they have averted rather than invited catastrophe. They are unlikely to kill again.

Psychiatrists have suggested that a matricidal man or boy can have an overt motive for murder (such as a wish for enrichment or revenge) and also a motive hidden from himself. He may be desperate to rid himself of an excessive attachment to his mother, for instance, or to cast out the intolerable emotions that she arouses in him: feelings of desire and hatred, a terror of engulfment or of dissolution. In myth and literature, matricidal impulses can take disguised forms. They have been identified not only in the Greek tragedy in which Orestes slays his mother because she has killed and betrayed his father, or in the 1950s novel in which Norman Bates murders his mother in a jealous rage, but also in Hamlet's feelings towards the 'incestuous' Gertrude, in Raskolnikov's attack on the old woman in *Crime and Punishment*, in the defeat of the Sphinx by Oedipus, the Gorgon by Perseus, the dragon by St George. In life, too, such impulses may be expressed in an attack not on the mother herself but on another woman.

It was clear that Robert had been disturbed by his mother and had become convinced that he needed to kill her, but to understand whether his fears were grounded in reality I needed to know if he ever again acted with such cruelty or became

gripped by such a fixation. I had to find out about his future
as well as his past. Though there seemed to be no information about him in the newspapers after September 1895, I was
able to glean a few facts from the files in Broadmoor's recently
opened archives. I was surprised by the gentleness of the regime
at the asylum at the turn of the twentieth century and by the
ways in which the institution had looked after Robert.

Broadmoor still houses some of the most disturbed
patients in England, and I spoke about Robert's case to a
psychiatrist who had worked there since 1998. She said that
it sounded as though Robert had experienced a psychotic
breakdown when he murdered his mother, complete with
auditory hallucinations, dissociation, disavowal, temporary
amnesia. Such a breakdown, she said, was likely to have
been provoked by extreme emotional strain. She told me
that almost every one of the men and women whom she had
treated at Broadmoor had suffered horribly as a child. They
may have been born susceptible to mental illness, but their
violent derangement was triggered by events in their lives. In
the course of their treatment, they were frequently assailed
by intense and painful emotions. Sometimes, they became
suicidal before they became stable.

The Broadmoor admissions register showed that Robert
was discharged to the Hadleigh colony in 1912, the doctors
having deemed him sane. I researched the colony's history at
the Salvation Army headquarters in London and I went to
Essex to look round the grounds, which were still in use as an
employment training centre.

It was more difficult to establish what happened to Robert
next. Only when I saw a photograph of his gravestone on a
website about Australian cemeteries did I realise that he had
emigrated and served in the Great War. Robert is buried in

Coffs Harbour, on the coast of northern New South Wales. His stone bears a metal plaque inscribed with his name and his date of death, the names of his battalions, and his military rank and number. With the help of the service records in Australian archives, I was able to trace his movements during the war. I pictured him on the ridges of Gallipoli, watching disaster unfold. As a stretcher-bearer he was obliged to bear witness to horrific events before scrambling forward to tend to the injured, to salvage something from a scene of catastrophe.

At first I could find little about Robert's life beyond 1919, apart from an approximate address and the circumstances of his death. My only lead was a phrase at the foot of the plaque on his gravestone: '*Always remembered by Harry Mulville & family*'. Though I did not imagine that the Harry Mulville who had known Robert would still be alive, I decided to try to track down his family. I found mentions of the name Mulville in the archives of the classified sections of the Coffs Harbour newspaper. I also found a phone number for an 'H. Mulville' in Coffs Harbour: I left a few messages but received no reply.

I next began to work my way through the numbers of all the Mulvilles in the New South Wales telephone directory, calling each one in the hope that he or she might be a relative. With my first call I struck lucky. A Mrs Mulville in Ulladulla, a coastal town south of Sydney, said, yes, she did have a family connection to a man called Harry Mulville who lived in Coffs Harbour, and she put me in touch with his daughter.

I emailed Harry Mulville's daughter, telling her that I was writing about Robert Coombes. I explained that Robert had killed his mother when he was a boy living in London, and that after his release from an asylum he had served with distinction in the Great War. I said that I did not know whether her father was aware of the earlier, darker period of his friend's life, and that I would understand if this was not something that she wanted to discuss with him. For several days I received no reply.

When I emailed again, she responded. 'My family have been very distressed at this news,' she wrote, 'and we are still trying to come to terms with it. I will have to discuss this more with my family. My father is almost ninety-four years old now and we as a family cannot speak to him about this. It would probably kill him.'

I apologised to Harry's daughter for causing such distress and I explained more about my research. She said that she would like to help me, but that her older brother and sister did not approve of my project. She asked me to speak to them. After my telephone conversations with Harry's older children, I understood why they had found the news of the murder quite so disturbing.

Henry Alexander Mulville, always known as Harry, was born on an island in the Clarence River in New South Wales on 15 February 1919. He spent his early childhood by the river, helping his father to work a hand-cranked punt that carried horses, carts and motorised vehicles back and forth between the large island of Woodford and the village of Tyndale, on the mainland. The Mulvilles lived in two rooms of a former butcher's shop near the Woodford jetty: one room was the kitchen and the other the bedroom. When the Clarence burst its banks in heavy rain, the water rushed into the building and the family was forced to take refuge with neighbours on higher ground until the flood subsided.

Harry's parents had married in 1917, when his father was fifty-six and his mother thirty-two. His mother, Bertha, brought an illegitimate daughter to the marriage, and she and Charles Mulville had four children together: after Harry came Percy, Alfred and Ellen. In 1925 Harry and his brother Percy fell ill with pneumonia. The five-year-old Percy died and was buried in the local Roman Catholic cemetery.

Harry grew into a spirited, cheeky boy with long, skinny legs, brown hair, a square jaw, blue eyes and big ears. His father, as well as running the vehicle ferry, had the concession to carry foot passengers across the Clarence by rowing boat, and Harry soon learnt to row the boat himself.

The land near the river was dense with vegetation, some of which had been cleared for dairying and sugarcane farming. Harry loved to watch the workers cutting the cane in the fields. The plants were hacked down by a team of Hindu labourers, then stripped with brush hooks, carried to the river by cart, loaded on to punts with a crane and towed by steamer to the sugar mill. Harry helped the cook take refreshments to the cutters when they broke for tea in the afternoon, and in return was invited to share their rock cakes and biscuits.

Harry was educated first at the Tyndale school, where two huge fig trees shaded the playground, and then, with his older half-sister Christabel, was driven to school in the village of Maclean on the family's horse and sulky (a light, two-wheeled cart). He enjoyed athletics, and did well in the sports competitions held at school on Empire Day. At home he helped to raise a small flock of poultry; the best of the family's Rhode Island Reds and Brown Leghorns won awards at the local agricultural fair. On Sundays, Harry sometimes

went to church with his mother, who played the pedal organ
at Anglican services.

Harry and Chrissie used to read the children's page in
the *Sydney Mail*, and in 1927 both wrote letters to the editor. Harry, aged eight, announced that he had won prizes
at school for English and arithmetic and asked to be put in
touch with a pen pal. Chrissie, who was thirteen, expressed
her enthusiasm for the Western adventures of the bestselling American novelist Zane Grey and asked for advice on
naming her kittens. The children's editor, 'Cinderella', suggested a suitable pen pal for Harry. She recommended the
names 'Mittens' and 'Muffet' for Chrissie's kittens, but was
dubious about her taste in literature: Zane Grey was 'rather
bloodthirsty', Cinderella thought; 'so many of his characters
meet a violent end'.

When Harry's father was laid up in bed with an illness
that year, Harry helped his mother to crank the vehicle punt
across the river. As a general store delivery van was driving off
the punt on to the jetty one day, the chain attaching the ferry
to the land slipped and the van fell through the gap into the
water, sinking twelve feet. The driver freed himself and swam
up, but most of his cargo floated down the Clarence. Charles
Mulville shortly afterwards lost his job as ferryman.

Bertha became unhappy. She attributed her difficulties
with her husband to religious differences. She was a native of
East London, and had been raised in the Church of England,
whereas Charles was an Irish-born Roman Catholic. Bertha
said that she did not like the Catholic priest calling at their
house. In 1928 she left the family home, with her two surviving sons and her two daughters, to take a job as housekeeper
to Harold William Smith, a farmer in his early fifties who lived
fifty miles south of the Clarence.

Smith had a dairy herd at a farm between Glenreagh and Nana Glen, villages in the Orara Valley. His first wife had died in 1920 and his second had left him in 1926 after three years of marriage. Smith hired Bertha to cook and clean for him and to look after his three-year-old daughter, Elizabeth. Bertha soon became her employer's lover and in 1929 she also became the mother of his next child.

In the year of the baby's birth, Charles Mulville's neighbours on Woodford Island sent word to Bertha that her husband was seriously ill with influenza, and Bertha despatched the ten-year-old Harry to tend to him. Within a few days of Harry's arrival, Charles developed pneumonia. He died in his son's arms, aged sixty-eight, and was buried alongside Harry's brother Percy in the Catholic cemetery. Harry returned to Nana Glen. A few months later Smith's marriage was dissolved and he and Bertha were able to marry.

Harold Smith was born in 1874 into a well-known and well-to-do family in the north of New South Wales, but he had not made a success of himself. Since being declared bankrupt in 1898 he had scratched a living as a horseman and share-farmer. A hard-drinking man, 'Tiger' Smith often sat at the dinner table with a horse whip and was quick to strike his stepchildren. He attributed his short temper to the effects of gassing in the war. In fact, he had served for only five months, all of which were spent in training or long-range patrolling with the 5th Light Horse in Egypt; he was invalided home with rheumatism in September 1916, having seen no combat. He had been aggressive before the war, in any case: in 1899 he had been convicted of assaulting a man with whom he had argued about a horse.

As the eldest boy, Harry bore the brunt of his stepfather's rage. One of Harry's jobs was to hold Smith's tools for him while he sharpened their blades. If he did not keep the tool's handle steady, Smith would raise his steel file and smack him on the head.

The Smiths' next-door neighbour was Robert Coombes, now in his mid-forties. Robert had settled in Nana Glen on his return from the Western Front. He may have chosen the district at the suggestion of Herbert Morrow, a Nana Glen farmer who had served with him in the 4th Division and who in 1918 had come back to Australia on the same ship. Robert's fellow bandsman and stretcher-bearer Casimir Collopy, a veteran of both the 13th and 45th Battalions, also farmed in this part of New South Wales. Robert lived in a rickety two-room house, next to which he grazed seven or eight cows and tended a plot of vegetables. He and Smith were both tenants of a farmer called Isaac Cundy.

Robert's house faced the dirt road that ran north from Nana Glen to the larger village of Glenreagh. Just across the track was a bright sweep of grazing pasture, stretching down to a line of trees along the Orara river. A range of wooded hills rose in the distance, separating the valley from the ocean. Behind the house was the dense web of the bush: the blackbutt and bloodwood trees, blue gum, bottlebrush, wattle and ironbark, twined with vines and creepers. Kookaburras and white cockatoos cackled and shrieked in the trees, giant frogs rasped in the river and creeks. The climate was mild, the temperatures rarely dropping below freezing point even in winter. In the warm, wet summers, the breeze carried a tang of camphor and gum.

The region around the Orara river had been inhabited by whites since the 1860s: first the timber-getters, who felled the much-prized red cedars, and then the gold-miners, who sunk shafts into the reefs near the river and panned for nuggets in the creeks. The gold mines had become unprofitable by the 1920s, but the timber business was still going strong. The local men used cross-cut saws, axes and wedges to chop down mammoth gums and white mahoganies. They sliced them into long logs and tethered them to teams of bullocks, which dragged their loads through the bush to the saw mills. Some of the land cleared by loggers had been claimed by banana growers and dairy farmers.

Robert milked the cows each day. He roped the cattle into sheds, pumped their milk into buckets by hand, skimmed off the cream with a separator and decanted it into cans. The cans were collected by a truck from the Orara Co-Op Dairy Society and delivered to the district town of Grafton, thirty-five miles north of Nana Glen. On the cream truck's return trip, the driver dropped off the empty cans along with supplies from Grafton. There were a handful of shops in Nana Glen itself: a bakery, a butcher, a general store, a post office, a combined billiards room and hairdresser, a pie shop, a saddlery. Robert bought tobacco with which to roll himself cigarettes.

In the evenings, Robert often dined on dampers: pancakes of flour, salt and milk baked in the hot ashes of a fire. He ate vegetables from his plot and drank the milk produced by the cows. Occasionally, he killed a calf for its meat, sharing or trading the veal with neighbours. Nana Glen had no electricity or running water. Most villagers kept kerosene lamps to light their homes at night and they washed their clothes in metal tubs by the creek.

Robert had once hankered after romance and riches in far-off lands, but in New South Wales he made a life free of either. In Nana Glen he formed no close friendships with other men, courted no women, accrued no property.

He seemed to have relinquished the desires for wealth and power that had animated him as a boy, along with the desires for sex and companionship that might have come to him as a man. His journey conformed only to the most innocent penny dreadful plot: that of the lad who flees the busy modern world for the rugged simplicity of the Australian bush. Instead of love and money, he had found peace and safety.

Robert became acquainted with Bertha and her children when they moved to the farm next to his in the late 1920s. He learnt that Bertha, a policeman's daughter, was born in East London in the 1880s and brought up in West Ham. Like Robert, she had emigrated to Australia early in 1914.

By 1930, the Smith family was under increasing financial strain. Harold was supporting six children: the baby he had with Bertha, the four children she had brought to the marriage, and his daughter Elizabeth. In the economic depression that had taken hold in Australia, work was scarce and the prices of dairy products were falling. Smith was running up a large debt at the general store in the neighbouring village of Glenreagh. To try to make ends meet, he killed most of his calves for their hides, and he took on a contract to build a dairy and a set of milking stalls at a farm twelve miles away. He left many of the tasks on the home farm to Harry.

Before milking Smith's half-dozen cows on winter mornings, Harry would warm his feet in a patch of grass on which a cow had lain overnight. Afterwards, he would often run barefoot the four miles to Nana Glen public school to make it in time for class; and run home again to do the afternoon's milking at the end of the school day. In the evenings, it fell to Harry to round up the calves and bring them close to home so that they would be safe from dingoes. If he couldn't find one of the calves in the bush, Smith was likely to beat him.

In the middle of 1930, Harold Smith's landlord Ike Cundy complained that the property was becoming overgrown with black wattle. He told Smith to cut the bush back. Harry helped Smith to fell the trees and stack them up for burning. They used an axe to chop the timber, and a brush hook – a scythe with a foot-long curved blade – to hack at the undergrowth. Harry was kept so busy with this work that he was hardly able to go to school at all.

When Cundy called round to inspect the land on 3 June 1930, Smith lost his temper and struck his sixty-eight-year-old landlord with a whip handle. Cundy was injured badly enough to need medical attention. He reported the assault to the police and threatened Smith with legal action.

Six days later, on Monday 9 June, Smith accused Harry of laziness and told him to get off the farm. Harry, now eleven, had been suffering from flu. When Smith found the boy still on the property in the afternoon, he attacked him, repeatedly hitting him with the handle of the brush hook and punching him in the face.

Harry was seriously injured. On Thursday he took himself to the police station at Glenreagh, four miles north along the track that ran past their house, and reported to the officer on duty that his stepfather had beaten him. Police Constable Lawrence Freebody dressed the boy's wounds, then put him in a car and drove him back to the farm. Smith was at the table, eating, when the policeman came in with Harry. Bertha was also in the room.

'This boy informs me that you assaulted him with a brush hook,' said Constable Freebody.

Smith carried on eating. 'Yes,' he said.

Freebody removed the bandages from Harry's right arm and asked Smith if he had caused the injuries with his brush hook, as Harry claimed, and punched him in the face with his closed fist. Smith, recanting, admitted only to having spanked him with an open hand while they were both milking. The cow, he said, had then kicked the boy.

Freebody asked him if he had hunted Harry away from the farm that day.

'Yes,' said Smith, 'I told him he would have to get out as he would not work.'

Bertha interrupted to say that Harry was not unwell because he had been beaten, but because he had influenza.

Freebody told Smith that he would be charged with assault. He then drove Harry to the district hospital in Grafton. A doctor treated the severe cuts and bruises on the boy's right elbow, his right eye, his nose, his left cheek and his legs. Harry was kept in hospital for a week.

On Friday 20 June, Harry was taken to give evidence against his stepfather at the children's court in Grafton.

Smith denied the assault. He said that he could not remember having told Freebody that he spanked Harry during the milking. 'The cow kicked him down,' he said, 'and I spanked him afterwards.' He admitted having hit Harry on the lower part of his body with an old axe handle that he had stuck on his brush hook, but insisted that the child's injuries had been caused by the cow trampling on him. Most of the time, said Smith, he and the lad got on well together.

Harry was then questioned by the magistrate. He said that he had been cutting bottlebrushes on 9 June when his stepfather, out of the blue and without saying a word, had started to beat him with the brush hook.

Bertha told the court that her son helped out on the farm and she believed that he always did his best but, of course, he was very young and had never lived on a farm before. Her husband was usually kind and considerate to all of her children, she added, and gave them everything he possibly could. She was eager to exculpate Smith, perhaps because she feared for her family's livelihood if he were convicted. But she acknowledged to the court that some of Harry's injuries were caused by his stepfather striking him with a brush hook.

The magistrate found Smith guilty of unlawful assault and fined him £5 with £7/7/6 in witness and medical expenses. He ordered him to deposit a further £20 with the court, which would be returned only if he remained on good behaviour for two years; the alternative was two months' imprisonment. The fine, said the magistrate, could be paid in instalments of £3 a month.

Upon learning what had happened to Harry, Robert Coombes decided to risk the careful, solitary life that he had created for himself: he offered to look after the boy. Harold Smith moved with his family to Grafton soon after his attacks on his landlord and his stepson. Harry stayed with Robert in Nana Glen.

Robert and Harry lived together in the house by the track. Though Harry helped out on the farm, Robert continued to milk the cows himself, and he made sure that Harry went back to school – he had been absent so long that he had to re-enrol at the end of June 1930. Sometimes Harry got a lift home in a neighbour's sulky or, to his delight, in one of the few cars in the village, such as Sam Green's Morris Cowley or Charles Wright's Chevy. In the afternoons, Robert helped him with his homework.

Towards the end of 1930, a bush fire spread across Ike Cundy's land, catching on the trees and dry grass and then on the hessian that clad Robert and Harry's house. The building and most of its contents were destroyed, including Robert's cornet and violin. His four military medals survived the blaze, though they were damaged by the fire and the ribbons were burnt away.

Robert and Harry slept in the cow stalls while they built themselves a shack, using the burnt iron from the old house as a roof. The owners of the farm across the road, the Playford family, gave them clothes and bedding to replace what they had lost, and at Christmas brought over cake, pudding and nuts.

The next year Robert found a new house on a small rise of land that belonged to Reginald Gill, an English-born farmer who lived about a mile south of Cundy's place. Gill's son ploughed the field so that they could plant a vegetable garden, and Robert agreed to give his landlord a quarter of his profits in return for the use of the house and land. At first the going was hard, as Robert and Harry had to fetch water for the garden from Coldwater Creek, a tributary of the Orara, and carry it several hundred yards up the hill in four-gallon kerosene cans. But Robert soon spotted a nice patch of flat land right by the creek and arranged with its owner to farm this plot while continuing to rent Gill's house.

Robert devoted himself to the garden. In the rich dark soil by the creek, he planted cauliflowers, cabbages, pumpkins, potatoes, tomatoes, cucumbers and peas. Most local families grew their own vegetables, but Robert's produce was so good that he was rarely short of customers. His peas and tomatoes were particularly fine. The O'Connells, who had a dairy farm in Nana Glen, used to send their eldest son down on a pony to buy Robert's tomatoes when the Catholic priest stopped by for lunch.

Harry hawked their vegetables around the neighbouring farms. At first he rode a bicycle, his wares thrown over his back in sugar sacks. Once a week or so he hitched a lift on the cream truck to Glenreagh, where he would sell vegetables until the truck came back through on its return trip. After a couple of years he and Robert acquired a brown mare, a sulky and harness so that Harry could drive himself up to Glenreagh with his goods. Harry supplemented the vegetables with fruit, buying watermelons and oranges from the Playfords to sell on at a profit. He also earned money by collecting mail from the post office and delivering it to neighbouring farms.

Harry always addressed Robert as 'Mr Coombes' and Robert called Harry 'Boy'. As with an army officer and a sol-dier, or an asylum attendant and a patient, there was never any doubt about who was in charge. It was Robert's duty to lead, protect and care for Harry, and the child's duty to obey his guardian. Robert grew fond of Harry, and he let the boy depend on him.

Robert was tidy in his habits. He trained Harry to wash the dishes and to clean the house thoroughly. They both wore shorts to work and had smarter outfits for best: Robert chose jackets for Harry at Mackelly's clothing store in Grafton. He could alter and repair their clothes himself, thanks to his train-ing in Charles Pike's tailoring shop at Broadmoor. Robert and Harry slept on folding stretcher beds in the bedroom. They kept a bull terrier as a pet, then two fox terriers. They shared their meals with the dogs.

In time, Robert restored the medals that had been damaged in the fire and he replaced their ribbons: the red, white and blue watered silk of the 1914–15 Star, the orange blaze of the

British War medal, the double rainbow of the Victory medal, the deep blue, white and crimson of the Military Medal. He bought a new violin and a new cornet, and would play the piano at neighbours' houses when he stopped by for tea. He taught music to children in the village.

Just over the creek from Robert's garden, also on the road to Glenreagh, were the village cricket pitch and two tennis courts. At weekends, Robert crossed the creek to play cricket or to watch the younger Nana Glen men compete against other teams. When electricity was run to a few buildings in Nana Glen in the mid-1930s, cricket enthusiasts were able to listen to broadcasts of international games on the radio in 'Pop' Thompson's pie shop.

Though the 45th Battalion had been dissolved in 1919, the band kept going. In the 1920s it was one of the few such bands regularly to compete in regional competitions, military gymkhanas and tattoos. Robert used to go by train to Sydney to perform in Armistice and Anzac Day parades. One April in the mid-1930s he took Harry with him to the Anzac parade and the Royal Easter Show. They stayed for two days in a small boarding house, eating their meals in a café across the road. On 25 April, the anniversary of the Gallipoli landings, Harry stood in the crowd to see his guardian play the cornet and march with his fellow veterans through the streets.

Robert impressed Harry as an educated, strong-minded man who could converse on any subject. He was a keen reader of books – novels and histories borrowed from the Grafton public library – and he followed the news, including the international cricket tests, in the *Sydney Morning Herald*. Robert also competed in chess tournaments at local clubs and by post. In the late 1920s the *Australasian* newspaper printed details of

three correspondence games that he had won against a clerk
from the town of Lismore, New South Wales.

In Holloway gaol, Robert had wept for his cats and his
mandolin. In the Australian bush, he took solace in his violin
and his dogs, in cricket, chess and books. And he had Harry, a
child to look after as he had tried to look after Nattie.

Nattie occasionally came to visit his brother. After being
demobilised in May 1919, when the *Swan* returned to
Sydney, he had settled in Newcastle, 300 miles south of Nana
Glen, and found work as a stoker on government boats that
dredged the state's rivers and harbours. He married a widow
called Mary May in 1928, when he was forty-five and she
forty-seven.

On one visit to the Orara Valley, Nattie stayed overnight
in the Glenreagh Hotel, a single-storey clapboarded building
where Robert and Harry joined him for dinner. Robert seemed
to bear his younger brother no grudge, despite the fact that
Nattie had testified against him in 1895. If Nattie had ever
resented Robert – for killing their mother, for upending their
lives, for disappearing to Broadmoor – he seemed to have laid
that to rest, too. Just as he had been chief witness to his brother's crime, Nattie had become the chief witness to his life: during the war, Robert had asked that he be notified of all his
injuries, promotions, decorations; and now he introduced him
to Harry.

Harry rarely saw his own family, but he learned later that
Harold Smith had continued to hurt and frighten his stepchildren. When Harry's younger brother Alf was helping to
fix a fence on a farm one day, Smith became furious with
him for holding the barbed wire incorrectly, and as punishment he tore the barbs through the boy's palms. On another
occasion, Smith ordered Alf to sharpen a piece of steel and

drive the spike through the heart of a sick horse. Alf was too distressed to carry out the task, so Smith made the boy hold the animal's head while he shot at its temple with a pistol; to Alf's horror, Smith missed, instead shooting off the horse's ears.

In October 1936, after a year of drought, bush fires were blown in to Nana Glen by fierce, fast winds. Robert and Harry were working in the garden by the creek when the flames shot to the tops of the surrounding bush, lighting the trees like beacons, and the sparks flew ahead to their house on the hill. They rushed to the building but were too late to save it. The farmers of the district battled for days and nights to quench the fires with water. Scores of cows and pigs were burnt to death in their sheds and sties, hundreds of miles of fencing were lost; pastures were scorched and plantations razed. The O'Connells barely escaped from their blazing farm: the parents bundled their three children into a sulky, wrapped in wet towels and blankets, and drove them out to safety through the burning trees.

This second fire marked the end of Robert and Harry's life together. While Robert started to piece together a shed of wood and iron at the garden by the creek, Harry was given shelter by the family of Herb Morrow, the soldier who had returned to Australia on the same ship as Robert, and he was then offered a room to rent in Reg Gill's house. He was seventeen, over six feet tall, and he felt ready to leave Robert's care.

Harry joined the 15th Light Horse Regiment of the AIF, a part-time militia that trained in nearby camps for several weeks a year, and he took a job as a road-builder for the forestry department, clearing land and laying tracks to ease the loggers' access to the bush. He would cycle twenty miles up the mountain to work on a Monday morning, stay in the bush for three nights, and cycle back to Nana Glen on Thursday night. At weekends, he spent time with Herb Morrow's niece Isabelle Rockey. Belle had been a fellow pupil at the Nana Glen school: Harry remembered that she and her best friend Maizee, an aboriginal girl, had read aloud to the class from the Australian children's classic *Dot and the Kangaroo*. Belle was a good tennis player, he now discovered, and an excellent dancer. Her parents gave Harry permission to take her to dances organised by the Methodist Church. The couple won a box of chocolates in a waltzing competition at the Cavalry Ball in the Nana Glen village hall in 1938, and two prizes at the Younger Set Ball the next year. The dance band was led by the Cowling brothers, Jack and Bill, local boys whom Robert had taught to play the drums and piano.

Robert continued to tend his garden and he now sold the vegetables himself. He carried his produce around the neighbourhood on the sulky, pulled by a small bay pony. His dark hair was greying and streaked with white.

When the Second World War broke out in 1939, Robert joined a volunteer defence corps in Nana Glen, composed chiefly of those too young or too old to join the army. The group met twice a week for training: in the village hall on one evening and at the sports ground each Sunday morning. Robert would take along his cornet to play for the small corps. Military service, for him, was an opportunity for music.

Just over a year into the war, Robert was able to join the army itself. The Australian government put out a plea at the end of 1940 for First World War veterans to form an emergency defence force to protect the coast of New South Wales in the event of a Japanese invasion. Robert volunteered for the 8th Garrison Battalion in February 1941. Since the unit would accept only men younger than fifty-five, Robert gave his age as fifty-four when he signed up (he was in fact fifty-nine). Before leaving home he wrote a will in which he left everything to Harry; his chief allegiance was no longer to his brother, but to his ward.

Robert and his fellow veterans were issued with uniforms and weapons, and sent to train in camps near Newcastle for three weeks at a time. The pay was six shillings a day, as it had been in the Great War. The 8th Garrison Battalion band led the Armistice Day parade in Newcastle in November 1941.

Harry was training as a gunner near Maitland, in southern New South Wales. On visits to Nana Glen he continued to court Belle Rockey and in September 1940 they became engaged. The following March the two were married in the Nana Glen Methodist church. Belle's health deteriorated soon afterwards, and in July 1941 the army discharged Harry on compassionate grounds, so that he could look after his wife. He worked in a Nana Glen sawmill, cutting timber for defence works.

Robert, too, became unwell. In February 1942 he developed heart problems and was discharged from the army. He returned to Nana Glen and resumed his gardening. Over the next few years he took part in local events – in 1946 he was a guest of honour at a meeting of the Orara Valley branch of the Returned Servicemen's League and a judge at a fancy-dress ball in the village hall. He kept at work on his land. Once or twice when Coldwater Creek burst its banks and the garden flooded he had to be rescued from the iron roof of his shack.

In 1945 Nattie fell ill with lung cancer, an occupational hazard for ships' stokers, and in September 1946 he died, aged sixty-three. He was cremated in Newcastle, New South Wales, and his estate of £103 passed to his widow.

Robert had a heart attack at the beginning of May 1949 and was taken to the hospital in Coffs Harbour, seventeen miles south-east of Nana Glen. Harry, who had recently moved to Coffs Harbour with his family, was notified of Robert's illness but did not manage to get to the hospital before his former guardian died on 7 May. The causes of Robert's death were given as chronic nephritis and arteriosclerosis, diseases of the kidneys and the heart. The assets he had bequeathed to Harry amounted to £3-worth of shares in the Orara Dairy Co-op, issued during his dairy-farming days. He had already given him his medals.

At the time of Robert's death, Harry was building a bungalow for his family and did not have the money to commission a gravestone. Robert was buried in an unmarked grave in the Church of England section of the town cemetery.

In the decades that followed, Harry worked at various sawmills, helped to raise his three children and to look after Belle, whose health was still poor: she suffered from kidney disease, severe stomach ulcers and anaemia. Harry accompanied her to Sydney for treatments; he once slept in his car for six weeks while she was recovering in a Sydney hospital from a stomach operation, as he could not afford a hotel. At home he made use of the skills that Robert Coombes had taught him: he cooked, washed up, cleaned and tidied, tended a bed of roses, petunias and marigolds in front of their house. In another plot he planted lettuce, squash, tomatoes and beans. Harry had adopted his wife's faith, and the family went regularly to Methodist services.

Harry used to talk to his children about Robert, and how he had rescued him from Harold Smith. He passed on to his son the war medals that Robert had entrusted to him. In the 1960s he appealed to the War Graves Commission for funds to erect a headstone for his former guardian, but the application was rejected on the grounds that Robert's military service had not caused his death.

Belle Mulville died in 1995, aged seventy-six, and the next year Harry decided at last to commission a headstone for Robert. It was almost half a century since he had died. When the stone and plaque had been installed in the Coffs Harbour cemetery, Harry took his youngest daughter to visit the grave. He placed a posy of plastic flowers on the tomb. His daughter, seeing that he was close to tears, remarked that it was a lovely thing that he had done for Mr Coombes. 'He looked after me very well,' Harry replied.

When I spoke to Harry Mulville's children in November 2012, I realised that Robert had been like a father to Harry, and a symbol of strength and kindness to them all. Harry's son told me that he had no wish to learn any more about Robert's past.

'What I want to retain,' he said, 'is Mr Coombes' goodness to my dad.'

He asked me not to speak to his father about the murder, though he wondered aloud whether the secret of the crime might not have been Robert's alone.

'The pertinent question is whether my father knew,' he said. 'I think there is a fifty-fifty chance that he knew.'

Though they did not want to talk to me further, Harry's son and older daughter told me that it would not affect their relationships with their sister if she chose to help me with my book.

Harry's younger daughter and I corresponded for more than a year. When she visited her father in his nursing home in Coffs Harbour, she would ask him about his life with Robert, and then email or telephone me to pass on his recollections. She sent me a photograph of Robert and several pictures of Harry. In this way, I gathered much of the information that I needed to put together a narrative of their years in Nana Glen.

In February 2014 I travelled to Australia. I visited a few libraries and archives in Canberra and Sydney to look up the diaries and letters of men who had served in Robert's battalions in the First World War. Then I flew from Sydney to Coffs Harbour. On the flight, I chatted to the man in the seat next to mine about why I was visiting the area, and he volunteered to trace some 'old-timers' from Nana Glen on my behalf. Within a couple of days, he had put me in touch with several men in their eighties and nineties who had seen Robert riding about with his vegetables when they were boys.

Maurice O'Connell described Robert's last home as a 'bloody old shack' next to a garden packed with 'beautiful veg' – it was Maurice's brother who used to ride over to buy tomatoes when the priest called round. Ernie Herd, who as a sixteen-year-old served in the Volunteer Defence Corps, recalled Robert as 'a gentlemanly sort of bloke' and a wonderful gardener and musician. Mick Towells described 'Bob' Coombes as a 'very quiet sort of chap' who 'stuck to himself' but would greet everyone with a friendly 'g'day'. Duncan McPherson said that he was 'a short, nuggety sort of bloke' – compact and stocky – who was very well liked in the neighbourhood. Len Goodenough told me that Robert taught music to the Cowling brothers, while Len Towells remembered that 'Coombesy' used to come across the creek from his shack to watch the cricket. The local lads had not known much about him: only that he was English, that he had served at Gallipoli, and that he had been awarded the Military Medal. If he seemed reticent about his past, so were many who had seen horrors in the Great War.

I visited Robert's grave in Coffs Harbour, in a grassy cemetery planted with tall palms and surrounded by eucalyptus trees. I noticed that Harold Smith, who had died in 1944, was buried only a few feet away. 'Lest we forget', read the inscription on his gravestone.

Harry's younger daughter took me to Nana Glen and showed me the places in which Robert and Harry had lived. She then offered to take me to meet her father. She had told him that an English writer was visiting Coffs Harbour to research the life of Robert Coombes, and he had agreed to see me.

We visited Harry in his nursing home in the morning of 5 March. He was sitting in a tall armchair in his room. His hair was white, his eyes bright and pale. He had just turned ninety-five. He did not ask me why I was writing Robert's story and I did not volunteer an explanation.

Harry answered my questions about his years in Nana Glen. He told me that his guardian had been a 'fine old gentleman', fair and steady. 'He kept an eye on me,' said Harry. 'He didn't punish me but he kept me on the straight and narrow.' I asked whether Robert spoke of the war. Harry replied that he talked only about the military band. Mr Coombes loved music, Harry said: in the shack by the creek at Nana Glen, he used to play his violin late into the night.

When I asked Harry about Harold Smith's assault on him, he expressed no bitterness: his stepfather had been a 'war wreck', he said. Harry believed that Smith was violent because he had been subjected to violence, that suffering had made him brutal.

Harry tilted his head to show me a scar above his right eyebrow, where Smith had hit him more than eighty years earlier. He pushed up a sleeve to expose a mark on his right elbow, rolled up a trouser leg to reveal a scar on his right shin. I saw how badly hurt he had been, and I imagined how frightened he had felt. His stepfather had sprung at him with the brush hook, whacking his body, punching his face. It was like the attack on Nattie that Robert had pictured as a child: their mother flaring up suddenly in fury and swinging a hatchet at the younger boy. Yet it was also like the terrible attack that Robert had made on his mother in the warm night of 8 July 1895, when he went at her with his knife and before she could speak or cry out cut her to the heart.

I believed that Robert had offered shelter to Harry in June 1930 because he recognised the boy's helplessness and fear, but also the rage of his assailant.

As I stood up to leave, Harry smiled and reached over to clasp my hand. He seemed glad to have told me what Robert had done for him. When I started work on this book, all that I had known about Robert Coombes was that he had stabbed his mother to death in the summer of 1895. It was astonishing to hold the hand of a man whom he had saved from harm. I still couldn't be sure whether Harry knew about the murder. I hoped that he did, and had loved Robert anyway.

NOTES

Most of the events in Part I are drawn from testimony given in the West Ham coroner's court, West Ham magistrates' court and Central Criminal Court at the Old Bailey between 18 July and 17 September 1895, as reported in newspapers including the *London Standard, London Daily News, The Times, Daily Telegraph, Morning Post, Daily Chronicle, Sun, Star, Illustrated Police News, Lloyd's Weekly Newspaper, News of the World, St James's Gazette, Manchester Times, Manchester Guardian, Reynolds's Newspaper, Forest Gate Gazette, Essex Newsman, Leytonstone Express and Independent, Chelmsford Chronicle, East Ham Echo, West Ham Herald and South Essex Gazette* and the *Stratford Express*. The same publications are the sources of most of the narrative in Parts II and III. Where the newspapers are quoted directly, dates are given in the Notes. Other sources include transcripts of witness depositions to the West Ham courts held at the National Archives in London (TNA: CRIM 1/42/9) and the transcript of the Old Bailey trial in the Old Bailey Session Papers (OBSP), online at www.oldbaileyonline.org.

Where not otherwise indicated, biographical details throughout are from census returns and records of birth, marriage, death and probate held by the National Archives in London (TNA) and the National Archives of Australia in Canberra (NAA), the electoral registers in the Newham Archives and Local Studies Library, London, the *1896 Post Office London Suburbs Street Directory of Plaistow* and the editions of *Kelly's Directory of Stratford* of 1894–5, 1895–6 and 1896–7.

ABBREVIATIONS

AWM	Australian War Memorial, Canberra
BRO	Berkshire Record Office, Reading, Berkshire
LMA	London Metropolitan Archives
ML	Mitchell Library, State Library of New South Wales, Sydney
NAA	National Archives of Australia, Canberra
NMM	National Maritime Museum, Greenwich, London

OBSP   Old Bailey Session Papers
PP   Parliamentary Papers
TNA   The National Archives, London

PART I: TEN DAYS IN JULY

CHAPTER I: THE THREE OF US

3   *already bright and warm*. . . The sun rose at 3.53 a.m. that morning, according to the *London Standard* of 8 July 1895, and set at 8.15 p.m. The *Standard* of 9 July reported that the temperature on Monday rose to 81 degrees Fahrenheit in the shade.

4   *pay the rent*. . . East London landlords and landladies traditionally called for the rent on a Monday morning and signed a rent book on receipt of the week's money. 'You just walk round on Monday mornings (or maybe you even drive in a trap),' reflects the novice landlord Jack Randall in Arthur Morrison's short story collection *Tales of Mean Streets* (1894), 'and you collect your rents'.

5   *the Gentlemen v Players match*. . . Account of the match from reports of 8, 9 and 10 July 1895 in the *Morning Post, London Daily News, Evening News* and *London Standard*; and from David Kynaston, *WG's Birthday Party* (2011).

7   *about average for the area*. . . See Jim Clifford, 'The Urban Periphery and the Rural Fringe: West Ham's Hybrid Landscape' in *Left History,* Spring/Summer 2008.

8   *'Light Ahead'*. . . From *The Era*, 28 November 1891, 21 January 1893, 22 June 1895 and 13 July 1895; and *Lloyd's Weekly Newspaper*, 29 November 1891.

9   *Among Robert's most recent purchases*. . . *Jack Wright and the Fortune Hunters of the Red Sea* was first published by the Boys' Star Library in New York in 1892 as *Jack Wright and his Submarine Yacht; or, The Fortune Hunters of the Red Sea*. The undated British reprint, which cost a penny, must have appeared on 3 or 10 July 1895, as it was number 51 in a weekly series that had been published by the Aldine Cheerful Library each Wednesday since July 1894, and it was found in 35 Cave Road on 17 July 1895. About 120 Jack Wright stories were printed between 1891 and 1904. The creations of the Cuban-American author Luis Senarens, they were even more wild, fantastical and racist than the adventures of the more famous dime novel hero Frank Reade Jr. For descriptions and images of Jack Wright and other early science-fiction heroes, see Jess Nevins's 'Fantastic Victoriana' (www. reocities.com/jessnevins/vicw) and John Adcock's 'Yesterday's Papers'

(john-adcock.blogspot.co.uk/2011/08/steam-men-and-electric-horses). Many of the British reprints are listed on Steve Holland's 'The British Juvenile Story Papers and Pocket Libraries Index' (www.philsp.com/homeville/bjsp/ostart).

11 *The horse-drawn trams.* . . These were the cheapest form of transport, usually a penny a ride. The tram rails enabled two horses to pull fifty passengers, twice the number that they could shift in an omnibus. See Jerry White, *London in the Nineteenth Century: A Human Awful Wonder of God* (2007).

11 *The route was busy with shops.* . . From *Plaistow Post Office Directory* (1896), *Kelly's Directory of Stratford 1894–95*, the West Ham electoral registers 1890–6 at the Newham Archives in Stratford and the 1894 ordnance survey map of West Ham and environs.

11 *a new public hall.* . . The Canning Town Library – the first library in the borough – was opened at 110 Barking Road in 1893, according to Donald McDougall (ed.), *Fifty Years a Borough, 1886–1936: The Story of West Ham* (1936); the library's electricity was generated next door at the Canning Town Public Hall from 14 February 1895.

11 *Over the previous two decades.* . . According to White, *London in the Nineteenth Century* (2007), the migration of the working classes to outer East London was also encouraged by the Cheap Trains Act of 1883, which compelled railway companies to run special low-fare trains for workmen. Thanks in part to the cheap tariffs offered by the Great Eastern Railway, which served most of 'London-in-Essex', the population of the eastern suburbs almost doubled between 1881 and 1901. For the development of West Ham in the late nineteenth century, see Archer Philip Crouch, *Silvertown and Neighbourhood: A Retrospect* (1900), McDougall (ed.), *Fifty Years a Borough*, and W. R. Powell (ed.), *A History of the County of Essex: Vol 6* (1973).

11 *'London over the Border'.* . . The phrase was coined by Henry Morley in his article 'Londoners over the Border', published in *Household Words* in 1857.

11 *Malays, Lascars, Swedes, Chinamen.* . . From an article by Robert Bontine Cuninghame Graham in *The Workers' Cry* of July 1891.

11 *'There is no seaport in the country.* . .' In Walter Besant, *East London* (1901), which also describes the noises of the docks.

12 *low and sluggish.* . . For description of the Thames, see *Evening News*, 4 July 1895.

13 *The sour, urinous scent.* . . See Roy Porter, *London: A Social History* (1994) and Harry Harris, *Under Oars: Reminiscences of a Thames Lighterman, 1894–1909* (1978), as well as Crouch, *Silvertown and*

Neighbourhood, McDougall (ed.), *Fifty Years a Borough* and Powell (ed.), *A History of the County of Essex.*

15 *John Fox visited two pawnbrokers.* . . Details of the pawnbroking trade from Melanie Tebbutt, *Making Ends Meet: Pawnbroking and Working-class Credit* (1983) and George Sims, *Living London: Its Work and its Play, its Humour and its Pathos, its Sights and its Scenes, Vol. I* (1901). The poorer classes often paid weekly visits to the pawnbroker, going in on a Monday to pledge clothes that had been worn over the weekend and returning to redeem the clothes when they received their wage packets on Friday. Women tended to visit a pawnbroker's shop on a Monday, to raise money for rent, whereas young men frequently came on a Wednesday or Thursday evening, to pledge a watch in exchange for beer money. The pawnbrokers that Fox visited in the Commercial Road were of a 'medium' grade, and catered to a relatively respectable and occasional clientele, most of whom pledged items worth five to ten shillings to tide them over in an emergency. The pawnbrokers' statutory opening hours were from 7 a.m to 8 p.m. in the summer months.

CHAPTER 2: ALL I KNOW IS THAT WE ARE RICH

17 *dozens of coffee shops.* . . The coffee in such shops was usually 'a dreadful draught', reported *Punch* magazine on 19 August 1882, 'served up in dirty crockery, accompanied by huge slabs of brown-crusted bread smeared with a yellow deposit of oily butter. Tea, too, is forthcoming upon call, a long-stewed, dingy-tinted potion of uncertain origin, flat as stale soda-water, nauseous as a sarsaparilla drench. Eggs which are musty, bacon which is rusty, steaks which are tough, and chops which are tainted, even sodden cuts from half-cooked joints, and wedges of flabby pastry, may be procured at the more pretentious Coffee-Houses, while at the humbler ones the sense is regaled with the strong savour of red-herrings and smoked haddocks' (see victorianlondon.org).

18 *A record 35,000 people.* . . The *Essex Newsman* of 8 June 1895 reported that about 9,000 visitors rode the electric trams and 8,000 the steamboats that Whit Monday. At Pier Hill fairground a north London man died after being struck in the ribs by a swing boat, two girls were injured after falling out of swings, a man sustained a bullet wound in the shooting gallery and several children cut their feet on broken bottles on the beach.

18 *They walked through the Pier Hill fairground.* . . Description of rides and stalls from the *Chelmsford Chronicle*, 21 September 1894.

18 *Little Elsie the Skirt Dancer. . . The Era* of 13 July 1895 reported that a burlesque actress, a clown and a group of jugglers were also to appear in the Pavilion that night.

18 *At low tide. . .* Account of the pier adapted from Walter Besant's description of a day trip to Southend in *East London* (1901).

19 *the most notorious murderer. . .* Account of James Canham Read's crime and conviction from the *London Standard* of 27 June, 9 July and 8 December 1894, *Morning Post* of 10 July 1894, *Chelmsford Chronicle* of 13 July 1894, *Essex Standard* of 14 and 21 July 1894, *Illustrated Police News* of 7 July, 14 July and 24 November 1894, *Evening News* of 15 and 16 November 1894 and *Reynolds's Newspaper* of 18 November 1894.

20 *When Robert learned. . .* In the Old Bailey, Robert's father said that Robert 'went to Southend to see Read' without specifying a date. Read appeared in the Southend police court on 9 and 16 July. Robert was on the register of Stock Street school at the time, but according to his headmaster did not attend after 7 July, the day of Read's arrest.

21 *The killer in 'The Bogus Broker's Right Bower'. . .* The preposterously titled *The Bogus Broker's Right Bower; or, Ralph Rolent's (Felon 26) Tigress Shadower* was one of the tuppenny magazines in Robert's collection, a sixty-four-page Aldine O'er Land and Sea story originally published by Beadle's Dime Library in New York on 14 March 1894.

22 *the Balaam Street recreation ground. . .* See McDougall (ed.), *Fifty Years a Borough*. The construction of the park cost £11,206, according to the *Chelmsford Chronicle* of 15 June 1894, and provided employment for some of the jobless labourers of West Ham.

22 *games of knocking down ginger. . .* In *The Love of a Brother: From Plaistow to Passchendaele* (2011), Percy Cearns recalls his childhood in the 1890s and 1900s: 'What terrors of Plaistow Park Road we lads must have been. I wonder how many fruitless journeys to open front doors we have caused ladies in the neighbourhood through our propensity to play a game, colloquially known as "knocking down ginger". "Kick can", "buttons", "egg cap", "leap frog", "robbers and thieves" were among other famous sports which we young ruffians were wont to pass our evenings.' Percy and his brother Fred shared a bedroom, where at night they read the 'forbidden fruit' of penny literature by candlelight. When their father found the magazines, he confiscated them and lectured his sons about their reading habits: 'Dad . . . always told us there were plenty of books in the bookcase to read "instead of such trash". I am afraid we neither of us took much notice of this advice however, as we would always replace the lost copies and impatiently await the next numbers.'

22 *From the front of the house.* . . . *Lloyd's Weekly Newspaper* of 21 July 1895 observed that Cave Road lay 'in the open part of Plaistow, looking across the flats and the river to the Kentish hills'.

22 *The German writer H. A. Volckers.* . . . In Part XII of 'A Journey to Europe', *Clarence and Richmond Examiner,* 31 July 1886.

23 *As the eldest son.* . . . For boys' chores, see Michael J. Childs, *Labour's Apprentices: Working-Class Lads in Late Victorian and Edwardian England* (1992) and Edward John Urwick (ed.), *Studies of Boy Life in Our Cities* (1904).

23 *There was no age restriction.* . . . In *East London,* Besant observed that East London boys smoked cheap cigarettes, known as 'fags', as a way of asserting their manhood. They also liked to read penny dreadfuls 'featuring the likes of Jack Harkaway knocking down the ship's captain on the quarter deck', and to play cards, known locally as 'darbs'. On boy smokers, also see Childs, *Labour's Apprentices.*

24 *When an overladen National Line vessel disappeared.* . . . In *Cattle Ships: Being the Fifth Chapter of Mr. Plimsoll's Second Appeal for Our Seamen* (1890), the MP Samuel Plimsoll reported that the widows of the lost *Erin* sailors told him that only the cashier had shown them kindness. Plimsoll recorded his name as 'Euston', presumably a mishearing of 'Hewson', since John Hewson was chief cashier of the National Line at the time.

24 *Dear Sir.* . . . A transcript of this letter is Exhibit A in TNA: CRIM 1/42/9.

25 *The weather had cooled off.* . . . See *London Daily News,* 15 July 1895.

25 *Buffalo Bill.* . . . The story found in Cave Road was probably *Buffalo Bill; or, Life and Adventures in the Wild West,* a reprint of a Beadle's Dime Library number, published in London in 1890 by the Aldine O'er Land and Sea Library. The young Billy's exploits are described in *Adventures of Buffalo Bill from Boyhood to Manhood,* published in New York by Beadle and Adams in about 1882. Bill Cody staged his 'Wild West' show at Earl's Court from June to October 1892.

26 *Over the weekend, the election campaigning.* . . . See *Stratford Express,* 17 July, and *West Ham Herald,* 20 July 1895.

26 *'to lift the weary load.* . . .' From a speech at an open-air meeting by the docks in Silvertown on Monday 8 July 1895, reported in *West Ham Herald,* 13 July.

27 *'feel that there is sunshine.* . . .' From an article by the socialist MP Robert Bontine Cuninghame Graham in *The Workers' Cry,* July 1891.

27 *In 1895 some 10,000 men.* . . . See Stephen Inwood, *City of Cities: The Birth of Modern London* (2005).

27 *Edward Leggatt had been prosecuted.* . . . See *Essex Newsman,* 6 July 1895, and *Barking, East Ham & Ilford Advertiser,* 13 July 1895.

27 *an activist had accidentally blown himself up.* . . . This incident inspired Joseph Conrad's novel *The Secret Agent* (1907).

27 *A donkey.* . . See *Stratford Express*, 17 July 1895.

27 *'West Ham Workers – Attention!.* . .' See *Evening News*, 15 July 1895.

28 *Robert's novelette 'Joe Phoenix's Unknown'.* . . *Joe Phoenix's Unknown; or, Crushing the Crooks Combination* was an American detective story featuring East London criminals first published by Beadle's Dime Library in New York in 1892 and reprinted in London in 1894 by the Aldine O'er Land and Sea Library.

28 *'I certify that Mrs Emily Coombes.* . .' A transcript of Griffin's note is Exhibit B in TNA: CRIM 1/42/9; the torn-off date is Exhibit C.

29 *Dear Pa.* . . A transcript of this letter and of the bill from Greenaway are Exhibits E and F in TNA: CRIM 1/42/9.

30 *'Sir,' wrote Robert.* . . A transcript of Robert's letter to the *Evening News* is Exhibit D in TNA: CRIM 1/42/9.

30 *'£2 wanted privately.* . .' *Evening News*, 4 July 1895.

32 *There was no running water.* . . See *London Standard*, 17 July 1895.

32 *As the polling deadline of 8 p.m. approached.* . . Account of election night from *West Ham Herald, Forest Gate Gazette* and *Leytonstone Express and Independent* of 20 July and *Stratford Express* of 17 July 1895.

32 *along roads lit by gas lamps.* . . According to McDougall (ed.), *Fifty Years a Borough*, there were 1,831 gas lamps in West Ham in 1886, lighting sixty miles of streets. Charles Masterman in *The Heart of Empire* (1902) describes other lights in the neighbourhood: 'At night long lines of barrows brilliant with flaring kerosene lamps contribute an element of weirdness. Past these drifts a continuous stream of tired women haggling for whelks and cauliflowers and other necessities of existence. Every corner sports the brilliantly lighted gin palace with its perpetual stream of pilgrims.' In *From the Abyss* (1903), he notices 'the wildly flaring naphtha lamps from strings of stalls in the gutters'.

CHAPTER 3: I WILL TELL YOU THE TRUTH

42 *The police discovered.* . . A list of the evidence gathered by the police is in TNA: CRIM 1/42/9.

PART II: THE CITY OF THE DAMNED

CHAPTER 4: THE MACHINE AND THE ABYSS

47 *The courthouse in West Ham Lane* . . . See Clare Graham, *Ordering Law: The Architectural and Social History of The English Law Court to 1914* (2003).

47   *The 'Sun'. . . the 'Star'. . .* On 18 July 1895.
48   *Ernest Baggallay.* . . . See 'Spy' caricature of Baggallay, captioned 'A Popular Magistrate', in *Vanity Fair* of 13 July 1905 and obituary of Baggallay in *The Times*, 11 September 1931.
48   *In Canning Town police court.* . . See *West Ham Herald*, 20 July 1895.
48   *Despite the passage of the Children's Act.* . . See Lionel Rose, *The Erosion of Childhood: Child Oppression in Britain, 1860–1918* (1991) and George K. Behlmer, *Child Abuse and Moral Reform in England 1870–1908* (1982).
51   *The 'Stratford Express' approved.* . . 20 July 1895.
51   *a street vendor in Northern Road.* . . See *West Ham Herald*, 27 July 1895, which reported that on 23 July the vendor was sentenced to a month's imprisonment with hard labour.
52   *Holloway gaol.* . . See Arthur Griffiths, *Secrets of the Prison House: Gaol Studies and Sketches* (1894); Philip Priestley, *Victorian Prison Lives: English Prison Biography 1830–1914* (1985); 'In Holloway "on Remand"', *Pall Mall Gazette*, 27 October 1892; and evidence given in 1894 by George Walker (the Holloway doctor), Lt-Col Everard Stepney Milman (the governor) and Rev. George Purnell Merrick (the chaplain) in the Departmental Committee on Prisons' *Report* and *Minutes of Evidence*, PP, C7702 (1895).
53   *Charles Carne Lewis.* . . . For his appointment as coroner, see *Chelmsford Chronicle*, 18 August 1882. For Florence Dennis inquest, see *Chelmsford Chronicle*, 6 July 1894. For sewage works inquest, see *Morning Post*, 19 July 1895.
54   *The room was furnished.* . . See *Evening News*, 29 July 1895.
55   *a double coffin.* . . See *Cassells Household Guide, Volume I* (1880).
56   *burial insurance.* . . See Maud Pember Reeves, *Round About a Pound a Week* (1913) and *Cassells Household Guide, Vol. I* (1880).
57   *Many of the headstones had fallen down.* . . See Mrs Basil Holmes, *The London Burial Grounds* (1896) and the page on Tower Hamlets Cemetery Park in www.londongardensonline.org.uk.
57   *At 1 p.m. Emily's body was lowered.* . . Burial details from *Daybook of Burials in Consecrated Ground, City of London and Tower Hamlets Cemetery*, LMA: CTHC 01/056.
58   *a fourteen-year-old boy had climbed a tree.* . . See *Illustrated Police News*, 8 and 15 July 1895.
58   *The penny paper 'Lloyd's Weekly'.* . . . The article was published on 21 July 1895, as was the *News of the World* piece. The *Forest Gate Gazette*, *West Ham Herald* and *Stratford Express* ran their first pieces about the crime on 20 July 1895.
60   *the British author Hugh E. M. Stutfield.* . . In an article entitled 'Tommyrotics', *Blackwood's Edinburgh Magazine*, June 1895. See

Sally Ledger and Roger Luckhurst (eds), *The Fin de Siècle: A Reader in Cultural History, c.1880–1900* (2000).

61 *An 'Illustrated London News' reporter.* . . See 'Picturesque Aspects of the East End III', 9 April 1892.

61 *The French novelist Emile Zola.* . . See *Manchester Guardian*, 3 October 1893.

61 *The English writer Ford Madox Hueffer.* . . In *The Soul of London* (1905).

61 *Walter Besant.* . . In *East London*.

61 *'As there is a darkest Africa. . .'* From William Booth, *In Darkest England and the Way Out* (1890).

62 *The American novelist Jack London.* . . 'Far better to be a people of the wilderness and desert, of the cave and the squatting-place, than to be a people of the machine and the Abyss,' writes London in *The People of the Abyss* (1903).

CHAPTER 5: A KISS GOODBYE

63 *an interview with Mary Jane Burrage.* . . See *Star*, 18 July 1895.

64 *certain rumours.* . . The *Illustrated Police News* of 27 July 1895 reported that Robert resented his mother for not giving him enough spending money, but the suggestion that Emily Coombes was a heavy drinker seems not to have appeared elsewhere in the press.

65 *he was declared bankrupt.* . . The petition against him was heard on June 1873 and his creditors received their first dividends (of 1/6d for every pound they were owed) in July 1874. See *London Gazette*, 27 June 1873 and 8 July 1874.

65 *Emily was born.* . . The Register for Births and Baptisms in India shows that she was born in India on 1 March 1858, the daughter of George and Tryphena Allen, both natives of Poole in Dorset. The story about the rescue on the river Indus was reported in the *Illustrated Police News*, 3 August 1895. Her father's naval service is detailed in United Kingdom Merchant Navy Seamen Records 1835–1941, TNA: BT113.

66 *Robert, their first son.* . . According to his birth certificate, Robert was born in 23 Edwards Street, ten minutes' walk north of his grandparents' house in Three Colt Street. At the age of seven, he was enrolled at Farrance Road board school, Limehouse, where Nattie joined him a year later. See Grange Road School Admissions Register 1888–1906, Newham Archives, Stratford Library. Upon the death of the boys' grandfather in 1882, their father temporarily moved the family into the house in Three Colt Street.

66   *The people of East London*. . . From Booth, *Life and Labour of the People in London*, Vol. 1 (1889). A docker's wife in Morrison's *Tales of Mean Streets* explains why she and her family are leaving Limehouse: 'My 'usband finds it too far to get to an' from Albert Docks mornin' and night. So we're goin' to West 'Am.'

66   *the National Line vessels 'England' and 'France'*. . . See N. R. P. Bonsor, *North Atlantic Seaway: An Illustrated History of the Passenger Services Linking the Old World with the New* (1955); Arthur J. Maginnis, *The Atlantic Ferry: Its Ships, Men and Working* (3rd edition, 1900); F. E. Chadwick, John H. Gould, J. D. J. Kelley, William H. Rideing, Ridgely Hunt and A. E. Seaton, *Ocean Steamships: A Popular Account of their Construction, Development, Management and Appliances* (1891); and John Kennedy, *The History of Steam Navigation* (1903).

66   *By 1895 the company had abandoned the passenger trade*. . . See *Leeds Mercury*, 29 December 1894.

66   *As a chief steward*. . . For details of rations, see NMM: RSS/CL/1895/60015 SS *France* and NMM: RSS/CL/1895/29996 SS *England*. For a steward's status and duties, see Frank Thomas Bullen, *The Men of the Merchant Service* (1900).

67   *Coombes was paid*. . . For pay of Coombes and his shipmates, see NMM: RSS/CL/1895/60015 SS *France* and NMM: RSS/CL/1895/29996 SS *England*.

68   *There was talk*. . . At the annual meeting, reported the *Sheffield Evening Telegraph* of 28 February 1895, some shareholders suggested that the company be wound up.

68   *a friend of Coombes*. . . This was probably his wife's brother-in-law John William Macy, an American master mariner who had married Emily's older sister Mary in 1866. Macy was said to be a good friend of Robert Coombes senior and he was in the United States at the time.

69   *he gave interviews to several newspapermen*. . . The reports appeared in the *New York Times*, *Pittsburgh Commercial Gazette* and *New York Tribune* on 22 July 1895. A fanciful article also appeared in the New York *Sun* that day, claiming that 'Mr Coombs stood on the porch of his little vine-covered cottage in Plaistow. . . and bade good-by to his wife and two sons', with the words, 'Boys, take care of your mother'.

72   *'I found him to be my apprentice. . .'* Letter published in *West Ham Herald* on 27 July 1895.

CHAPTER 6: THIS IS THE KNIFE

73   *At six o'clock*. . . For the routine at Holloway, see note to p.52.

73 *In the prison register.* . . Walker described his form of mental debility as 'recurrent mania' and the 'probable cause' as '?injury to head at birth'. See *Report of the Commissioners of Prisons and the Directors of Convict Prisons 1895–96, for the Year Ended 31 March 1896,* PP, 1896, XLIV, 235.

74 *'London Standard'.* . . 22 July 1895.

74 *'Evening News'.* . . 22 July 1895.

74 *Charlie Sharman.* . . Sharman was born in Great Baddow, Essex, in 1850; his father was a schoolteacher and his mother, who was blind, played organ in the village church. As a young clerk, Sharman worked in Chelmsford, Essex, but was driven out of town in 1887 after being accused of indecent assaults – see *Chelmsford Chronicle,* 8 May 1891. For his law suits against his former clerk, see *Essex Newsman* of 2 May 1891, *Chelmsford Chronicle* of 15 May 1891 and *Whitstable Times and Herne Bay Herald* of 16 May 1891. For his defence of the Walthamstow verger, see *Chelmsford Chronicle* of 23 March 1894. For his success in the general election see *Chelmsford Chronicle* of 20 November 1896.

76 *'Star'.* . . 25 July 1895.

76 *'Evening News'.* . . 26 July 1895.

76 *To wear a shirt with a collar.* . . In *The Nether World* (1889), George Gissing notes that navvies, scaffolders, costermongers and cab touts usually went collarless, while shopmen and mechanics were likely to sport collars.

78 *On the ground floor, Orpwood explained.* . . According to the criteria laid out in Joseph Rowntree's survey of working-class housing in York in 1900, the Cave Road terrace was of the type designed for relatively well-off working-class families. The best workmen's dwellings were slightly larger, with five rather than four rooms, but like the Coombes residence they had a bay window, cornicing, a small railed garden to the front, frontages of fifteen to seventeen foot and a scullery behind the back parlour. The front parlour in such houses was used on Sundays as a room in which to receive guests, and otherwise only occasionally – for letter-writing or music practice, for instance. See John Burnett, *A Social History of Housing 1815–1985* (1986).

78 *'Sun'.* . . 29 July 1895.

80 *'News of the World'.* . . 28 July 1895.

90 *'Illustrated Police Budget'.* . . 27 July 1895.

90 *'Daily Chronicle'.* . . Quoted in *Evening News,* 27 July 1895.

90 *Cesare Lombroso.* . . For instance, in *The Criminal Man* – the third edition, published in 1884, drew heavily on theories of degeneration.

91 *'Evening News'.* . . 26 July 1895.

91 *the wicked Mr Hyde.* . . In *Strange Case of Dr Jekyll and Mr Hyde* (1886), Robert Louis Stevenson describes Hyde as like 'a schoolboy'

who casts off his burden of respectability to 'spring headlong into the sea of liberty'. He has 'the light step, leaping pulses and secret pleasures' of youth, as well as being an atavistic, 'ape-like' creature. See Claudia Nelson, *Precocious Children and Childish Adults: Age Inversion in Victorian Literature* (2012).

91 *A group of doctors*. . . Quoted in *Evening News*, 27 July 1895.

92 *'the profoundest impression*. . .' See Ernest Jones, *The Life and Work of Sigmund Freud* (1964).

92 *'East London Advertiser'*. . . Interview published on 3 August 1895.

92 *'Cockney Bob's Big Bluff '*. . . Published by Beadle's Dime Library in New York on 2 May 1894, as *Fire-Eye: the Thugs' Terror; or, Cockney Bob's Big Bluff*, and reprinted in London in 1895 by the Aldine O'er Land and Sea Library.

CHAPTER 7: CHRONICLES OF DISORDER

95 *'Leytonstone Express'*. . . 3 August 1895.

97 *'Sun'*. . . 29 July 1895.

100 *'India in London'*. . . See *Daily Telegraph*, 2 July 1895, and *Evening News*, 3 July 1895.

104 *The Children's Act of 1889*. . . *Law of Parent and Child*, a guide of 1895, quoted Lord Coleridge: 'It is not enough to show neglect of reasonable means for preserving and prolonging the child's life; but to convict of manslaughter it must be shown that the neglect had the effect of shortening life.' For the Peculiar People cases, see also Behlmer, *Child Abuse and Moral Reform in England*.

104 *Lewis announced that he was 'sick and tired'*. . . See *Evening News* and *Daily Chronicle*, 26 July 1895.

104 *Lewis berated the parents*. . . See *Barking, East Ham & Ilford Advertiser*, 3 August 1895.

108 *penny dreadfuls*. . . For the history of the penny dreadful, see John Springhall, *Youth, Popular Culture and Moral Panics: Penny Gaffs to Gangsta Rap, 1830–1997* (1999); E. S. Turner, *Boys Will be Boys: The Story of Sweeney Todd, Deadwood Dick, Sexton Blake, Billy Bunter, Dick Barton, et al* (1948); Robert J. Kirkpatrick, *From the Penny Dreadful to the Ha'penny Dreadfuller: A Bibliographical History of the Boys' Periodical in Britain, 1762–1950* (2013); Kelly Boyd, *Manliness and the Boys' Story Paper in Britain: A Cultural History, 1855–1940* (2002); Charles Ferrall and Anna Jackson, *Juvenile Literature and British Society 1850–1950: The Age of Adolescence* (2009); Joseph Bristow, *Empire Boys: Adventures in a Man's World*

(1991); and Troy Boone, *Youth of Darkest England: Working-Class Children at the Heart of Victorian Empire* (2005).

108   *penny bloods*. . . 'Bloods is what we calls 'em in the trade,' a London shopkeeper told the journalist John Foster Fraser in 1899 – quoted in Fraser's *Vagabond Papers* (1906). '"Penny bloods" is the trade name for penny dreadfuls', reported the *Bristol Mercury* on 27 September 1895.

108   *'Tons of this trash. . .' Motherwell Times*, 2 March 1895

109   *proper novels for boys*. . . See *Freeman's Journal*, 6 November 1895 and *Fortnightly Review*, November 1895.

109   *a 'St James's Gazette' journalist*. . . His articles were published on 25, 26, 29 and 30 July 1895. He reported that the authors of penny dreadfuls were paid three and a half to four shillings per thousand words. The speed at which the bloods were composed is apparent in some of the stories in Robert's collection. William G. Patten's *Cockney Bob's Big Bluff*, published by Beadle's in 1894, is laden with errors of typing, spelling, grammar and punctuation, as if written in a tremendous rush and printed without being read over: 'Her eyes unclosed,' writes Patten, 'at the very instant when his fingers were present over her lips' (that is, the heroine opened her eyes just as the villain was about to touch her lips); 'The open air was grateful to the lovers after the time they had spent in the mysterious cottage.'

110   *The adventure yarns*. . . Quotes from John Tosh, *A Man's Place: Masculinity and the Middle-Class Home in Victorian England* (1999).

110   *New York dime novels*. . . On 16 November 1895 the *Marlborough Express* in New Zealand compared 'these vile, flaringly coloured, cheap novels' to undesirable immigrants and suggested that they should be destroyed by the Customs authorities.

110   *'The Secret of Castle Coucy'*. . . A story by the British New Yorker Frederick Whittaker, published by Beadle's Dime Library in 1881 as *The Severed Head; or, The Secret of Castle Coucy, A Legend of the Great Crusade* and reprinted by the Aldine O'er Land and Sea Library in about 1894.

111   *The novelist James Joyce*. . . 'An Encounter' is the second story in *Dubliners*, a collection completed in 1905 though not published until 1914.

111   *In an article of 1888*. . . 'About Penny Dreadfuls', *Pall Mall Gazette*, 29 June 1888.

111   *Every month, it seemed*. . . The reports cited here are from the *Gloucester Citizen*, 29 March 1889, *Dundee Courier*, 29 November 1892; *Manchester Evening News*, 31 October 1893; *Yorkshire*

Evening Post, 17 November 1892; *Coventry Evening Telegraph*, 8 January 1894.

112 *In 1888 two eighteen-year-olds.* . . See *London Daily News*, 15, 18, 26, 27 October and 15 December 1888.

113 *the publishing magnate Alfred Harmsworth.* . . In an article in the *Sunday Times* in 1948, A. A. Milne remarked that Harmsworth eventually 'killed the "penny dreadful" by the simple process of producing the ha'penny dreadfuller'. Harmsworth also owned the bestselling *Evening News*, in which Robert had planned to place an advertisement, and in 1896 founded the *Daily Mail*.

113 *'Union Jack'.* . . Justice Kennedy referred to issues of this magazine being found in Cave Road (see *News of the World*, 22 September).

113 *the press had often pointed out.* . . For instance, Edward G. Salmon in *Juvenile Literature as It Is* (1888) argued that the dreadfuls were dangerous because they 'are patronised chiefly by the sons of working-men, who are the future masters of the political situation'. For the national anxiety about penny dreadfuls, see especially Springhall, *Youth, Popular Culture and Moral Panics*, which includes a discussion of the Coombes case.

114 *'Pall Mall Gazette'.* . . 4 November 1886.

114 *'agents for the overthrow of society'.* . . Francis Hitchman in the article 'Penny Fiction': 'We have cast out the unclean spirit of ignorance from the working-class mind, and left it empty, swept, and neatly garnished with "the three Rs". Let us beware lest the unclean spirit returns with seven other spirits more wicked than himself, and turn the class we have made our masters into the agents for the overthrow of society.' Quoted in Boone, *Youth of Darkest England*.

CHAPTER 8: HERE GOES NOTHING

115 *It was common for a parent.* . . See Rose, *The Erosion of Childhood*.

116 *She switched between surrendering her authority.* . . In *Studies of Childhood* (1895) the psychologist James Sully warned against 'alternations of gushing fondness with almost savage severity, or fits of government and restraint interpolated between long periods of neglect and *laisser faire*'.

116 *'The Rock Rider'.* . . A story by Frederick Whittaker, author of *The Secret of Castle Coucy*, first published in 1880 by Beadle's Dime Library in New York and reprinted by the Aldine O'er Land and Sea Library in London in 1894.

117 *Robert and Nattie's father spent a week in New York.* . . Details of employment of cattlemen and of the ship's schedule in NMM:

RSS/CL/1895/60015 *SS France*. For life on a cattleship, see Plimsoll, *Cattle Ships*; W. H. Davies, *The Autobiography of a Super-Tramp* (1908); I. M. Greg and S. H. Towers, *Cattle Ships and our Meat Supply* (1894); Chadwick et al., *Ocean Steamships*; and *Report of the Departmental Committee of the Board of Trade and the Board of Agriculture on the Transatlantic Cattle Trade*, C6350 (PP, 1890–91, vol. LXXVIII).

118 *From the mouth of the Thames, wrote Joseph Conrad. . .* In Conrad's *Heart of Darkness* (1899). H. G. Wells describes the 'monstrous variety of shipping' on this stretch of the river: 'great steamers, great sailing-ships, trailing the flags of all the world. . . witches' conferences of brown-sailed barges, wallowing tugs, a tumultuous crowding and jostling of cranes and spars, and wharves and stores' (*Tono-Bungay*, 1909).

118 *'The river runs. . .'* In Hueffer's *The Soul of London*. Joseph Conrad writes that the Thames near the city 'flows oppressed by bricks and mortar and stone, by blackened timber and grimed glass and rusty iron, covered with black barges, whipped up by paddles and screws, overburdened with craft, overhung with chains, overshadowed by walls making a steep gorge for its bed, filled with a haze of smoke and dust' (*The Mirror of the Sea*, 1906).

118 *On Sunday the 'France' docked. . .* See NMM: RSS/CL/1895/60015 *SS France*. In *The Atlantic Transport Line 1881–1931: a History with Details on All Ships* (2012), Jonathan Kinghorn notes that in the 1890s cattle could be landed only at the Deptford wharf; the meat was sold at Smithfield Market. By 1896, more than 200,000 head of cattle a year were being landed in London (see Paula Young Lee, *Meat, Modernity and the Rise of the Slaughterhouse*, 2008). In 'The Feeding of London', published in *The Leisure Hour* in 1889, W. J. Gordon describes the process of transporting and slaughtering cattle (online at victorianlondon.org).

118 *Canon Basil Wilberforce delivered a sermon. . .* See *East Ham Echo*, 16 August 1895.

119 *Lawrence explained in his letter. . .* In *West Ham Herald*, 27 July 1895.

119 *John William Fox was born. . .* He was born on 19 April 1850 to Hannah Fox, who signed his birth certificate with a cross, in 4 Bell Yard, off Gracechurch Street. She was resident in the Flower Pot pub in Bishopsgate when he was sent to the Hanwell School, and she had married a shoe-maker in Shoreditch, East London, by the time he was apprenticed to Lawrence – see LMA: CBG/359/006 and LMA: CBG/361/003.

119 *industrial school in West London. . .* See Central London District Poor Law School admission and discharge register, 14 Apr 1857–20 Jul 1863: LMA: CLSD/165 7.

120   *apprenticeship* . . . See City Board of Guardians Register of Apprentice-
       ship and Service Papers 1866–97, LMA: CBG/36, apprentice bundles
       LMA: CBG/359/006 and LMA: CBG/361/003, and City of London Union
       Minute Books, March to Dec 1866 (2 volumes, LMA: CBG/47 and LMA:
       CBG/48). See also *London City Press*, 28 April and 20 October 1866.

120   *a fire broke out*. . . Account of fire on *Egypt* from *Manchester Courier
       and Lancashire General Advertiser*, 26 July 1890.

121   *on which Fox had also once served*. . . Fox joined the *Erin* at Gravesend
       in August 1885 as a captain's servant on a voyage to New York (NMM:
       RSS/CL/1885/50274 *SS Erin*).

121   *'Evening News'*. . . Interview conducted on 3 August and published
       13 August 1895.

122   *The new home secretary*. . . See *Manchester Courier*, 17 August 1895.

123   *'Leeds Times'* . . . 3 August 1895.

123   *'Lancet'*. . . 17 August 1895.

123   *'Penny Dreadfuls Again'*. . . See *Evening News*, 27 August 1895.
       The same headline was given in the *Nottingham Evening Post* on
       10 September to an article about a fifteen-year-old from Shepherd's
       Bush, West London, who had poisoned himself with carbolic acid.
       His father had given him a 'good hiding', the paper reported, because
       he had been out of work for a month. The boy left a note reading 'I
       wish you to know the reason I did it is because I could not work', but
       the judge none the less ascribed his death to his consumption of 'liter-
       ary offal'.

124   *Hugh Chisholm*. . . In 'How to Counter-act the Penny Dreadful',
       Fortnightly Review, November 1895.

124   *Wilde's decadent productions*. . . See also Merrick Burrow, 'Oscar
       Wilde and the Plaistow Matricide: Competing Critiques of Influence
       in the Formation of Late-Victorian Masculinities', *Culture, Society
       and Masculinities*, 1 October 2012.

124   *twenty boys at a north-west London board school*. . . See *Hampshire
       Advertiser*, 21 August 1895.

124   *'epidemic of suicide'*. . . See *Evening News*, 25 July, and *The People*,
       28 July 1895.

125   *childhood had been prized*. . . See Sally Shuttleworth, *The Mind of
       the Child: Child Development in Literature, Science, and Medicine,
       1840–1900* (2010), Henry Maudsley, *The Pathology of Mind* (edi-
       tion of 1895), James Crichton-Browne, 'Education and the Nervous
       System' in Malcolm A. Morris (ed.), *The Book of Health* (1883), and
       Sully, *Studies of Childhood*.

126   *interview to the 'Evening News'*. . . Published on 16 September 1895.

127   *Sir Forrest Fulton*. . . Fulton had been elected Conservative MP for
       West Ham North in 1886. When unseated by a Liberal in 1892, he was

appointed Common Serjeant of London, deputy to the most senior permanent judge at the Old Bailey.

129   *Kennedy proceeded to hear. . .* See OBSP.

129   *a fifth of Londoners. . .* According to White's *London in the Nineteenth Century*, one in five Londoners was a regular churchgoer in the 1890s. The proportion in the east of the city was even lower: Besant reported in *East London* that in a census on church attendance in 1886 just 7 to 8 per cent of East Londoners said that they took part in a form of worship on a Sunday.

130   *Francis Longsdon Shaw. . .* See *Clergy List* of 1896, *Crockford's Clerical Directory* of 1898, and Nigel Scotland, *Squires in the Slums: Settlements and Missions in Late Victorian Britain* (2007). Shaw's conversion was reported in the *North Wales Chronicle* of 30 August 1890 and his ordination in the *Chelmsford Chronicle* of 25 May 1894. For a photograph of the vicar and curates of St Andrews, including Shaw, see TNA: 1/436/885.

130   *Allen Hay. . .* See *Crockford's Clerical Directory* of 1898.

130   *a mandolinist called Miss Halfpenny. . .* From *West Ham Herald*, 16 June 1894.

PART III: THESE TENDER TIMES

CHAPTER 9: COVER HER FACE

135   *taken from their cells. . .* For the trip to Newgate and Old Bailey, see Departmental Committee on Prisons, *Report* and *Minutes of Evidence*, PP, C7702 (1895).

135   *Paul Koczula. . .* See *Haydn's Dictionary of Dates and Universal Information* (1895) and *Morning Post*, 15 August 1894.

136   *the Old Bailey courthouse. . .* For Old Bailey building and procedures, see Sims, *Living London, Vol. I*; R. Thurston Hopkins, *Life and Death at the Old Bailey* (1935); Anon, *London Characters and the Humorous Side of London Life* (1870); Anon, *The Queen's London: A Pictorial and Descriptive Record of the Streets, Buildings, Parks, and Scenery of the Great Metropolis in the Fifty-Ninth Year of the Reign of Her Majesty Queen Victoria* (1896): Montagu Williams, *Round London: Down East and Up West* (1894); and the page on the Old Bailey on Lee Jackson's website www.victorianlondon.org.

136   *'Star'. . .* 16 September 1895.

137   *'pea-soupers'. . .* See Inwood, *City of Cities*.

137   *Justice William Rann Kennedy. . .* See obituary in *The Times*, 18 January 1915, entry in *Oxford Dictionary of National Biography*

and report in *Liverpool Echo*, 28 October 1892. The National Portrait Gallery in London has a photograph of him in the early 1900s: NPG x35957.

137   *The case against Robert and Fox*. . . The prosecution case had been prepared by Frederick Frayling, a clerk in the joint office of the Director of Public Prosecutions and Solicitor to the Treasury. The total cost of the case to the Crown, from its inception on 19 July to its conclusion on 17 September 1895, was £63 10/ 10d – see *Report of the Commissioners of Prisons and the Directors of Convict Prisons 1895–96, for the Year Ended 31 March 1896*, PP, 1896, XLIV, p. 235.

137   *Charles Gill*. . . See obituary in *The Times*, 23 February 1923, and portrait by 'Spy' in *Vanity Fair*, 9 May 1891.

137   *Horace Avory*. . . See entry in *Oxford Dictionary of National Biography* and caricature by 'Spy' in *Vanity Fair*, June 1904.

139   *the Crown had made the fullest possible inquiries into Robert's state of mind*. . . This arrangement dated from 1886, when the offices of the Director of Public Prosecutions and Solicitor to the Treasury were merged, and the Treasury solicitor was required to ensure that any evidence about a prisoner's sanity was placed before the court. See Tony Ward, *Psychiatry and Criminal Responsibility in England 1843–1939* (DPhil thesis, 1996).

140   *In reply to his questions* . . . The examination of the witnesses is drawn from newspaper reports and the transcript of their testimony in OBSP. In places, a barrister's question has been inferred from his witness's response.

140   *trajectory of degeneration* . . . Bénédict Morel, *Traité des Dégénérescences physiques, intellectuelles et morales de l'espèce humaine* (1857).

141   *'Sun'*. . . 16 September 1895.

145   *Newgate*. . . See Griffiths, *Secrets of the Prison House*; Anon, *The Queen's London*; Priestley, *Victorian Prison Lives*; and the Departmental Committee on Prisons' *Report* and *Minutes of Evidence*, PP, C7702 (1895).

146   *W. T. Stead in 1886*. . . In 'My First Imprisonment', quoted in Priestley, *Victorian Prison Lives*. Stead was a renowned investigative journalist and crusader against child prostitution. He was a passenger on the *Titanic* in 1912, and died after the ship hit an iceberg.

146   *'Saturday Review'*. . . 21 September 1895.

148   *'Spectator'*. . . 21 September 1895.

148   *a wax worker was offering models*. . . In an advertisement in the *Era*, 27 July 1895.

148   *a melodrama about the murder*. . . See *Spectator*, 21 September 1895.

CHAPTER 10: THE BOYS SPRINGING UP AMONGST US

151 *'Evening News'*. . . 17 September 1895.

151 *'London Daily News'*. . . 18 September 1895.

151 *'Sun'*. . . 17 September 1895.

151 *From nine o'clock to twelve o'clock*. . . For the board school regime, see Anna Davin, *Growing Up Poor: Home, School and Street 1870–1914* (1986); Hugh B. Philpott, *London at School: The Story of the School Board, 1870–1904* (1904); and Rose, *The Erosion of Childhood*.

152 *endeavoured to train their young charges not to drop the 'h's*. . . See Charles Morley, *Studies in Board Schools* (1897). In *The Soul of London*, Hueffer identified south Essex as the source of the 'extraordinary and miasmic dialect' of East London. As well as dropping and misplacing aitches, the late-nineteenth-century East Londoner would replace 'e' for 'a' in such words as 'catch', according to White's *London in the Nineteenth Century*, 'v' for 'th' in words such as 'they' or 'there' and 'ff' for 'th' in 'three' and 'thank you'. He or she would typically use double negatives ('I don't know nuffing'), double superlatives ('more quicker'), pronounce 'gate' as 'gite' and 'Victoria' as 'Victawia'. Most of the witnesses' dialect in the Coombes case was standardised by the court reporters, but the occasional Cockney idiom slips through, for instance, in Mrs Hayward's phrase 'on the look' or in an unaltered transcription of Nattie's brief exchange with Robert after the murder: 'I done it'; 'You ain't done it.' Some of Robert's penny bloods revelled in the street slang of East London. Cockney Bob in *Cockney Bob's Big Bluff* is full of ripe expostulations: 'Blow me, but you are a stunner', 'Oh, drop it, darling', 'Capital!', 'Well, I should smile!'

152 *an academic 'standard'*. . . See William W. Mackenzie, *A Treatise on the Elementary Education Acts, 1870–1891 (with the Acts in an Appendix)* (1892).

152 *'oases', as one commentator described them*. . . Masterman, *The Heart of Empire*.

152 *The Coombes boys' first school*. . . Details of Robert and Nattie's changes of school are in the Grange Road School Admissions Register 1888–1906, Newham Archives. Robert reached the fourth standard in October 1892, according to this register, and left Grange Road for Stock Street in November 1893. Nattie left in July 1894 to attend the school at Cave Road, which opened that month. For the West Ham board schools, see Powell (ed.), *A History of the County of Essex: Vol. 6*. The National Archives has files on individual schools: Grange Road ED 21/5644; Stock Street ED 21/5679; Cave Road ED 21/5629.

152 *'Each school. . .'* In Booth (ed.), *Life and Labour of the People in London, Vol. 1*.

155   *'Singularly precocious. . .'* In the 1895 edition of Maudsley's *The Pathology of Mind*. Victorian ideas of precocity are discussed in Shuttleworth, *The Mind of the Child*, and in Nelson, *Precocious Children and Childish Adults*. As well as Little Father Time, Nelson cites the Artful Dodger in *Oliver Twist* (1838) and Jim Hawkins in *Treasure Island* (1883) as literary examples of the precocious child in Victorian England. Their counterpart was the childish man, exemplified by the simple, sweet-hearted Mr Dick in *David Copperfield* (1850) – a figure as benign and innocent as John Fox.

155   *'Dictionary of Psychological Medicine'*. . . Edition of 1892, ed. Daniel Hack Tuke.

155   *The latest instalment of Thomas Hardy's new novel*. . . The serial ran in twelve instalments under the title *The Simpletons* and then *Hearts Insurgent* in *Harper's New Monthly Magazine* between December 1894 and November 1895; in November it was published as the novel *Jude the Obscure*.

155   *Little Time is an old soul*. . . See '"Done because we are too menny": Little Father Time and Child Suicide in Late-Victorian Culture' by Sally Shuttleworth in Phillip Mallett (ed.), *Thomas Hardy: Texts and Contexts* (2003).

157   *The Thames Iron Works*. . . See Booth (ed.), *Life and Labour of the People in London, Vol. I*; A. J. Arnold, *Iron Shipbuilding on the Thames: An Economic and Business History* (2000); and the National Maritime Museum's illustrated history of the Thames Iron Works at www.portcities.org.uk/london/server/show/ConNarrative.59/Thames-Ironworks.

157   *the 'Fuji Yama'*. . . The ship's construction was described in the *Thames Iron Works Gazette* of 29 June 1895, the edition that also announced the formation of the football club that later became West Ham United. The vessel was launched in September as the *Fuji*.

157   *she had withstood years of relative hardship* . . . For the role of boy workers in the family, see Childs, *Labour's Apprentices*, Ellen Ross, *Love and Toil: Motherhood in Outcast London, 1870–1918* (1993), and Clare Rose, 'Working Lads in Late-Victorian London' in *Childhood and Child Labour in Industrial England: Diversity and Agency, 1750–1914* (2013).

157   *A couple of decades earlier*. . . For the decline of the apprentice system see Urwick (ed.), *Studies of Boy Life in our Cities*. In *Manchester Boys: Sketches of Manchester Lads at Work and Play* (1905), C. E. B. Russell observes that the working lad was usually 'set to some work which only calls for intelligence of the meanest kind. . . At this work he remains for week after week, year after year, his mind dormant, his hands moving with the precision and dullness of a machine.'

158   *Coombes brought home £9 2/-*. . . See NMM: RSS/CL/1895/60015 SS *France*.

CHAPTER 11: IT IS ALL OVER NOW

161 '*Star*'. . . 17 September 1895.

161 '*Sun*'. . . 17 September 1895.

162 *Wynn Westcott*. . . In *Suicide: Its History, Literature, Jurisprudence, Causation and Prevention* (1885).

162 *cerebral irritation*. . . In 1892 the *Journal of Nervous & Mental Disease* (vol. 19) reported on research by Dr Jules Simon into children with cerebral irritation. They were often melancholy, mentally unsteady, cruel to animals, oversensitive and capricious, said Simon. Sometimes they experienced epileptoid attacks, sometimes violent localised pains or impulsive movements. He recommended treating the condition with increasing doses of bromide of potassium.

164 *sailed to New York on the SS 'England'*. . . The *New York Times* of 22 July 1895 reported that the pair sailed on the *England* in 1895; the ship's voyage of January to March tallies with the dates of Robert's absence from school. For dates and crew, see NMM: RSS/CL/1895/29996 *SS England*.

164 *The ship was pelted with rain*. . . Details of outward journey from New York *Evening World* of 7 February 1895. The *Western Daily Press* of 15 February 1895 claimed that the Atlantic crossing that month was the worst on record. In the Rudyard Kipling poem 'Mulholland's Contract', which appeared in the *Pall Mall Gazette* on 6 June 1895, the narrator describes cattle ships as 'more like Hell than anything else I know'.

166 *The Englands' two older sons*. . . See Grange Road School Admissions Register 1888–1906 in Newham Archives.

167 *George Walker had been a prison doctor*. . . For Walker's background and his work at Holloway, see his testimony in the Departmental Committee on Prisons' *Report* and *Minutes of Evidence*, PP, C7702 (1895). For his evidence in other Old Bailey trials see OBSP.

167 *The insanity plea had become increasingly common*. . . See Ward, *Psychiatry and Criminal Responsibility in England 1843–1939*; Martin J. Wiener, 'Judges v Jurors: Courtroom Tensions in Murder Trials and the Law of Criminal Responsibility in Nineteenth-Century England' in *Law and History Review*, Autumn 1999; Ruth Harris, *Murders and Madness: Medicine, Law and Society in the Fin de Siècle* (1989); and Joel Peter Eigen, 'Diagnosing Homicidal Mania: Forensic Psychiatry and the Purposeless Murder', *Medical History*, October 2010. Both Ward and Eigen discuss the Coombes case.

168 *The 'right from wrong' test, said Maudsley*. . . At the annual meeting of the British Medical Association on 1 August 1895, published in the *Journal of Mental Science* of October 1895. In 1890, the lunacy

law expert Wood Renton claimed that a 'silent revolution' had taken place, whereby the 'knowing right from wrong' test was frequently ignored by judges and juries. See Ward, *Psychiatry and Criminal Responsibility in England 1843–1939*.

168 *'The brain is always compressed. . .'* The Dictionary of Psychological Medicine (1892) warned that clumsily applied forceps could cause brain damage.

170 *'Homicidal mania'.* . . See Etienne Esquirol, *Mental Maladies: a Treatise on Insanity* (1845), and Eigen, 'Diagnosing Homicidal Mania'.

170 *the sole marker of insanity.* . . See, for instance, 'Insanity of Conduct' by George H. Savage and C. Mercier in the *Journal of Mental Science*, April 1896, which argues that an act of violence can be 'the one insane symptom'.

173 *Walker had frequently been permitted.* . . Ward, in *Psychiatry and Criminal Responsibility in England 1843–1939*, notes that medical witnesses were meant to testify only to the facts on which they based their opinions of a prisoner's state of mind and not to the opinions themselves, but observes that this rule was honoured largely in the breach by the late 1880s.

174 *a 'hysterical' woman.* . . According to the *Dictionary of Psychological Medicine* (ed. Daniel Tuke, 1892), hysteria was characterised by an 'undue prominence of feelings uncontrolled by intellect' and was often attributed to 'dammed-up sexual emotions'.

175 *'bromism'.* . . In *The Diagnosis of Psychosis* (2011), Rudolf N. Cardinal and Edward T. Bullmore report that high doses of bromide, which was prescribed in the late nineteenth century as a sedative and anti-epileptic, can cause a neurotoxic condition in which the patient may become psychotic.

175 *The last witness for the defence.* . . For methods of attendance officers, see Philpott, *London at School* and David Rubinstein, *School Attendance in London 1870–1904: A Social History* (1969).

177 *Since 1882 the law had stipulated.* . . In 1882 Queen Victoria objected to the fact that Roderick Maclean, who had shot at her with a pistol, was found 'not guilty by reason of insanity', as the insanity verdict was then phrased. As a result, the wording of the verdict was changed to 'guilty but insane'. While Sherwood's argument might have had some merit before 1883, an insane defendant was now technically guilty of a crime.

177 *'Star'.* . . 17 September 1895.

177 *'Lloyd's Weekly'.* . . 22 September 1895.

179 *a strong recommendation to mercy.* . . Juries had successfully pleaded for mercy on account of a defendant's age in the trial of a twelve-year-old boy who had killed his grandfather with poison in 1847,

and in the trial of a sixteen-year-old who had killed a fellow apprentice in 1867. In both cases, the death sentence was commuted to life
imprisonment.

179   *Edis was keen to make clear*. . . On 20 September 1895, Harry Edis
wrote to the *London Daily News* to reiterate the jury's position: 'you
say that Fox gets the benefit of the contention raised by counsel – that
the insane can do no wrong, consequently there can be no accessory
after the fact. Now, in fairness to Fox, I think it necessary to state that
the verdict was not guilty upon the evidence.'

CHAPTER 12: BOX HIM UP

181   *'Broadmoor!'*. . . From 'Christmas Day at Broadmoor: an Ex-Warder's
Story' by R. J. Tucknor, *Reynolds's Newspaper*, 20 December 1896.

181   *newspapers and journals*. . . Those quoted in this chapter include
the *Star* of 17 September, *The Times*, *St James's Gazette*, *London
Daily News*, *Pall Mall Gazette*, *Evening News* and *Daily Chronicle*
of 18 September, the *Saturday Review*, *Lancet* and *Spectator* of 21
September, and the *News of the World* of 22 September 1895.

185   *The 'Journal of Mental Science'*. . . In January 1896.

185   *Others pointed out*. . . On 5 October 1895, the *Graphic* noted that
'The "penny dreadful" scare, one notices with relief, appears to be
slightly abating. . . The cheap romance of blood has really proved
sometimes on a closer inspection to be not so very much more sangui-
nary than some of the modern classics of adventure.'

185   *The Duchess of Rutland*. . . *Evening Telegraph*, 3 December 1895.

186   *The 'Child's Guardian'*. . . See Monica Flegel, *Conceptualizing Cruelty
to Children in Nineteenth-Century England: Literature, Representation
and the NSPCC* (2009), which refers to the Coombes case.

187   *'Was he, too, insane?'*. . . The journal seemed to ridicule the idea that
both boys were mad, but the phenomenon of *folie à deux*, a type of
madness described in the *Journal of Mental Science* in April 1895,
could conceivably have afflicted Robert and Nattie. This was a form
of shared insanity that relied on the two sufferers having a similar pre-
disposition and a deep and protracted intimacy – an affinity that was
possible between siblings. It usually manifested itself in a shared perse-
cutory paranoia that had some plausibility, as the Coombes boys' terror of their mother might have done if her punishments were severe.

188   *In a booklet*. . . Quoted in Behlmer, *Child Abuse and Moral Reform
in England*. According to Behlmer, of more than 10,000 families
investigated by the NSPCC between 1889 and 1891, only about 400
had a weekly income below 20/-. More than 3,000 had an average
family income of 27/-, well above the average weekly wage of 21/-.

This indicated that abuse was by no means confined to very poor households. 'The motive of cruelty is often the cruel person's own self-loathing,' observed an NSPCC report. 'Generally speaking, the faults with which children are credited by cruel people are the illusions of bad minds. Hating the child, hateful things are seen in it. The devil in *them* sees a devil in the *child*.'

188 The *'Illustrated Police News'*. . . On 27 July and 3 August 1895.

189 the *'Times' critic J. F. Nisbet*. . . In *The Human Machine* (1899).

189 *Pierre Janet*. . . Quoted in Nelson, *Precocious Children and Childish Adults*.

189 *Frederic Myers*. . . See his essay 'The Subliminal Consciousness' in *Proceedings of the Society for Psychical Research*, 1892.

PART IV: THE MURDERERS' PARADISE

CHAPTER 13: THOSE THAT KNOW NOT WHAT THEY DO

195 *Broadmoor asylum*. . . The Broadmoor archives are held at the Berkshire Record Office, Reading, Berkshire (BRO). For the layout, rules and routines at the asylum, see *Rules for the Guidance of Officers, Attendants, and Servants of Broadmoor Criminal Lunatic Asylum* (1869); Mark Stevens, *Broadmoor Revealed: Victorian Crime and the Lunatic Asylum* (2013) and *Life in the Victorian Asylum: the World of Nineteenth Century Mental Health Care* (2014); and the Superintendent's annual reports 1895–1912, BRO: D/H14/A2/1/1.

195 *'Hampshire Telegraph'*. . . 28 September 1895.

195 *His occupation*. . . See Admission Registers, 1863–1900, BRO: D/H14/D1/1.

196 *the sun shone*. . . See *London Standard*, 27 September 1895.

196 *an undulating landscape*. . . See George Griffith, *Sidelights on Convict Life* (1903) and 'Warmark', *Guilty but Insane: A Broadmoor Autobiography* (1931).

197 *'When questioned as to the murder. . .'* Note in Robert Coombes's file, BRO: D/H14/D2/2/1/1671, dated 24 September 1895. Under the current protocol between the Berkshire Record Office and the West London Mental Health Trust, Robert's case file is closed until 2042 (160 years after his birth), but the Trust allowed the BRO to disclose some of its contents.

197 *Broadmoor was built in the early 1860s*. . . For the history of the asylum, see Harvey Gordon, *Broadmoor* (2012); Stevens, *Broadmoor*

Revealed; and Ralph Partridge, *Broadmoor: A History of Criminal Lunacy and its Problems* (1953).

197 *the institution now held.* . . Figures from the Superintendent's annual report for 1895 in BRO: D/H14/A2/1/1.

197 *joined in the admissions ward.* . . From Admission Registers, 1863–1900, BRO: D/H14/D1/1.

197 *Henry Jackson.* . . See trial at OBSP; and Ward, *Psychiatry and Criminal Responsibility in England 1843–1939*.

198 *Carmello Mussy.* . . See his case file, BRO: D/H14/D2/2/1/1674, and his trial at OBSP.

198 *'Sheffield Independent'.* . . 19 September 1895.

199 *housed in single chambers.* . . In a meeting at Broadmoor reported in the *Journal of Mental Science* of April 1901, both the superintendent and his predecessor argued against the dormitory system and in favour of single rooms for intractable and well-behaved patients alike.

199 *An attendant drew the bolts.* . . See 'Warmark', *Guilty but Insane*.

200 *A few attendants kept watch.* . . See Frederick Dolman's article about Broadmoor in *Cassell's Magazine* of February 1899.

200 *The allotments were planted.* . . See G. W. Steevens, *Things Seen: Impressions of Men, Cities, and Books* (1900).

200 *Thomas Henry Townsend.* . . Quoted in John Edward Allen, *Inside Broadmoor* (1953).

200 *A typical dinner.* . . See Superintendent's annual reports in BRO: D/H14/A2/1/1.

201 *the attendants had snipped out any articles.* . . See Frederick Dolman's piece in *Cassell's Magazine* of February 1899.

201 *'Jude the Obscure'.* . . See Hayden Church, 'The Strange Case of Dr Minor: II', *The Strand*, January 1916.

202 *Throughout the night.* . . See 'A Visit to Broadmoor: a Day among Murderers', *Pall Mall Gazette,* 17 February 1886.

202 *an outspoken opponent of criminal anthropology.* . . In Nicolson's inaugural address as president of the Medico-Psychological Society, delivered in July 1895 and published in the *Journal of Mental Science* in October.

202 *'an insane man. . .'* and *'I prefer to train up. . .'* See Nicolson's evidence of 6 December 1894 in Departmental Committee on Prisons' *Report* and *Minutes of Evidence*, PP, C7702 (1895).

203 *Some of the patients.* . . See Charles Arthur Mercier, *The Attendant's Companion: The Manual of the Duties of Attendants in Lunatic Asylums* (1892).

203 *no mechanical restraints.* . . See 'Broadmoor Asylum and Its Inmates' in *The Green Bag: an Entertaining Magazine for Lawyers* (1893).

204 *The attendants at Broadmoor.* . . . Information on staff at Broadmoor
from the Defaulters Book, 1867–1922 (BRO: D/H14/B1/3/1/3); Order
Book: Attendants, 1863–1900 (BRO: D/H14/A2/1/7/1); Register of
Staff Appointments, 1862–1920 (BRO: D/14/B2/1/1); Staff Payments,
1863–1973 (BRO: D/H14/B3/1/1/3 and BRO: D/14/B3/1/1/4); and the
Superintendent's annual reports in BRO: D/H14/A2/1/1. Details of
the staff's ages, origins and families are chiefly from census returns;
Broadmoor patients are included in the returns, too, though from
1901 they are identified only by their initials.

204 *He would remind visitors.* . . . Such as Frederick Dolman, whose article
about Broadmoor was published in *Cassell's* in February 1899.

205 *the mental condition of Oscar Wilde.* . . . See Harford Montgomery
Hyde, *Oscar Wilde: the Aftermath* (1963).

205 *George Steevens.* . . . See Steevens, *Things Seen*; the chapter on
Broadmoor was first published as 'During Her Majesty's Pleasure' in
the *Daily Mail*, 24 November 1897.

205 *Robert Coombes was the youngest inmate.* . . . According to Gordon's
Broadmoor, one boy under sixteen had been admitted in the 1860s,
one in the 1870s and one in the 1880s. Of the three, two had been
convicted of arson. The ten-year-old arsonist who arrived in 1885
(who had turned twenty by the time of Robert's arrival) became the
longest-serving inmate of Broadmoor, remaining there until his death
in 1962.

206 *Nathaniel Currah.* . . . See BRO: D/H14/D2/2/1/1442; TNA: CRIM1/321;
and articles in *London Standard*, 24 June 1889, *Western Times*, 25
June 1889, and the *Era*, 29 June 1889. His examination by the alienist
Lyttelton Forbes Winslow is described in Winslow's *Mad Humanity:
Its Forms Apparent and Obscure* (1898). Though Sims does not
name him, he describes their encounter in *Cassell's Saturday Journal*,
reprinted in the *Otago Witness* of 10 December 1902 as 'Life Sketches
in Sunshine and Shadow: Broadmoor'. Currah died in Broadmoor in
1915.

207 *Several of Robert's fellow Block 2 inmates.* . . . The assignment of
some patients to the block is detailed in the Daily Log of Admissions,
Removals and Deaths, Male, January 1898–April 1913 (BRO: D/H14/
D1/7/1/1) and in the records of individual patients.

207 *Richard Oakes.* . . . See his case file, BRO: D/H14/D2/2/1/1492, and
OBSP. Oakes' suicide note is reproduced in William Booth's *In
Darkest England*.

208 *George Pett.* . . . See his case file, BRO: D/H14/D2/2/1/1689, and *Sussex
Advertiser*, 17 February 1896.

208 *'From time to time.* . . .' See 'Warmark', *Guilty but Insane*. The book's
author, George Penny, was not admitted to Broadmoor until 1923,

but he reported that the delusional doctor was the 'doyen' of Block 2, having been there for more than forty years.

209   *Archibald Campbell.* . . See his case file, BRO: D/H14/D2/2/1/1798.

209   *Isaac Jacob Mauerberger.* . . See *Reynolds's Newspaper*, 30 January 1887, and *Leeds Times*, 5 February 1887. He died in Broadmoor in 1925.

209   *Roderick Maclean.* . . Maclean's case file (BRO: D/H14/D2/2/1/1095, closed until 2022) reportedly suggests that he was resident in blocks other than Block 2, but he played for the Block 2 team several times in the early 1900s, according to the asylum's cricket books (BRO· D/H14/G1/1/1 and D/H14/G1/1/2). He seems to have been in the Block 2 day room during the visit by Sims in 1902 (Sims notices that a man who had shot at the Queen is reading a copy of *Punch* in the day room occupied by the most affluent inmates). His sonnet-writing in Broadmoor is described in an article by Julius M. Price in the *Westminster Budget* of 21 January 1898 – Price, too, seems to have seen him in the Block 2 day room. Maclean's case is described in Paul Thomas Murphy, *Shooting Victoria: Madness, Mayhem, and the Rebirth of the British Monarchy* (2012). Maclean died in the asylum in 1921.

209   *William Chester Minor.* . . See Simon Winchester, *The Surgeon of Crowthorne: A Tale of Murder, Madness and the Love of Words* (1998); Church, 'The Strange Case of Dr Minor: II' in *The Strand* of January 1916; and Stevens, *Broadmoor Revealed*.

210   *Some wore frock coats* . . . See Stevens, *Things Seen*.

210   *On one of his visits.* . . From Sims's article in *Cassell's Saturday Journal* in 1902.

210   *George Sims was invited into a bedroom.* . . See *Daily Mail*, 21 November 1905.

210   *Alfred Gamble.* . . See *Morning Post* of 12, 15 and 21 October 1895; *London Standard*, 15 October, 4, 5 and 13 December 1895; *Reynolds's Newspaper*, 29 October and 8 December 1895; *Lloyd's Weekly*, 8 December 1895. The Daily Log of Admissions, Removals and Deaths, Male, January 1898–April 1913 (BRO: D/H14/D1/7/1/1) indicates that he was discharged to the Salvation Army colony in Hadleigh in 1917.

211   *pronounced him an imbecile.* . . See OBSP.

211   *'Journal of Mental Science'.* . . In April 1896.

211   *Sherlock Hare.* . . See his case file, BRO: D/H14/D2/2/1/1553.

211   *the queen's sixtieth jubilee.* . . See *Reading Mercury*, 3 July 1897.

212   *swine fever.* . . See Superintendent's annual report of 1899 in BRO: D/H14/A2/1/1.

212   *the Boer War.* . . See *Reading Mercury*, 18 November 1899 and 17 March 1900.

212 *Jonathan Lowe.* . . See BRO: D/H14/D2/2/1/1779 and TNA: HO144/558/A60060. Lowe was in Block 5, the other of the two privilege blocks, when he wrote his letter, and was later transferred to Block 2. Another inmate who liked Broadmoor better than the world beyond its walls was August Deneis (or Denies), a Dutchman who was detained in the asylum in 1886, having attacked his wife with a mallet. He was discharged as sane in 1895, and entrusted to the care of his children in France, but in November 1896 he turned up at the asylum gates, begging to be readmitted. He died in Broadmoor in 1903. See Deneis' case file, BRO: D/H14/D2/2/1/1714.

213 *Lloyd's Weekly.* . . 7 August 1898.

213 *A former inmate.* . . Brailsford's letter is in Lowe's case file, BRO: D/ H14/D2/2/1/1779.

214 *One elderly inmate.* . . See 'A Visit to Broadmoor: a Day among Murderers', *Pall Mall Gazette*, 17 February 1886.

214 *'those that know not what they do. . .'* See Steevens, *Things Seen*. The inmate was alluding to Christ's words on the Cross, cited in the Gospel According to Luke: 'Father, forgive them; for they know not what they do.'

214 *the lunacy commissioners.* . . See Partridge, *Broadmoor*.

215 *Thomas Cutbush.* . . See his case file, BRO: D/H14/D2/2/1/1523. Cutbush died in the asylum in 1903.

215 *Arthur Gilbert Cooper.* . . See *Morning Post*, 16 November 1887. He died in the asylum in 1927.

215 *One morning in May.* . . See Pett's case file, BRO: D/H14/D2/2/1/1689.

215 *In November 1898, at the age of sixteen.* . . See Daily Log of Admissions, Removals and Deaths, Male, January 1898–April 1913 (BRO: D/H14/ D1/7/1/1).

CHAPTER 14: TO HAVE YOU HOME AGAIN

217 *a letter written by Emily Coombes.* . . Exhibit J in TNA: CRIM 1/42/9.

218 *'the nice little home. . .'* In Urwick (ed.), *Studies of Boy Life in Our Cities*, Reginald Bray reflects on the working-class ideal of 'the little home', which consisted not of the rented house itself but its moveable contents – the tables and chairs and pictures and ornaments. He notes the 'pride and affection' that the typical working family took in 'the little home that they have got together'.

218 *'your mother or Annie'.* . . That is, her husband's mother Mary Coombes and his widowed sister Anne, who lived together in Lockhart Street by Bow cemetery.

218 *'Mrs Cooper. . .'* Robert at first pretended that his mother was visiting a Mrs Cooper when his aunt confronted him in the back parlour on 17 July 1895.

219 *That Sunday's newspapers. . .* For instance, *Lloyd's Weekly* of 7 July 1895 reported that meat prices were 'still depressed' but 'firmer than last week'. The same paper carried an advertisement for *Light Ahead* at the Theatre Royal in Stratford, the play that Robert and Nattie were to attend two days later.

219 *hazy with heat. . .* See *Evening News* and *London Daily News*, 8 July 1895.

219–20 *presumably to sell or pawn. . .* It was common practice to pawn blankets and coats in the summer, with the intention of redeeming them in winter. See Tebbutt, *Making Ends Meet*.

CHAPTER 15: IN THE PLASTIC STAGE

221 *Robert was allowed back. . .* See Daily Log of Admissions, Removals and Deaths, Male, January 1898–April 1913 (BRO: D/H14/D1/7/1/1).

221 *worked in the tailors' shop. . .* Notes in his file (BRO: D/H14/D2/2/1/1671) indicate that he was working there in May 1896 and on 18 November 1904. 'Shows a fair degree of application at work in tailor's shop,' according to a note dated 5 April 1897. In total, according to the Superintendent's reports, about forty-five men worked in the various workshops.

221 *They cut the winter jackets. . .* See Superintendent's annual reports in BRO: D/H14/A2/1/1 and 'Warmark', *Guilty but Insane*.

222 *an eighth of the going rate. . .* See Griffith, *Sidelights on Convict Life*.

222 *Charles Leach Pike. . .* His appointment as master tailor was announced in the *London Gazette* of 2 January 1895. The *Reading Mercury* noted his participation in many shows and concerts over the next twenty years.

222 *vice-captain of the Broadmoor Cycling Club. . .* Reading Mercury, 18 March 1899.

222 *The costumes for the shows. . . Reading Mercury*, 2 January 1904.

222 *an enthusiastic member of the asylum's brass band. . .* Notes in Robert's file (BRO: D2/2/1/1671) in 1905, 1907 and 1911 indicate that he was playing in the 'asylum band', presumably the brass band, and in 1907 he was said to take a 'great interest' in it. Since he emerged from Broadmoor able to play the violin and piano as

well as the cornet it is likely that he also played with the string band, which was accompanied by the tailor Charles Pike and included Block 2 staff such as Coleman and Block 2 patients such as Frank Rodgers.

222 *The editor of 'The British Bandsman'.* . . Sam Cope, quoted in Trevor Herbert, *The British Brass Band: A Musical and Social History* (2000).

223 *a concert on the Broadmoor cricket pitch.* . . *Reading Mercury*, 2 June 1900.

223 *his impersonation in November 1900.* . . *Reading Mercury*, 24 November 1900.

224 *Sherlock Hare.* . . See his case file, BRO: D/H14/D2/2/1/1553.

224 *the death of Queen Victoria.* . . *Reading Mercury*, 26 January and 9 February 1901.

225 *the coronation.* . . *Reading Mercury*, 13 December 1902.

225 *a fireball.* . . *Reading Mercury*, 16 June 1900.

225 *an attendant's three-year-old son.* . . *Reading Mercury*, 30 June 1900.

225 *an attendant was invalided out.* . . *Reading Mercury*, 8 November 1902.

225 *Coleman hurried to the aid of William Chester Minor.* . . Minor was discharged to the care of his brother in America in 1910.

225 *'RAC rather depressed. . .'* Noted in his case file, BRO: D/H14/ D2/2/1/1671.

225 *excelled at billiards.* . . Noted in 1902 in his case file, BRO: D/H14/ D2/2/1/1671, and reported in Martin Smith's blog streathambrixtonchess.blogspot.co.uk.

225 *a frayed old table.* . . See Griffith, *Sidelights on Convict Life.* 'I should say that it dates from somewhere in the Fifties,' observes Griffith. 'At any rate, it looks a great deal older than the asylum itself, although, of course, it amply fulfils its purpose, and is quite as suitable for the playing of a match between a homicide and an incendiary as the most up-to-date exhibition table would be.'

225 *taking bets in batches of tobacco.* . . See Sims's article of 1902 in *Cassell's Saturday Journal.*

226 *allotted an ounce of tobacco.* . . See Griffith, *Sidelights on Convict Life.*

226 *Dr Brayn used to tell.* . . See Hargrave Lee Adam, *The Story of Crime: From the Cradle to the Grave* (1908).

226 *played chess.* . . According to a note in his case file, BRO: D/H14/ D2/2/1/1671, reported in streathambrixtonchess.blogspot.co.uk.

226 *Edward Oxford.* . . *and Richard Dadd.* . . See Stevens, *Broadmoor Revealed*, Murphy, *Shooting Victoria*, and streathambrixtonchess. blogspot.co.uk.

226 *Reginald Saunderson.* . . See TNA: CRIM1/41/4 and Winslow, *Mad Humanity*. For his chess prowess, and details of the match in which he and Robert competed between 1903 and 1904, see Tim Harding,

Correspondence Chess in Britain and Ireland 1824–1987 (2010) and streathambrixtonchess.blogspot.co.uk. Reginald Treherne Bassett Saunderson died in Broadmoor in 1943.

228 *both Robert and Saunderson played cricket. . .* For cricket players, see cricket score books at BRO: D/H14/G1/1/1 (July 1904 to Aug 1906) and D/H14/G1/1/2 (June 1907 to July 1908).

228 *the asylum's strictures on cricket. . .* See *Rules for the Guidance of Officers, Attendants, and Servants of Broadmoor Criminal Lunatic Asylum.*

228 *the Reverend Hugh Wood. . .* See cricketarchive.com. Wood left Broadmoor in 1906 and was succeeded by the Reverend Albert Whiteley, a Yorkshire grammar-school boy and Cambridge graduate who remained at the asylum until 1934.

229 *the laying of a new pitch. . .* See Partridge, *Broadmoor.*

229 *Sandhurst Royal Military College and the Windsor police. . .* See cricket score book 1907–08, BRO: D/H14/G1/1/2.

229 *listed in the local paper. . . Reading Mercury,* 6 July 1907.

229 *George Melton. . .* See *London Standard,* 13 March 1896, and BRO: D/H14/D2/2/1/1695.

229 *Henry Spurrier. . .* See *Hampshire Advertiser,* 18 February 1899. According to the admissions register (BRO: D/H14/D1/1), he was discharged to the care of the Salvation Army in 1923.

229 *Kenneth Murchison. . .* One of the best gunners in South Africa, Murchison had played a decisive part in the battle of Cannon Kopje at the beginning of the siege of Mafeking. When the Boers prepared to attack Mafeking on 31 October 1899, Colonel Baden-Powell sent about fifty men to fight them off from a small hill outside the walls. Murchison was put in charge of a seven-pounder cannon, which he used to tremendous effect, and by the end of the day the small band of British soldiers had defeated a force of about a thousand Boers. The next evening, Murchison dined at Dixon's Hotel in Mafeking with a British war reporter. The pair drank heavily and in the course of the meal Murchison's companion began to taunt him, accusing him of knowing nothing about guns; as they left the hotel, the journalist followed the lieutenant out into the town square, still goading him. Murchison suddenly pulled out his pistol and shot the man dead. Afterwards Murchison was bewildered and distraught, claiming to have no memory of the shooting. Pending his court-martial, he was confined in a gaol in Mafeking, from which he was temporarily released – with a rifle – when the Boers launched a heavy attack on the town in May 1900. He helped to drive back the enemy by nightfall and then returned to his cell. In June 1900, after the relief of Mafeking, Murchison was court-martialled by Baden-Powell, found guilty and

sentenced to death. Thanks to a petition by his friends, the sentence was commuted to life imprisonment and he was sent to Parkhurst prison on the Isle of Wight. In 1902, the South African war ended with a British victory over the Boers. After further pleas for clemency, Murchison was deemed to have been insane at the time of his crime, and was transferred to Broadmoor. See *Oxford Journal*, 11 August 1900, *Lloyd's Weekly*, 3 June 1900, *Warwick Argus*, 22 September 1900, and TNA: HO144/946/A61992. He died in Broadmoor in 1917.

229   *Thomas Shultz*. . . See trial in OBSP. Shultz was discharged to the care of his father in 1910.

229   *Frank Rodgers*. . . Account of his crime from the *Cambridge Daily News*, 3 and 4 June 1904, and the *Herts and Cambs Reporter and Royston Crow*, 14, 15, 16, 21 and 29 April 1904, reproduced on meldrethhistory.org.uk. Details of his crime and his time in Broadmoor from TNA: HO144/995/119149.

232   *Thomas Anstey Guthrie's 'Vice Versa'*. . . The boy in this novel is discussed in Nelson, *Precocious Children and Childish Adults*.

233   *Granville Stanley Hall's 'Adolescence'*. . . Quotes from Ferrall and Jackson, *Juvenile Literature and British Society 1850–1950*. Hall claims that psychoses and neuroses are especially common in early adolescence. He reminds his readers of 'the omnipresent dangers of precocity' in 'our urbanised hothouse life, that tends to ripen everything before its time', and recommends that a child be encouraged to visit nature, the 'wild, undomesticated stage from which modern conditions have kidnapped and transported him'. Quoted in Shuttleworth, *The Mind of the Child*.

235   *He was one of 175 patients*. . . See Partridge, *Broadmoor*.

235   *Patrick Knowles*. . . See TNA: T1/11342 and TNA: HO144/11429.

236   *In his fifteen years in charge*. . . See Partridge, *Broadmoor*.

236   *In the most recent of these*. . . See Gwen Adshead, 'A transient frenzy?', *British Medical Journal*, 1 August 1998.

237   *The band played*. . . *Reading Mercury*, 3 February 1912.

238   *Dr Brayn had taken the view*. . . In a report in Robert's case file (BRO: D/H14/D2/2/1/1671) dated 20 July 1905, Brayn assessed his mental condition as 'rational and tranquil', but replied 'yes' when asked whether his insanity might recur if he were discharged. A Home Office note in the file suggests that the same assessment was made each May between 1906 and 1911.

238   *As Brayn told a visiting journalist*. . . See Griffith, *Sidelights on Convict Life*.

238   *Baker wrote to the home secretary*. . . Letter in Robert's case file, BRO: D/H14/D2/2/1/1671.

238 *'He is not likely to trouble the Broadmoor authorities. . .'* From 'Mustard & Cress', a column written by George Sims under the alias Dagonet, *Sunday Referee,* 22 September 1895.

239 *he handed back his uniform. . .* For the discharge process, see 'Warmark', *Guilty but Insane.*

239 *in the custody of Charles Pike. . .* According to a note in Robert's case file, BRO: D/H14/D2/2/1/1671.

PART V: WITH TRUMPETS AND SOUND OF CORNET

CHAPTER 16: SMOOTH IN THE MORNING LIGHT

243 *An Essex woman. . .* See *Chelmsford Chronicle,* 15 March 1912.

244 *Colony at Hadleigh. . .* For a history of the colony, see H. Rider Haggard, *The Poor and the Land: Report on the Salvation Army Colonies in the United States and at Hadleigh, England, with Scheme of National Land Resettlement* (1905) and *Regeneration: Being an Account of the Social Work of the Salvation Army in Great Britain* (1910); Mark Sorrell, 'The Farm Colony at Hadleigh, Essex' in *Essex Journal,* spring and winter 1992; Anon, *Hadleigh: The Story of a Great Endeavour* (Salvation Army Press, 1902); Walter Besant, 'The Farm and the City', *Living Age,* 29 January 1898; Anon, 'Up from Despair: the Salvation Army Industrial Colony at Hadleigh' in *Boston Evening Transcript,* 4 May 1901; Gordon Parkhill and Graham Cook, *Hadleigh Salvation Army Farm: A Vision Reborn* (2008).

244 *The Salvation Army. . .* See Pamela J. Walker, *Pulling the Devil's Kingdom Down: The Salvation Army in Victorian Britain* (2001) and Boone, *Youth of Darkest England.*

245 *8,000 of the 11,000 Mancunians who volunteered for service. . .* See Urwick (ed.), *Studies of Boy Life in Our Cities,* which also reported that 30 per cent of young men examined for the Army nationwide were rejected as unfit, and a further 40 per cent were thrown out in their first two years of service. The decline in men's health was attributed by the author to the massive shift of population over the previous fifty years from the country to the town.

245 *'We came down in a farm wagon. . .'* Quoted in an illustrated guide to the Hadleigh farm colony published by the Salvation Army in 1926.

245 *despatched to Canada. . . Essex Newsman,* 29 March 1912.

247 *he wrote to the chief steward*. . . Robert's requests and acknowl-
edgements, addressed to Alexander Sayer at Broadmoor from Castle
House in Hadleigh, are in his case file, BRO: D/H14/D2/2/1/1671.

247 *He could see*. . . Description of the view adapted from the Salvation
Army publication *Hadleigh: the Story of a Great Endeavour*.

247 *Robert's father had moved out*. . . When he left London as chief steward on the *France* on 10 October 1895, he gave his address as 509
Barking Road, Plaistow – see NMM: RSS/CL/1895/60015 SS *France*.

248 *found time to visit his son*. . . A note in Robert's case file, BRO:
D2/2/1/1671, shows that his father visited on 26 November 1895 – no
further visits were recorded from him or anyone else, but the case
files rarely include such records and no visitors' log from the period
survives.

248 *Charlie Sharman was declared bankrupt*. . . For his bankruptcy and
theft from clients, see *Essex Newsman*, 12 September 1896, and
Chelmsford Chronicle, 20 November 1896. For his alleged assault,
see *Chelmsford Chronicle*, 19 February 1897. For his career in organised crime, see James Morton, *East End Gangland* (2009). He was
convicted of theft at the Old Bailey in 1925, at the age of seventy-five,
and sentenced to three years' penal servitude. He died in 1933, five
years after his release from Dartmoor prison.

249 *Nattie remained the smaller*. . . See his Royal Navy record, TNA:
ADM 188/500/306663.

249 *'the lowest class of sailorman'*. . . Robert Machray, *The Night Side of
London* (1902).

249 *Nattie had been scarred*. . . See his Royal Navy and Royal Australian
Navy records, TNA: ADM 188/500/306663 and NAA: A6770,
Coombes NG.

249 *The stokers 'come and go*. . .' In Chadwick et al., *Ocean Steamships*.

250 *He had been lent*. . . See Nattie's RAN record of service, NAA: A6770,
Coombes NG.

250 *HMAS 'Australia'*. . . See Vince Fazio, *The Battlecruiser HMAS
Australia, First Flagship of the Royal Australian Navy: A Story of
Her Life and Times* (2000) and www.navy.gov.au/hmas-australia-i.

250 *'I have been down many coal mines*. . .' See *Maitland Daily Mercury*,
27 September 1913 .

250 *hailed by the defence minister*. . . See www.navy.gov.au/hmas-australia-i.

250 *to execute his father's will*. . . When probate was granted on 11
October 1913, Robert gave his occupation as 'tailor' and his address
as 'West View, Hadleigh' – West View was a two-storey dormitory
with its own library, which had been built in 1912.

250 *He sailed on 2 January 1914*. . . See passenger list for SS *Otranto* in
TNA: Passenger Lists Leaving UK 1890–1960 (BT 27).

251 *She sailed out to the Atlantic.* . . . See *Sydney Evening News* and *Perth Daily News*, 3 February 1914.

251 *Nattie had lodgings.* . . . For Nattie's address in Australia, see RAN record of service, NAA: A6770, Coombes NG. He gave his next of kin as his cousin Robert Macy, the son of his aunt Mary, who had moved to Newcastle, NSW, a few years earlier.

251 *He found work.* . . . See 13th Battalion embarkation roll, AWM: 8/23/30/1.

CHAPTER 17: SUCH A HELL OF A NOISE

253 *When war broke out.* . . . See Peter Pedersen, *The Anzacs: Gallipoli to the Western Front* (2007).

253 *About a quarter.* . . . See Peter Hart, *Gallipoli* (2011).

253 *Robert trained in a series of camps.* . . . Account of training camps from Thomas A. White, *The Fighting Thirteenth: The History of the 13th Battalion AIF* (1924); Arthur Graham Butler, *Official History of the Australian Army Medical Services, 1914–1918, Volume I – Gallipoli, Palestine and New Guinea* (2nd edition, 1938); Winsome McDowell Paul, *Blessed with a Cheerful Nature: a Reading of the Letters of Lieutenant George Stanley McDowell MC, 13th Battalion AIF 1914–1917* (2005); and diary of Charles Francis Laseron, ML: MSS 1133, at Mitchell Library, State Library of New South Wales.

254 *Robert was assigned to the 13th Battalion.* . . . For his service with the 13th Battalion, from September 1914 to December 1915, see 13th Battalion embarkation roll (AWM: 8/23/30/1) at Australian War Memorial in Canberra (awm.gov.au) and his AIF record (NAA: B2455, Coombes RA) at National Archives of Australia in Canberra (naa.gov.au).

255 *Robert was one of about twenty-eight men selected.* . . . A picture of the band was published in *Sunday Times*, Sydney, 29 November 1914.

255 *the band marched through Melbourne.* . . . See diary of Byron Hobson, AWM: 2DRL/0694.

255 *During the six-week voyage.* . . . Account of life on board from diaries of the 13th Battalion soldiers William Frederick Shirtley (AWM: 2DRL/0792), Byron Hobson (AWM: 2DRL/0694), Charles Francis Laseron (ML: MSS 1133) and Eric Susman (ML: CY4933 1–98). See also *Barrier Miner,* 5 February 1915, and Bea Brewster and Marie Kau (eds), *Diary of Bandsman H. E. Krutli, D Company, 14th Battalion, 4th Infantry Brigade Australian Imperial Forces (AIF): September 1914 to April 1916* (2009). Krutli played with the 14th Battalion band, which travelled on the same transport as the 13th.

257   *The 13th trained hard*. . . Account of 13th in Egypt from diaries of
      Laseron, Shirtley, Susman and Hobson (see above), 13th Infantry
      Battalion war diaries November 1914–December 1915 (AWM:
      4, 23/30/1–14) and White, *The Fighting Thirteenth*.
257   '*The Terror*'. . . See photographs by Joseph Cecil Thompson at www.
      flickr.com/photos/eethompson.
257   *the same penny fiction*. . . A few commentators connected the spirit
      of the dreadfuls to the practice of war. 'Do not grow indignant when
      you see an errand boy with his eyes glued to a penny dreadful!' cau-
      tioned the *Aberdeen Evening Express* on 23 May 1917. 'We have seen
      in the heroism of our battlefield the result of the love of courage and
      adventure it engenders and keeps alive.' In the *Century Magazine* of
      November 1916, St John G. Ervine described the armed insurrection
      in Dublin in Easter 1916 as an accident that grew out of romantic
      fantasies: 'It was as if boys, letting their imaginations feed too fat on
      penny dreadfuls, had forgotten that they were only pretending to be
      wild Indians attacking Buffalo Bill, and had suddenly scalped a com-
      panion or halved his skull with a tomahawk.'
257   *At the start of a night march*. . . Described by the 13th Battalion
      bandmaster, Percy 'Richo' Copp, *Reveille*, 1 May 1940.
258   *their battalion's stretcher-bearers*. . . Account of training from George
      M. Dupuy, *The Stretcher Bearer* (1915).
258   *On 11 April, recalled Sergeant Charles Laseron*. . . Account of trip to
      Gallipoli mainly from Laseron's diary (see above), and his article in
      the *Sunday Times*, Sydney, on 11 July 1915. In the newspaper version,
      he softened the punchline of the song about Major Ellis, replacing
      'May God strike him dead' with 'Something strike him red'. Details
      also drawn from White, *The Fighting Thirteenth*; diaries of Susman,
      Hobson and Shirtley (see above); Copp's reminiscences in *Reveille*,
      1 May 1940; and recollections of Lt W. H. Mankey in *Sunday Times*,
      Perth, 11 June 1916.
259   *Gallipoli*. . . Account of Gallipoli campaign chiefly from Charles
      Bean, *The Story of Anzac, Vols I & II* (11th edition, 1941); Pedersen,
      The Anzacs; Hart, *Gallipoli*; Butler, *Official History of the Australian
      Army Medical Services, 1914–1918, Vol. I*. Details of 13th Battalion
      at Gallipoli from White, *The Fighting Thirteenth*; the battalion's
      war diaries November 1914–December 1915 (AWM: 4, 23/30/1–14);
      Thomas Ray Crooks's war diary, 11 February 1915 to 24 May 1918
      (ML: MSS 838); and diaries of Laseron, Hobson, Shirtley (see
      above).
260   *The bearers were kept busy*. . . See Butler, *Official History of the
      Australian Army Medical Services, 1914–1918, Vol. I*; Emily Mayhew,
      Wounded: From Battlefield to Blighty, 1914–18 (2013); Mark

Johnston, *Stretcher-Bearers: Saving Australians from Gallipoli to Kokoda* (2015); Joseph Lievesley Beeston, *Five Months at Anzac: a Narrative of Personal Experiences of the Officer Commanding the 4th Field Ambulance, Australian Imperial Force* (1916); and war diary of Frederick Wray, chaplain to 4th Brigade, AWM: PR00247.

261 *'The stretcher-bearers are great. . .'* From letter to the editor of the *Sydney Morning Herald* by Harold G. Massey, cited in P. Cochrane, *Simpson and the Donkey: the Making of a Legend* (1992).

261 *Private Ray Lingard. . .* Letter printed in *Newcastle Morning Herald and Miners' Advocate*, 16 July 1915.

262 *James Dow. . .* See transcript of Dow's letter at ddoughty.com. According to his AIF record (NAA: B2455, Dow, JG), Dow was invalided home with neurasthenia in April 1916. According to Ben Shephard's *A War of Nerves: Soldiers and Psychiatrists in the Twentieth Century* (2000), the troops most vulnerable to shell shock in the First World War were those who were obliged to endure enemy assaults without being able to retaliate.

263 *'It was just hell pure and simple. . .'* George McClintock, quoted in Pedersen, *The Anzacs*.

263 *'Some of these are very ghastly. . .'* Quoted in Pedersen, *The Anzacs*.

263 *'We have been fighting now. . .'* Quoted in Hart, *Gallipoli*.

264 *'There is not a front line. . .'* In a letter to Sorrell's parents in Lithgow, reproduced in *Sydney Morning Herald*, 29 June 1915.

265 *'Grenades like showers of peas. . .'* Quoted in Hart, *Gallipoli*.

267 *Robert had escaped serious injury. . .* He had been blown up twice on Gallipoli and also sustained a gunshot wound, according to the information he gave on being discharged – see repatriation case file NAA: C138/ R30557.

267 *Robert's fellow bearer James Dow. . .* See ddoughty.com.

268 *About 10,000 AIF soldiers. . .* See Butler, *Official History of the Australian Army Medical Services, 1914–1918*, *Vol. I.*

268 *Nattie was also serving. . .* Some 850 Royal Navy men were serving with the Royal Australian Navy at the outbreak of the war, comprising about a fifth of the RAN. Nattie's war career is detailed in NAA: A6770, Coombes NG. For the fortunes of the *Australia* see Arthur Wilberforce Jose, *Official History of Australia in the War of 1914–1918 Volume IX: The Royal Australian Navy, 1914–1918* (9th edition, 1941) and Fazio, *The Battlecruiser HMAS Australia*.

268 *'The perspiration dripped. . .'* See *Richmond River Herald*, 4 January 1916.

268 *rabbit-skin coats. . .* See *Graphic*, 9 June 1916.

268 *transferred to one of the sanitary sections. . .* Robert was assigned to the 3rd Sanitary Section in February and transferred to the 4th

Sanitary Section when the 4th Division was created in March. For his service with the 4th Sanitary Section, from March to October 1916, see NAA: B2455, Coombes RA; the 4th Sanitary Section war diaries (AWM: 4 26/79); and Butler, *Official History of the Australian Army Medical Services, 1914–1918, Vol. II – The Western Front* (1941).

269   *building box-latrines*. . . Charles Bean, *The Story of Anzac, Vol. III: the Australian Imperial Force in France, 1916.*

269   *the first anniversary of the Gallipoli landings*. . . See McDowell Paul, *Blessed with a Cheerful Nature.*

270   *recommended for a Military Medal*. . . See www.awm.gov.au/people/rolls/R1583110.

271   *incidence of shellshock*. . . 236 cases were diagnosed in the 4th Division in 1916, compared to three in the 3rd Division, according to Butler's *Official History of the Australian Army Medical Services, 1914–1918, Vol. II*; the author points out that this may have been in part because the 4th's Medical Officer was more inclined to diagnose the condition.

271   *Sergeant Rodgers*. . . See Frank Rodgers's record (regimental number 47019) in TNA: British Army WW1 Service Records, 1914–20 and his medal card at TNA: WO 372/17/65366. The record indicates that Frank's life after the war was rockier. In 1929 he was remanded at Marylebone police court on a charge of larceny and receiving. He died in Lambeth in 1965.

271   *45th Battalion*. . . For Robert's service with the 45th Battalion, from October 1916 to October 1918, see NAA: B2455, Coombes RA; the 45th Battalion diaries (AWM: 4 23/62); Butler, *Official History of the Australian Army Medical Services, 1914–1918, Vol. II*; and J. E. Lee, *The Chronicle of the 45th Battalion, AIF* (1927).

272   *the 'London Gazette' announced*. . . On 27 October 1916. See www.awm.gov.au/people/rolls/R1542612.

272   *'It was too bad!'*. . . *Cairns Post*, 28 April 1919.

272   *Robert proved an effective bandmaster*. . . According to the reminiscences of Henry Herbert Neaves of the 45th Battalion (AWM: 2DRL/0752), Robert 'proceeded to lick the bandsmen into shape'. In his history of the 45th Battalion, J. E. Lee reported, 'The men soon became very proud of their band whose influence in assisting to maintain the morale of the unit in the strenuous months ahead was invaluable.'

273   *William Alabaster*. . . See NAA: B2455, Alabaster W, and letters from Alabaster to his family, AWM: 1DRL/0016.

273   *The AIF no longer used its musicians*. . . In 'The Stretcher-Bearer Tradition', an essay in *As You Were: A Cavalcade of Events With the Australian Services From 1788–1947* (1947), Charles Bean explained, 'Until the First Battle of the Somme many battalions had used their bandsmen as stretcher-bearers. After that battle this

system generally was abandoned. For one thing, after such battles the band was too badly needed for cheering up the troops! A battle like Pozières sometimes made a clean sweep of the regimental bearers. Also, on its side, the work of the bearers was too important to be left to unselected men; they were now specially selected for their physique and guts.'

273   *marching out to meet the troops.* . . In a diary entry of 26 February 1917, Thomas Ray Crooks records, 'Our Band came up from "Dernancourt" this afternoon and gave the Bn some music, cheered the boys up a little' (ML: MSS 838).

273   *it struck camp once every five days.* . . See Lee, *The Chronicle of the 45th Battalion, AIF.*

273   *the band sometimes led the way.* . . In diary entries of 27 February 1917, for example, Thomas Crooks and James Vincent of the 45th record that the band led the battalion from Mametz to Bècourt (Crooks diary, ML: MSS 838, and Vincent diary, AWM: PR90/025).

273   *The mechanisms in the men's rifles.* . . See E. P. F. Lynch, *Somme Mud: The Experiences of an Infantryman in France, 1916–1919,* a fictionalised memoir by a 45th Battalion soldier, composed in the 1920s, edited by Will Davies and published in 2006.

274   *On the coldest nights.* . . See G. D. Mitchell, *Backs to the Wall: A Larrikin on the Western Front* (1937).

274   *Christmas Day 1916.* . . See war reminiscences of H. H. Neaves, AWM: 2DRL/0752.

274   *'We live in a world of Somme mud. . .'* From Lynch, *Somme Mud.*

275   *Herring recommended him for the Military Medal. . .* See www.awm.gov.au/people/rolls/R1594096. The award was announced in the *London Gazette,* 16 August 1917 – see www.awm.gov.au/people/rolls/R1520876.

275   *'We're a pretty casual sort of army. . .'* From Lynch, *Somme Mud.*

275   *Robert and his friend Bill Alabaster.* . . Robert told Red Cross staff that he had spent a leave with Alabaster and knew his people in Forest Gate (Red Cross wounded and missing roll, AWM: 1DRL/0428).

276   *A photographer took a series of pictures.* . . The photographs were taken at Meteren on 6 March 1918. See AWM: E01790 and E01791.

276   *On 5 April he was hit by a shell.* . . See Red Cross wounded and missing roll, AWM: 1DRL/0428.

277   *the Grand Theatre.* . . They performed at the Grand Theatre du Havre on 15 and 16 August 1918. See AWM: PUBS002/004/001/001/015.

277   *granted special leave.* . . See NAA: C137/ R30557.

277   *He and the other soldiers were greeted.* . . See *Sydney Morning Herald,* 30 December 1918.

277   *Of the 32,000 men.* . . See Anthony MacDougall, *ANZACs: Australians At War* (1991).

EPILOGUE: ANOTHER BOY

280   *'the air was electrical'*. . . See Morrison, *Tales of Mean Streets*. 'Several large and successful movements had quickened a spirit of restlessness in the neighbourhood,' he writes, 'and no master was sure of his men.'

280   *'a stirring and an agitation*. . .' From Masterman, *The Heart of Empire*.

281   *it has remained a very rare crime*. . . See C. M. Green, 'Matricide by Sons', *Medicine, Science and the Law*, 21 (1981); and Federal Bureau of Investigation, *Crime in the United States* (1998).

281–2   *Adolescent boys who kill their mothers*. . . See Kathleen M. Heide and Autumn Frei, 'Matricide: a Critique of the Literature' in *Trauma, Violence, & Abuse II* (2010); Kathleen M. Heide, *Understanding Parricide: When Sons and Daughters Kill Parents* (2012); B. F. Corder, B. C. Ball, T. M. Haizlip, R. Rollins and R. Beaumont, 'Adolescent Parricide: A Comparison with Other Adolescent Murder', *American Journal of Psychiatry*, 133 (1976); K. M. Heide, *Why Kids Kill Parents: Child Abuse and Adolescent Homicide* (1992); D. J. Scherl and J. E. Mack, 'A Study of Adolescent Matricide', *Journal of the American Academy of Child Psychology*, 5 (1966); D. H. Russell, 'A Study of Juvenile Murderers of Family Members', *International Journal of Offender Therapy & Comparative Criminology*, 28 (1984); Frederic Wertham, *Dark Legend: a Study in Murder* (1941); E. Tanay, 'Adolescents who Kill Parents: Reactive parricide', *Australian and New Zealand Journal of Psychiatry*, 7 (1973).

282   *Psychiatrists have suggested*. . . See Wertham, *Dark Legend*, Green, 'Matricide by Sons', Scherl and Mack, 'A Study of Adolescent Matricide'.

282   *in myth and literature*. . . See Gilbert Murray, *Hamlet and Orestes* (1914); M. Kanzer, 'Dostoevsky's Matricidal Impulses', *Psychoanalytic Review*, 35 (1948); Green, 'Matricide by Sons'; Wertham, *Dark Legend* and 'The Matricidal Impulse: Critique of Freud's Interpretation of *Hamlet*', *Journal of Criminal Psychopathology*, 2 (1941); Aeschylus, *Oresteia* (circa 458 BC); Robert Bloch, *Psycho* (1959); Fyodor Dostoevsky, *Crime and Punishment* (1861); William Shakespeare, *The Tragedy of Hamlet, Prince of Denmark* (circa 1600).

283   *a psychiatrist*. . . Carine Minne, consultant psychiatrist in forensic psychotherapy at Broadmoor Hospital, Berkshire, and the Portman Clinic, London.

283   *a photograph of his gravestone*. . . On austceindex.com.

285   *Henry Alexander Mulville*. . . Account of his life from a handwritten memoir by Harry Mulville and from conversations and emails with his youngest daughter and her husband.

285   *a hand-cranked punt*. . . Charles Mulville paid £135 a year for the right to run the Tyndale ferry – see Lismore *Northern Star*, 18 January 1918. Harry said that he took £15 a month in fares.

287   *Sydney Mail*. . . 29 June 1927.

288   *Smith's marriage was dissolved*. . . The dissolution of his marriage to Pearl May Smith (née Garland) was announced in the *Sydney Morning Herald*, 15 January 1930. Entry on Harold William Smith, Pearl May Smith and Victor Rose (co-respondent) in the Matrimonial Causes files at the New South Wales State Library in Sydney (8/3110, 482.1928 and 8/3110, 1543.1928). 'I would not go back to Smith again,' Pearl told the official who served divorce papers on her. For his marriage to Bertha, see Grafton *Daily Examiner*, 10 May 1930.

288   *a well-known and well-to-do family*. . . See obituaries of his father and mother, William and Elizabeth Smith of Wollongbar House, in Lismore *Northern Star*, 25 April 1923 and 13 May 1925.

288   *declared bankrupt in 1898*. . . See *Sydney Mail and New South Wales Advertiser*, 19 February 1898.

288   *he had served for only five months*. . . He was a part-time trooper with the New South Wales Lancers from 1900, and volunteered for the AIF in November 1915. See NAA: B2455, Smith W. See also Jean Bou, *Light Horse: a History of Australia's Mounted Arm* (2009).

288   *convicted of assaulting a man*. . . See Lismore *Northern Star*, 11 March 1899.

289   *Robert had settled in Nana Glen*. . . He appears in New South Wales electoral registers as a farmer in Glenreagh and Nana Glen from 1920 to 1949. For the experience of soldiers in the aftermath of the Great War, see Stephen Garton, *The Cost of War: Australians Return* (1996).

289   *the dense web of the bush*. . . For history of the flora and fauna of the Orara Valley see *Orara River Rehabilitation Project, Landholders Booklet*, published by Coffs Harbour City Council in 2012.

289   *The region around the Orara*. . . For history of the area, see Mary and Clarrie Brewer, *Looking Back: Nana Glen, 1879–1979* (1979), Annette Green and Margaret Franklin, *A History of Nana Glen Primary School, 1892–1992* (1992), Elizabeth Webb, *Glenreagh: a Town of Promise* (1998), John Vader, *Red Gold: the Tree that Built a Nation* (2002), Nan Cowling (ed.), *Coffs Harbour Time Capsule Book: 1847–2011* (2011).

290   *The cans were collected*. . . Account of the Orara to Grafton cream truck run in *Sydney Morning Herald*, 29 March 1932. For dairy industry, see Terry Kass, *Regional History of the North Coast* (1989).

291   *Nana Glen public school.* . . Harry enrolled at the school in September
        1928, according to the Nana Glen Public School Register 1928–1981
        at the Coff's Harbour District Family History Society.
292   *Cundy was injured.* . . Grafton *Daily Examiner*, 30 July 1930.
292   *Harry was seriously injured.* . . See Grafton *Daily Examiner*, 21 June
        1930, and *Sydney Morning Herald*, 23 June 1930. None of the family
        is identified in these reports.
294   *Harold Smith moved with his family to Grafton.* . . Smith was found
        guilty of assaulting Isaac Cundy, and fined a further £7 plus £10 9/- in
        medical and witness expenses. See Grafton *Daily Examiner*, 30 July
        1930.
294   *he had to re-enrol.* . . See Nana Glen Public School Register 1928–
        1981, Coff's Harbour District Family History Society.
297   *the band kept going.* . . In 1925, for instance, the 45th Battalion band
        performed in a competition in Taree, 150 miles south of Nana Glen,
        in a military tattoo to welcome the American fleet to Sydney, and
        in the Sydney Armistice Day parade (*Cessnock Eagle and South
        Maitland Recorder*, 5 May 1925, *Sydney Morning Herald*, 31 July
        and 10 November 1925). From 1928, the band also played at battalion
        reunions. The popularity of brass bands in Australia faded after the
        advent of radio in the 1920s. See Duncan Bythell, 'The Brass Band
        in the Antipodes: the Transplantation of British Popular Culture', in
        Herbert, *The British Brass Band*.
297   *competed in chess tournaments.* . . See *Australasian*, 26 November
        1927 and 14 January 1928.
299   *after a year of drought.* . . See *Barrier Miner*, Brisbane *Courier-Mail*,
        Grafton *Daily Examiner* and Lismore *Northern Star*, 29 October
        1936, and Brewer, *Looking Back*. In 1945 Robert wrote to the AIF to
        request replacements for the discharge papers that had been destroyed
        in the blaze (see NAA: B2455, Coombes RA). He said that since he
        did not have his birth certificate he needed the papers for 'some legal
        formalities' – he may have been applying for a pension: if he had been
        born in 1886, as he had claimed when he joined the Army in 1940, he
        would have been about to turn sixty.
299   *the 15th Light Horse Regiment.* . . The Light Horse had just doubled
        its troopers' pay to eight shillings a day. See Bou, *Light Horse*.
300   *The couple won.* . . See Grafton *Daily Examiner*, 14 October 1938 and
        6 June 1939.
301   *Robert volunteered for the 8th Garrison Battalion.* . . See NAA: B884,
        N105727. Call for recruits and terms of service in *Newcastle Morning
        Herald*, 21 November 1940.
301   *led the Armistice Day parade.* . . See *Newcastle Morning Herald*,
        10 November 1941.
301   *Harry was training.* . . See his service records, NAA: B883, NX46646.

301 *in 1946 he was guest of honour.* . . Grafton *Daily Examiner*, 7 March and 13 June 1946.

302 *died on 7 May.* . . See death certificate, repatriation case file NAA: C138, R30557 and obituary in Grafton *Daily Examiner*, 13 May 1949.

302 *The assets he had bequeathed to Harry.* . . See deceased estate files at State Records Authority of New South Wales: NRS 13340/B29325/20/4740.

303 *he appealed to the War Graves Commission.* . . See NAA: C138, R30557.

305 *Harold Smith, who had died in 1944.* . . See obituary in Grafton *Daily Examiner*, 21 December 1944.

SELECT BIBLIOGRAPHY

For details of newspapers and periodicals, unpublished papers, parliamentary papers, websites and 'penny dreadfuls', see Notes.

Adam, Hargrave Lee, *The Story of Crime: From the Cradle to the Grave* (London, 1908)

Anon, *Hadleigh: The Story of a Great Endeavour* (London, 1902)

Anon, *The Queen's London: A Pictorial and Descriptive Record of the Streets, Buildings, Parks, and Scenery of the Great Metropolis in the Fifty-Ninth Year of the Reign of Her Majesty Queen Victoria* (London, 1896)

Arnold, A. J., *Iron Shipbuilding on the Thames: An Economic and Business History* (London, 2000)

August, Andrew (ed.), *The Urban Working Class in Britain, 1830–1914: Vol. I: Home and Community* (London, 2013)

Bean, Charles, *The Story of Anzac, Vols I, II & III* (Sydney, 1941)

Beeston, Joseph Lievesley, *Five Months at Anzac: A Narrative of Personal Experiences of the Officer Commanding the 4th Field Ambulance, Australian Imperial Force* (Sydney, 1916)

Behlmer, George K., *Child Abuse and Moral Reform in England 1870–1908* (Stanford, 1982)

—, *Friends of the Family: The English Home and its Guardians 1850–1940* (Stanford, 1998)

Besant, Walter, *East London* (London, 1901)

—, *All Sorts and Conditions of Men: An Impossible Story* (London, 1882)

Bonsor, N. R. P., *North Atlantic Seaway: An Illustrated History of the Passenger Services Linking the Old World with the New* (Prescot, Lancs, 1955)

Boone, Troy, *Youth of Darkest England: Working-Class Children at the Heart of Victorian Empire* (London, 2005)

Booth, Charles, *Life and Labour of the People. Vol. I* (London, 1889)

Booth, William, *In Darkest England and the Way Out* (London, 1890)

Boyd, Kelly, *Manliness and the Boys' Story Paper in Britain: A Cultural History, 1855–1940* (Basingstoke, Hants, 2002)

Brewer, Mary and Clarrie, *Looking Back: Nana Glen, 1879–1979* (Coffs Harbour, NSW, 1979)

Bristow, Joseph, *Empire Boys: Adventures in a Man's World* (London, 1991)

Bullen, Frank Thomas, *The Men of the Merchant Service* (London, 1900)

Burnett, Frances Hodgson, *The Secret Garden* (London and New York, 1911)

Burnett, John, *A Social History of Housing 1815–1985* (London, 1986)

Butler, Arthur Graham, *Official History of the Australian Army Medical Services, 1914–1918, Vols I and II* (Canberra, 1938 and 1941)

Cantlie, James, *Degeneration amongst Londoners* (London, 1885)

Cardinal, Rudolf N. and Bullmore, Edward T., *The Diagnosis of Psychosis* (Cambridge, 2011)

Cearns, Percy, *The Love of a Brother: From Plaistow to Passchendaele* (Loughton, Essex, 2011)

Childs, Michael J., *Labour's Apprentices: Working-Class Lads in late Victorian and Edwardian England* (London, 1992)

Conrad, Joseph, *The Secret Agent* (London, 1907)

—, *Heart of Darkness* (London, 1899)

Corder, B. F., Ball, B. C., Haizlip, T. M., Rollins R. and Beaumont, R., 'Adolescent Parricide: A Comparison with Other Adolescent Murder', *American Journal of Psychiatry*, 133 (1976)

Cowling, Nan (ed.), *Coffs Harbour Time Capsule Book: 1847–2011* (Coffs Harbour, NSW, 2011)

Cox, J. Randolph, *The Dime Novel Companion: A Source Book* (Westport, CT, 2000)

Crouch, Archer Philip, *Silvertown and Neighbourhood: A Retrospect* (London, 1900)

Davies, W. H., *The Autobiography of a Super-Tramp* (London, 1908)

Davin, Anna, *Growing Up Poor: Home, School and Street 1870–1914* (London, 1996)

Deans, Richard Storry, *The Law of Parent and Child, Guardian and Ward, and the Rights, Duties and Liabilities of Infants; with the Practice of the High Court of Justice in Relation Thereto* (London, 1895)

Dupuy, George M., *The Stretcher Bearer* (London, 1915)

Eigen, Joel Peter, *Unconscious Crime: Mental Absence and Criminal Responsibility in Victorian London* (Baltimore, MD, 2003)

—, *Witnessing Insanity: Madness and Mad-Doctors in the English Court* (New Haven and London, 1995)

—, 'Diagnosing Homicidal Mania: Forensic Psychiatry and the Purposeless Murder', *Medical History*, October 2010

Esquirol, Etienne, *Mental Maladies: A Treatise on Insanity* (London, 1845)

Fazio, Vince, *The Battlecruiser HMAS Australia, First Flagship of the Royal Australian Navy: A Story of Her Life and Times* (Garden Island, NSW, 2000)

Ferrall, Charles and Jackson, Anna, *Juvenile Literature and British Society 1850–1950: The Age of Adolescence* (London, 2009)

Flegel, Monica, *Conceptualizing Cruelty to Children in Nineteenth-Century England: Literature, Representation and the NSPCC* (Farnham, Surrey and Burlington, NC, 2009)

Garton, Stephen, *The Cost of War: Australians Return* (Melbourne, Vic, 1996)

Gissing, George, *The Nether World* (London, 1889)

Goose, Nigel and Honeyman, Katrina (eds), *Childhood and Child Labour in Industrial England: Diversity and Agency, 1750–1914* (Farnham, Surrey, 2013)

Gordon, Harvey, *Broadmoor* (London, 2012)

Graham, Clare, *Ordering Law: The Architectural and Social History of the English Law Court to 1914* (Aldershot, Hants, 2003)

Green, Annette and Franklin, Margaret, *A History of Nana Glen Primary School, 1892–1992* (Nana Glen, NSW, 1992)

Green, C. M., 'Matricide by Sons', *Medicine, Science and the Law*, 21 (1981)

Greg, I. M. and Towers, S. H., *Cattle Ships and our Meat Supply* (London, 1894)

Griffith, George, *Sidelights on Convict Life* (London, 1903)

Griffiths, Arthur, *Secrets of the Prison House: Gaol Studies and Sketches* (London, 1894)

Haggard, H. Rider, *The Poor and the Land: Report on the Salvation Army Colonies in the United States and at Hadleigh, England, with Scheme of National Land Resettlement* (London, 1905)

—, *Regeneration: Being an Account of the Social Work of the Salvation Army in Great Britain* (London, 1910)

—, *King Solomon's Mines* (London, 1885)

—, *She: A History of Adventure* (London, 1886)

Hall, Granville Stanley, *Adolescence: Its Psychology and its Relations to Physiology, Anthropology, Sociology, Sex, Crime, Religion and Education* (New York, 1904)

Harding, Tim, *Correspondence Chess in Britain and Ireland 1824–1987* (Jefferson, NC, 2010)

Hardy, Thomas, *Jude the Obscure* (London, 1895)

Harris, Harry, *Under Oars: Reminiscences of a Thames Lighterman, 1894–1909* (London, 1978)

Harris, Ruth, *Murders and Madness: Medicine, Law and Society in the Fin de Siècle* (Oxford, 1989)

Hart, Peter, *Gallipoli* (Oxford, 2011)

Heide, Kathleen M., *Understanding Parricide: When Sons and Daughters Kill Parents* (New York, 2012)

Heide, Kathleen M. and Frei, Autumn, 'Matricide: a Critique of the Literature' in *Trauma, Violence, and Abuse II* (2010)

Herbert, Trevor, *The British Brass Band: A Musical and Social History* (Oxford, 2000)

Holmes, Mrs Basil, *The London Burial Grounds* (London, 1896)

Hopkins, Eric, *Childhood Transformed: Working-Class Children in Nineteenth-Century England* (Manchester, 1994)

Hopkins, R. Thurston, *Life and Death at the Old Bailey* (London, 1935)

Howarth, Edward G. and Wilson, Mona, *West Ham: a Study in Social and Industrial Problems* (London, 1907)

Hueffer, Ford Madox, *The Soul of London* (London, 1905)

—, *The Mirror of the Sea* (London, 1906)

Inwood, Stephen, *City of Cities: The Birth of Modern London* (London, 2005)

Johnston, Mark, *Stretcher-Bearers: Saving Australians from Gallipoli to Kokoda* (Melbourne, Vic, 2015)

Joyce, James, *Dubliners* (London, 1914)

Kennedy, John, *The History of Steam Navigation* (Liverpool, 1903)

Kirkpatrick, Robert J., *From the Penny Dreadful to the Ha'penny Dreadfuller: A Bibliographical History of the Boys' Periodical in Britain, 1762–1950* (London, 2013)

Kynaston, David, *WG's Birthday Party* (London, 2011)

Ledger, Sally and Luckhurst, Roger (eds), *The Fin de Siècle: A Reader in Cultural History, c.1880–1900* (Oxford, 2000)

Lee, J. E., *The Chronicle of the 45th Battalion, AIF* (Sydney, 1927)

Lombroso, Cesare, *The Criminal Man* (London, 1884)

London, Jack, *The People of the Abyss* (New York, 1903)

Lynch, E. P. F., ed. Will Davies, *Somme Mud: The Experiences of an Infantryman in France, 1916–1919* (Milsons Point, NSW, 2006)

MacDougall, Anthony, *ANZACs: Australians at War* (Balgowlah, NSW, 1991)

McDougall, Donald (ed.), *Fifty Years a Borough, 1886–1936: The Story of West Ham* (West Ham, 1936)

Machray, Robert, *The Night Side of London* (London, 1902)

Mackenzie, William W., *A Treatise on the Elementary Education Acts, 1870–1891 (with the Acts in an Appendix)* (London, 1892)

Maginnis, Arthur J., *The Atlantic Ferry: Its Ships, Men and Working*, 3rd edition (London, 1900)

Masterman, Charles, *The Heart of Empire* (London, 1902)

—, *From the Abyss* (London, 1903)

Maudsley, Henry, *The Pathology of Mind* (London, 1895)

Mayhew, Emily, *Wounded: From Battlefield to Blighty, 1914–18* (London, 2013)

Meacham, Standish, *A Life Apart: The English Working Class, 1890–1914* (London, 1977)

Mercier, Charles Arthur, *The Attendant's Companion: The Manual of the Duties of Attendants in Lunatic Asylums* (London, 1892)

Mitchell, G. D., *Backs to the Wall: A Larrikin on the Western Front* (Sydney, 1937)

Morley, Charles, *Studies in Board Schools* (London, 1897)

Morrison, Arthur, *Tales of Mean Streets* (London, 1894)

Murphy, Paul Thomas, *Shooting Victoria: Madness, Mayhem, and the Rebirth of the British Monarchy* (London, 2012)

Nelson, Claudia, *Precocious Children and Childish Adults: Age Inversion in Victorian Literature* (Baltimore, MD, 2012)

Newland, Paul, *The Cultural Construction of London's East End: Urban Iconography, Modernity and the Spatialisation of Englishness* (Amsterdam, 2008)

Nisbet, J. F., *The Human Machine: An Inquiry Into the Diversity of Human Faculty in Its Bearings Upon Social Life, Religion Education, and Politics* (London, 1899)

Nordau, Max, *Degeneration* (London, 1895)

Parkhill, Gordon and Cook, Graham, *Hadleigh Salvation Army Farm: A Vision Reborn* (London, 2008)

Partridge, Ralph, *Broadmoor: A History of Criminal Lunacy and its Problems* (London, 1953)

Pedersen, Peter, *The Anzacs: Gallipoli to the Western Front* (Camberwell, Vic, 2007)

Pember Reeves, Maud, *Round About a Pound a Week* (London, 1913)

Philpott, Hugh B., *London at School: The Story of the School Board, 1870–1904* (London, 1904)

Pick, Daniel, *Faces of Degeneration: A European Disorder, c. 1848–1918* (Cambridge, 1989)

Pittard, Christopher, *Purity and Contamination in Late Victorian Detective Fiction* (Farnham, Surrey, 2011)

Plimsoll, Samuel, *Cattle Ships: Being the Fifth Chapter of Mr. Plimsoll's Second Appeal for Our Seamen* (London, 1890)

Porter, Roy, *London: A Social History* (London, 1994)

Powell, W. R. (ed.), *A History of the County of Essex: Vol. 6* (London, 1973)

Priestley, Philip, *Victorian Prison Lives: English Prison Biography 1830–1914* (London, 1985)

Rose, Jonathan, *The Intellectual Life of the British Working Classes* (New Haven and London, 2001)

Rose, Lionel, *The Erosion of Childhood: Child Oppression in Britain, 1860–1918* (London, 1991)

Ross, Ellen, *Love and Toil: Motherhood in Outcast London, 1870–1918* (London, 1993)

Rubinstein, David, *School Attendance in London 1870–1904: A Social History* (Hull, 1969)

Russell, C. E. B., *Manchester Boys: Sketches of Manchester Lads at Work and Play* (Manchester, 1905)

Russell, D. H., 'A Study of Juvenile Murderers of Family Members', *International Journal of Offender Therapy and Comparative Criminology*, 28 (1984)

Salmon, Edward G., *Juvenile Literature as It Is* (London, 1888)

Scherl, D. J. and Mack, J. E., 'A Study of Adolescent Matricide', *Journal of the American Academy of Child Psychology*, 5 (1966)

Schneer, Jonathan, *London 1900: The Imperial Metropolis* (New Haven, 1999)

Scotland, Nigel, *Squires in the Slums: Settlements and Missions in Late Victorian Britain* (London, 2007)

Scull, Andrew, *Madness in Civilization: A Cultural History of Insanity* (Princeton, NJ, 2015)

Shephard, Ben, *A War of Nerves: Soldiers and Psychiatrists in the Twentieth Century* (London, 2000)

Shuttleworth, Sally, *The Mind of the Child: Child Development in Literature, Science, and Medicine, 1840–1900* (Oxford, 2010)

Sims, George, *Living London: Its Work and its Play, its Humour and its Pathos, its Sights and its Scenes, Vol. I* (London, 1901)

Smith, Roger, *Trial by Medicine: Insanity and Responsibility in Victorian Trials* (Edinburgh, 1981)

Springhall, John, *Youth, Popular Culture and Moral Panics: Penny Gaffs to Gangsta Rap, 1830–1997* (Basingstoke, Hants, 1998)

—, *Coming of Age: Adolescence in Britain, 1860–1960* (Dublin, 1986)

Steevens, G. W., *Things Seen: Impressions of Men, Cities, and Books* (Edinburgh, 1900)

Stevens, Mark, *Broadmoor Revealed: Victorian Crime and the Lunatic Asylum* (Barnsley, Yorks, 2013)

—, *Life in the Victorian Asylum: The World of Nineteenth Century Mental Health Care* (Barnsley, Yorks, 2014)

Stevenson, Robert Louis, *Strange Case of Dr Jekyll and Mr Hyde* (London, 1886)

—, *Treasure Island* (London, 1883)

Stokes, John, *In the Nineties* (Hemel Hempstead, Herts, 1989)

Sully, James, *Studies of Childhood* (London, 1895)

Tanay, E., 'Adolescents who Kill Parents: Reactive parricide', *Australian and New Zealand Journal of Psychiatry*, 7 (1973)

Tebbutt, Melanie, *Making Ends Meet: Pawnbroking and Working-class Credit* (London, 1983)

Tosh, John, *A Man's Place: Masculinity and the Middle-Class Home in Victorian England* (New Haven and London, 1999)

Tuke, Daniel Hack (ed.), *Dictionary of Psychological Medicine* (London, 1892)

Turner, E. S., *Boys Will be Boys: The Story of Sweeney Todd, Deadwood Dick, Sexton Blake, Billy Bunter, Dick Barton, et al* (London, 1948)

Urwick, Edward Johns (ed.), *Studies of Boy Life in Our Cities* (London, 1904)

Walker, Pamela J., *Pulling the Devil's Kingdom Down: The Salvation Army in Victorian Britain* (Berkeley, 2001)

Ward, Tony, *Psychiatry and Criminal Responsibility in England 1843–1939* (DPhil thesis, 1996)

'Warmark' [George Penny], *Guilty but Insane: A Broadmoor Autobiography* (London, 1931)

Webb, Elizabeth, *Glenreagh: A Town of Promise* (Glenreagh, NSW, 1998)

Wells, H. G., *The Time Machine* (London, 1895)

—, *Tono-Bungay* (London, 1909)

Wertham, Frederic, *Dark Legend: A Study in Murder* (New York, 1941)

—, 'The Matricidal Impulse: Critique of Freud's Interpretation of Hamlet', *Journal of Criminal Psychopathology*, 2 (1941)

Westcott, W. Wynn, *Suicide: Its History, Literature, Jurisprudence, Causation and Prevention* (London, 1885)

White, Jerry, *London in the Nineteenth Century: A Human Awful Wonder of God* (London, 2007)

White, Thomas A., *The Fighting Thirteenth: The History of the 13th Battalion AIF* (Sydney, 1924)

Wiener, Martin J., 'Judges v Jurors: Courtroom Tensions in Murder Trials and the Law of Criminal Responsibility in Nineteenth-Century England', *Law and History Review*, Autumn 1999

Williams, Montagu, *Round London: Down East and Up West* (London, 1894)

Williams, Paul (ed.), *Aggression: From Fantasy to Action* (London, 2011)

Winchester, Simon, *The Surgeon of Crowthorne: A Tale of Murder, Madness and the Love of Words* (London, 1998)

Winslow, Lyttelton Forbes, *Mad Humanity: Its Forms Apparent and Obscure* (London, 1898)

ACKNOWLEDGEMENTS

Thanks above all to the late Harry Mulville, who died in Coffs Harbour in August 2014, to his daughter Joy Northcott and her husband, John, for their tremendous trust and generosity, and to Harry's other children, who made it possible for their sister to help me. I was also helped in Australia by Iain Couper in Coffs Harbour, Rachel Hollis at the State Records Authority of New South Wales, the Bloomsbury team in Sydney, and the staff of the Australian War Memorial, the National Library of Australia, the Mitchell Library, the State Library of New South Wales, the Coffs Harbour District Family History Society and the Coffs Harbour City Library.

Mark Stevens at the Berkshire Record Office gave me invaluable information about Broadmoor, as did Amlan Basu, Sheena Ebsworth and Estelle Morris at Broadmoor Hospital and, especially, Carine Minne at the Portman Clinic in London. Thank you to the staff of the British Library, the London Library, the National Archives, the Wellcome Library, the London Metropolitan Archives, Reading Central Library, Stratford Library, the Museum of London Docklands and the National Maritime Museum. I am grateful to Steve Holland for his research on penny dreadfuls, to Martin Smith for his knowledge about chess at Broadmoor, to Saul David and Mark McKenna for their help on the Great War, and to Sally Shuttleworth for her guidance on childhood in Victorian England. For excellent advice, thank you to Deborah Cohen, Chris Hilliard, Chris Hilton and Rada Vlatkovic.

Huge thanks to my friends and my family, particularly to Sam Randall and to those who read or talked to me about this book as I was writing, among them Philippa Barton, Lorna Bradbury,

Cristina Bruno, Alex Clark, Toby Clements, Will Cohu, Hal Currey, Tamsin Currey, Miranda Fricker, Manuela Grayson, Stephen Grosz, Victoria Lane, Sinclair McKay, Ruth Metzstein, Chris Michallet, Kathy O'Shaughnessy, Robert Randall, John Ridding, Fotini Roberts, Martha Stutchbury, Wycliffe Stutchbury, Claire Sturge, Ben Summerscale, Juliet Summerscale, Lydia Syson, Georgia Vuksanovic and Keith Wilson.

Thank you again to my agent, David Miller, to the rest of the brilliant team at Rogers, Coleridge & White, including Laurence Laluyaux, Stephen Edwards, Peter Robinson and Federica Leonardis, to Julia Kreitman at The Agency and to Melanie Jackson at MJA. I am grateful to my wonderful editors, Alexandra Pringle and Anna Simpson in London and Virginia Smith Younce in New York. Thank you also to Kate Johnson for her superb copy-editing; to Vicky Beddow, Richard Charkin, Madeleine Feeny, David Mann, Nigel Newton and Rachel Nicholson at Bloomsbury; and to Ann Godoff and Scott Moyers at Penguin Press. And my thanks to the other publishers who have supported this book – Dominique Bourgois in Paris, Sofia Ribeiro in Lisbon, Nikolay Naumenko in Moscow, Andrea Canobbio in Turin and Henk ter Borg in Amsterdam.

INDEX

A NOTE ON THE TYPE

The text of this book is set in Linotype Sabon, a typeface named after the type founder, Jacques Sabon. It was designed by Jan Tschichold and jointly developed by Linotype, Monotype and Stempel in response to a need for a typeface to be available in identical form for mechanical hot metal composition and hand composition using foundry type.

Tschichold based his design for Sabon roman on a font engraved by Garamond, and Sabon italic on a font by Granjon. It was first used in 1966 and has proved an enduring modern classic.